THE STAGE OF HER LIFE

Conversations
with Actress Lea Koenig
on Theater and Her Life

The book is published with the kind support of
The Peres Academic Center
The Rena Costa Center for Yiddish Studies, Bar-Ilan University
The Itzhak Akavyahu Fund, Department of Literature of the Jewish People, Bar-Ilan University

דער רנה-קאָסטאַ-צענטער פֿאַר ייִדיש-לימודים
The Rena Costa Center for Yiddish Studies
המרכז ללימודי יידיש ע"ש רנה קוסטה

The Rena Costa Center for
Yiddish Studies,
Bar Ilan University

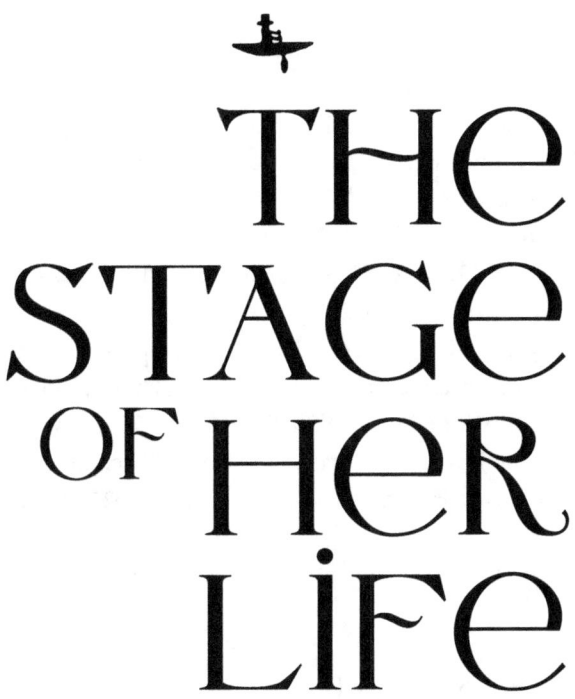

THE STAGE OF HER LIFE

Conversations
with Actress Lea Koenig
on Theater and Her Life

Yaniv Shimon
Goldberg

ACADEMIC STUDIES PRESS
BOSTON
2025

Library of Congress Cataloging-in-Publication Data

Names: Goldberg, Yaniv author | Koenig, Lea, 1929- interviewee
Title: The stage of her life : conversations with actress Lea Koenig on theater and her life / Yaniv Shimon Goldberg.
Description: Boston: Academic Studies Press, [2025] | Includes bibliographical references.
Identifiers: LCCN 2025025364 (print) | LCCN 2025025365 (ebook) | ISBN 9798897830305 hardback | ISBN 9798897830312 adobe pdf | ISBN 9798897830329 epub
Subjects: LCSH: Koenig, Lea, 1929- | Actors--Israel--Interviews | Jewish actors--Interviews | Theater--Israel | LCGFT: Biographies
Classification: LCC PN2919.8.K64 A5 2025 (print) | LCC PN2919.8.K64 (ebook) LC record available at https://lccn.loc.gov/2025025364 LC ebook record available at https://lccn.loc.gov/2025025365

Copyright © Academic Studies Press, 2025. Paperback 2026

ISBN 9798897831296 (Paperback)
ISBN 9798897830312 (Adobe PDF)
ISBN 9798897830329 (ePub)

Book design by PHi Business Solutions
Cover design by Ivan Grave. Photograph by Yechiam Gal

Published by Academic Studies Press
1007 Chestnut Street
Newton, MA 02464, USA
press@academicstudiespress.com
www.academicstudiespress.com

Vifl mol ich zey dich schpieln
Farlieb ich in dir oyfsnei.

Every time I see you on stage
I fall in love with you again.

Zvi (Hirshl) Stolper, Tel Aviv, April 23, 1976

Contents

Introduction	1
Chapter 1	7
Knowing Where I Came from	7
The Parents	8
Yiddish or Hebrew	13
Theatrical Education of Yiddish Actors	17
What about Talent?	18
A Mother's Review of the Game	19
Criticism of Acting Today	21
Chapter 2	23
World War II—From Czernowitz (Chernivtsi) to Samarkand	23
Bucharest—I'm Becoming an Actress	29
Personality and Charisma in Working on a Role	31
There Are Small Roles and There Are Big Roles	34
Chapter 3	37
Father and Stepfather	37
Zvi (Hirshl)	39
Why I Don't Have Children	40
Chapter 4	43
Playing Anne Frank and Holocaust Remembrance	43
Creating a Role	52
Chapter 5	57
The Beginning of a Career in Israel	57
Learning Hebrew	57
Schund and Intrigue in Israel	60
Lea at Habima	63
Master Puntila and His Man Matti	63
Bereshit—the Great Success	66

The Klausner Prize	68
Growing Up on Stage	70
Bereshit	70
The Life before Us	73
Driving Miss Daisy—the Stage as a Reflection of Life	74
Chapter 6	**78**
King Lear	78
The Chairs and the Theater of the Absurd	79
Mother Courage and Mother Dina	84
Yiddish Concert Tours Abroad	88
Chapter 7	**90**
The Parents	90
Character Actress	93
Grocery Store	94
Between *King Lear* and *Mirele Efros*, the Jewish Queen Lear	98
Chapter 8	**103**
Mirele Efros and the Israel Prize	103
The Israel Prize	109
Lea Koenig and Miriam Zohar Alternate in the Roles of Mirele Efros and Machle	110
A Tour Guide to Warsaw	112
Hirshl (Zvi)	114
Chapter 9	**119**
Feeling Israeli	119
Chapter 10	**123**
Entering the Stage and Performing	123
The Old Lady's Visit	123
Speaking on Stage	126
Acting Development and Professionalism	128
Chapter 11	**131**
Being Old	131
I'm a Comedian	133
Being a Partner on Stage and Dedication to the Profession	135

Chapter 12 — 141
The Theater Taught Me How to Live — 141
- Hanoch Levin — 141
- Understanding the Stage Space — 147
- What about Television and Cinema? — 152
- Each Role Left Its Mark — 161
- Survival — 164

Chapter 13 — 169
Four Years Later: Reflections — 169

Epilogue — 178
Lea Koenig—The First Lady of the Theater and Always Dina's Daughter — 178
- Between the Two Languages — 178
- The Defining Childhood — 181
- Passing the Baton from Mother to Daughter — 182
- The Choice—Hebrew — 183
- The Pursuit of Truth — 186
- The Yiddish Actress Is Making a Comeback — 188
- The Ghosts Echoing in the Theater — 190
- Breakthroughs in Artistic Life in Israel — 194

Appendices — 196
- Dina Koenig. A Short Biography — 196
- Yosef Kamien. A Short Biography — 201
- Lea Koenig's Theater Roles — 206
  - Romania — 206
  - Israel — 208
- Lea Koenig's Music Albums — 213
- From Lea's Photo Album — 214

Bibliography — 245
- Hebrew and Yiddish Sources (Translated) — 245
- English and Other Sources — 245
- Newspaper and Magazine Articles — 246
- Literary Sources — 247
- Electronic Sources — 247

Introduction

The art of acting on stage is a deceptive art. Why do we go to the theater? What attracts us to the actor we see on stage? Why are there actors who leave a huge impression on us and others who are forgotten as soon as they leave the stage and, sometimes, even while they are still on it? There are few unforgettable actors; actors whose talent erupts from them on stage, shakes the audience, moves them, makes them laugh, saddens them, and ensures their persona goes with them even after they leave the theater.

Lea Koenig is one such actress. From the first moment I saw her on stage, I couldn't help but fall in love with her. It seemed as if all the stage lights turned on when Lea Koenig walked on stage. Over the years, we became good friends and, as our personal friendship deepened, my appreciation for her increased both professionally and personally. During the course of her career, Lea has been interviewed many times about her personal life and her theatrical work. Countless articles have appeared in newspapers, she has appeared on television often, and a variety of documentaries and other programs have been made about her. And yet, I felt that not everything had been revealed and the hidden prevailed over the visible, both in the professional and personal aspects. Only after many years of personal acquaintance and private conversations between us about the theater and her life could I approach her with the idea of writing this book. I suggested that we talk about the theater, but that the conversations would also include her life story.

I didn't want to write a biography about the actress Lea Koenig. I wanted to bring our conversations to life because the insights she shared in all her conversations, whether they were private or public, like the words she chose to use or the music of her speech and its rhythm, were instructive and educational.

In this book, the transcripts of the conversations we had and recorded from 2018 to 2024 are presented. They discover that the course of Lea's life is intertwined with the roles she played. Life penetrates the stage and the stage affects life. The book seeks to trace the family and cultural origins of the actress Lea Koenig in an attempt to understand how she became a great actress. The explanation of her work as an actress in the many roles she played reveals more and more biographical details, and, as you progress along the timeline, more complex and fascinating aspects of her personality are revealed.

The Stage of Her Life

Those who have seen her on stage cannot forget the experience. In her roles, Lea was moving and exciting, she had a wonderful sense of humor, her timing was precise, and she always left an enduring impression on the audience. Today, after a career of more than seventy years and a fascinating list of roles, which she performed with great success, Lea can be said to be a legendary actress. She made an indelible mark on Israeli theater.

Lea Koenig is one of the last Yiddish actors who learned directly from the Yiddish actors of before World War II, and she is the last to pass on the tradition of this style of acting. She has also improved over the years, making her acting more modern. Taken together, this makes Lea one of the greatest Jewish actresses of all time.

Lea's mother tongue is Yiddish. She studied theater and started acting in Yiddish. After she arrived in Israel in her 30s, Lea learned Hebrew and started acting in Hebrew. The main tool of expression for actors is language. They must have control of it in order to be able to transfix the audience not only through the text of their role in the play, but also the subtext, the hidden text, the meaning behind the spoken words. Lea Koenig, during her extraordinary career in Israel, has managed to do this in a language that wasn't her mother tongue. While she faced the difficulties of the new language, she was not ready to let this bring her down despite the constant temptations to act only in Yiddish. When she allows herself to act in Yiddish, you can see, even today, how free she is in her acting, how she acts without fear of forgetting a word and not being able to find a replacement for it. In the Yiddish space, her safe language, she has always been like a fish in water. From this, you can learn about the great sacrifice she made to act in Hebrew in Israel, a not-so-small sacrifice over the years.

Some of the roles she played during her career were also performed by great actresses around the world and the comparison between them reveals her greatness and enormous talent. There are very few actors in the world on her level, but that is not the only reason why Lea is unique. Lea also carries the history of Jewish theater on her shoulders. Her parents, her father's brother, her stepfather, and her husband were all actors, and her grandparents worked as tailors in the theater in Lodz. She grew up in the theater. From her first day, she breathed and absorbed Jewish theater and culture. As a curious and observant person, Lea assimilated the Jewish language, melody, and wisdom that surrounded her, and she brings this rich history to the stage, performance after performance.

My personal acquaintance with Lea began when I was working on my doctorate dealing with the play *The Dybbuk* by S. An-sky. Lea's father, Yosef (Osya/Oscar) Kamien (Józef Kamień), and his brother, Eliyahu (Alex/Alyusha) Stein, acted in the first production of *The Dybbuk* staged in Warsaw in December 1920 by the theater troupe from Vilna (Vilnius), the Vilna Troupe. Lea's mother, the actress Dina Koenig, also played the role of Leah in *The Dybbuk* in the same production, after joining the troupe. Lea shared her memories of her parents with me as well as her perception of the play and her interpretation of it, which was different from the well-known interpretation in the monumental production of the Habima Theater with Hanna Rovina. A few weeks after that meeting, Lea called me and invited me to come see her Yiddish show at the Storytelling Festival in Givatayim (Tel Aviv Metropolitan area). Over time, I realized that this was her way. She knew how to draw people in, those whom she wanted near, with warmth and love. As our friendship deepened, I came to know that her special personality and also her unforgettable presence on stage intrigued me as a theater researcher, as a person, and as a friend. I ended that first conversation between us about *The Dybbuk* and her parents with the words, "It was a fascinating conversation." Lea reacted instinctively, half joking, half serious, with "I am a fascinating woman . . ." This sentence echoed in my head for a long time. In her personal life, Lea is a warm and humble person; she knows her own worth professionally, but I have never seen her proud or condescending to others. In all the years I have known her, I have never seen her abuse her position or her publicity. The statement, "I am a fascinating person," I realized, turned out to be a sentence expressing a simple truth. Lea is indeed a fascinating person! She is a person who is not afraid to recognize her own worth, but there is no trace of pride in this self-recognition. All her life, Lea has strived to find the absolute truth in her life and in the roles she plays, and she is equally precise when she talks about herself or when trying to define who she is, where she came from, and what her purpose is in this world. In one of our meetings, I told her that I intended to teach a course on the history of the theater and I said that I would like to have been able to show a segment of her performance, but unfortunately, it hadn't been filmed. Lea responded, "What's the problem? I'll come and do the part." And, to my surprise, she added, "It's called friendship. You need help and I can help you."

This offer and Lea's visit to the university launched a program of which to be proud. Thanks to Lea, the Brookdale Program at Bar-Ilan University presents a Lifetime Achievement Award to actors who have left their mark on culture and art in Israel, with the intention of honoring the artist later in life. A program was also founded that honors and remembers deceased artists. Lea's simple and humble agreement to come to the class and help me with the lecture added another layer to my understanding that there is a very large gap between the 'theater actress, Lea Koenig' persona, who is seen at least among some of the Israeli public as a beloved and popular actress, the 'queen of the theater' or the 'first lady of the theater in Israel,' and the personal persona of a modest woman, who is ready to dedicate her time and appear for a few minutes as a volunteer for a friend.

Lea jokingly doubts the title 'First Lady of the Theater' and says that perhaps she isn't the first, but the fifth because there are many who are standing in line ... and there is more than a grain of truth in this joke. Lea is a wonderful actress who has won the love of her audience and critics over the years, and yet she appreciates other good female actresses and supports them.

One of my greatest experiences in the theater was when I spoke to Lea a few minutes before the show *The Life before Us* started. During the play, in which I sat in the first row of the theater, I found myself forgetting that the character of Madame Rosa, whom I see on stage, is the actress, Lea Koenig, and I believed that she was indeed Rosa. It was an unforgettable experience. Lea, the actress, managed to strip herself of her own personality and put on the personality of Madame Rosa. She created a complete identification with the stage character, shaping and presenting the elusive truth that the theater strives to reach.

As mentioned, Lea's mother tongue is Yiddish. Even when Lea speaks Hebrew, her syntax is Yiddish. She thinks in Yiddish and, very quickly, our conversations began to be conducted in this language, especially in places where it was important for her to clarify the facts or her thoughts. I tried very hard to keep Lea's special language and almost not edit it so I could share her thought process and the music of her speech with the reader. However, minimal editing was performed due to the associative nature of some of the conversations and the fact that they were written down.

Because the conversations were conducted in person, it is sometimes possible to see certain things being repeated. These are events that were seen as important and warranted emphasis for Lea. I believe that there is value in this repetition viewed through the window that Lea opened into her life. Through it, she discovered things that she had never told anyone until then. In the early days of the Habima Theater, it was believed that the actor should remain mysterious to be able to convince the audience of the character he is portraying (although almost all the actors made sure to write at least one autobiography). I believe that precisely this window that Lea opened to her soul and life allows us to appreciate her greatness even more as an actress and as a person. This book tells the personal story of the actress Lea Koenig, but it also tells us about the lives of actors, about coping and survival, about being displaced from a country and culture, about the pursuit of truth, and about life. This is the stage of Lea Koenig's life.

I would like to thank the Habima Theater management; Hani Seligsohn, the founder of the Habima National Theater Archive; Rami Semo, the director of the archive; Dr. Olga Levitan, former chair of the Israel Center for the Documentation of the Performing Arts at Tel Aviv University, and the archive staff for their kind and heartfelt help. Thanks also to photographers Yechiam Gal, Rachel Hirsch, Pesi Girsch, and Gérard Allon for their kindness and assistance with the photographs; to Lea's co-actors, colleagues, and friends who filled me in with details and stories to get the full picture; to Darryl Egnal for editing the manuscript with patience; to my family; and, last but not least, to actress Lea Koenig Stolper, who opened her heart to me and taught me what good theater and great friendship are.

Yaniv Shimon Goldberg

Chapter 1

Knowing Where I Came from

Yaniv: Let's talk about theater.

Lea: Theater? I thought you wanted to talk about me?

Yaniv: It's not the same?

Lea: What do you think?

Yaniv: I'm trying to understand who Lea Koenig is. And maybe, along the way, understand what you went through in life and why the theater became a part of your life in such a significant way.

Lea: And why is it interesting to you?

Yaniv: I think the answer will be the same for everyone who has seen you on stage. You have intrigued me since the first moment I saw you, and, since we got to know each other personally, my curiosity has only grown. I see how you construct a role, how you understand theater, and how you relate to this whole art called theater, and I feel that I must understand this phenomenon called Lea Koenig. Your approach to theater is very different from the acting concept I studied, and, therefore, you intrigue me even more. Sometimes it seems to me that you act contrary to everything I know and believe about theater, and yet you fascinate me on stage.

Lea: I'm not so sure that I'm really that far off from the approaches you know.

Yaniv: We'll get to that later, but, for now, I don't understand your motivation for this book. After all, many films have been made and articles written about you, so why a book? What is there to tell that has not yet been told?

Lea: This time, it is very important for me to share my story about where I came from, not only the geography, but, more importantly, the culture I came from. It is important for me to talk about my parents and the Yiddish actors in the Yiddish theater in Eastern Europe. They were great actors, but in Israel they were treated with great disdain. It's time someone told their story and I can do that through telling mine. You have a PhD in Yiddish, you research Yiddish theater and love it, so you are a good person to tell my story to.

The Parents

Yaniv: Let's start from the beginning. Shaul Tchernichovsky said, "Man is but the imprint of his native landscape," and man is, first of all, a product of his parents, so let's start with your parents. Who was your father?

Lea: Honestly, I constantly feel the need to dedicate everything to them. It hurts me very much that they were interesting artists, artists who devoted so much to their work, and they are being forgotten. There are people who still remember them to this day, but they are getting fewer and fewer, and those types of people, who devoted so much to their work for so many years, they deserve to have something left of them. Certainly, the main limitation is that they appeared in Yiddish and not in Polish or other languages and this limited them, this prevented them from becoming famous and becoming more successful in the profession. My heart hurts all the time because there were wonderful actors in the Yiddish theater who just disappeared, who are not remembered, who are not talked about. I constantly have the feeling that I am not dedicating enough to them, so it is important for me to leave a legacy for them. My desire is to do research on Yiddish theater. The population that grew up in these areas loved them so much and the actors loved it and devoted their lives to Yiddish theater and art. I'm not only talking about theater, but also about music and literature. Yiddish literature, in general, has been forgotten and is not recognized here. The truth is that, due to the circumstances of the years and because of World War II, I was not interested enough, I did not ask enough, and I miss that, and, as time passes, I feel a bigger need to devote my time to them.

Yaniv: Let's start changing that. Who was your father?

Lea: My father, the actor Yosef Kamien, was born in Vilnius to the Stein family. They had a law firm called Stein.

Yaniv: So how did Stein become Kamien?

Lea: *Stein* in Yiddish means 'stone,' and, in Russian, it is *kamen'*. My father's brother, Alex Stein,[1] was also an actor and he and my father acted together in the most important theater group in Eastern Europe, the Vilna Troupe. My father changed his name from Stein to Kamien so people could differentiate between them.

Yaniv: Your father died in 1942, but your parents divorced before that and your father remained in Poland while you and your mother lived in Czernowitz (Chernivtsi), Bukovina. What do you remember about him?

Lea: I remember him well. Sometimes, like in a picture, I can see his smile. My father had to have his leg amputated due to an illness and I vaguely remember his heavy prosthesis.

Yaniv: How did it affect you?

Lea: It startled me. Without a doubt. It left a big impression on me. The truth is that I don't know enough about why my parents got divorced. I once asked my mother why, and she said, "I think we were young and didn't know how to overcome it." I think my mother thought about it too, but it was no longer possible to turn back the wheel.[2] I certainly missed my father's presence. He was an impressive man. He had grace and a sense of humor, and, somehow, I don't know, when you miss something, the longing is inside you and not just in your head. I think my mother, when she looked at me, was very aware that I looked similar to my father. I think I inherited a lot of his talent and humor from him, thank God.

Yaniv: Who was your mother?

Lea: My mother was a more dramatic actress. I remember that my mother did not say, "Oh, you look so much like your father." My mother was a very smart and very restrained person. She was not some *yenta* (a woman who is a gossip or busybody) who said, "Oh, my child is the best." She was very realistic

---

1 Eliyahu (Alex/Alyusha) Stein, Yosef Kamien's older brother, was part of the Vilna Troupe. He was the first Honen in the first production of The Dybbuk staged by the Vilna Troupe in 1920 in Warsaw. (I have the playbill for the first show, YSG.)
2 For a brief biography of Lea's parents, Yosef Kamien and Dina Koenig, see the appendices.

when she looked at me and thought about who I am and what I am. And because I was with her all the time, I was very influenced by her. The more I think about her, the more I appreciate her. My mother was not only an excellent actress, but also a realistic person with her feet on the ground. She had so much wisdom. And she had something about her; for example, when I immigrated to Israel, she warned me about things she couldn't have known and no one had any information about. We lived in a time and place where there was no information about Israel, but her instinct and wisdom guided me to the right place to make sure I didn't make mistakes.

Yaniv: What do you mean?

Lea: Some people think that I immigrated to Israel and started acting in Yiddish. This is not true. I acted in Israel for the first time in Yiddish only three years later when Hirshl[3] wrote his first play, *Hochma Ligt in Keshene* (Wisdom lies in the pocket). The father of the actor Yossi Kantz, who also acted in Yiddish, asked in an article he wrote why we acted in Yiddish after we had already acted at the Habima in Hebrew. He, a Yiddish actor, wrote against acting in Yiddish.

Yaniv: How did your mother know to tell you not to act in Yiddish plays in Israel?

Lea: My mother understood. I was very successful at the State Jewish Theater (the State Yiddish Theater) in Bucharest, Romania. My success was immediate and my mother said that, if I change my status, I won't go back. She somehow realized that acting in Yiddish would not get me anywhere.

Yaniv: How did she feel about it when you were in Romania?

Lea: We all felt it. The State Jewish Theater in Romania was excellent, but, when we traveled by train, we spoke Romanian and not Yiddish. We would go on vacations and the guys in the theater wouldn't say, "I'm from the State Jewish Theater." They would say, "I'm from the State Theater." When people heard the word, "Jewish" (*evreiesc* in Romanian), you would see them swallow. In other words, Yiddish was still considered inferior to Romanian.

---

3   Hirshl—Zvi Hirshl Stolper, Lea's husband, actor and director. In this book, sometimes he will be called Zvi (Hebrew) and sometimes Hirshl (Yiddish).

Yaniv: Did your mother not have an opportunity to act in the Romanian theater?

Lea: She never tried. My mother was a prodigy in Poland and she performed in Polish. The actor Shimon Finkel, saw her and never forgot her. Then she acted with Esther Rachel Kamińska (a central figure of Eastern European Yiddish theater at the end of the nineteenth century and the beginning of the twentieth), who told her that she should never change her name, but should always remain Koenig ("king" in Yiddish) and that she should always act in Yiddish. After that, my mother did just that, she acted only in Yiddish. She didn't speak Romanian very well, certainly not enough to act on stage in Romanian, and she was already a very well-known Yiddish actress.

Yaniv: After the war, was it out of the question to move back to Poland so she could act in Polish?

Lea: She was already married to Isak (Yitzhak) Havis, who was not from Poland. He was from Bălți (Belz) in Moldova and they couldn't move to Poland. Besides, my mother already well-known in Romania and that was very important because they liked to hire well-known actors. My mother felt that acting in the Yiddish theater had stunted her career and, therefore, she told us that, when we get to Israel, we should act in Hebrew, the official language, the language of the majority, and not in Yiddish, the minority language.

Yaniv: Actually, your mother told you to do in Hebrew what she didn't dare to do in Romanian, something you would then go on to do.

Lea: Not only that, she said that the State Jewish Theater in Bucharest was a repertory theater[4] with government support, good directors, and proper sets. It wasn't like the Yiddish theater, which was private and poor. She knew the private Yiddish theaters. They were called *'schund* theaters'[5] and she told both me and Hirshl that we shouldn't go to a *schund* theater, that we may fail. She told us to only go to a repertory theater.

---

4   Repertory theater: A public theater in which a resident acting company presents works from a specified repertoire, usually in alternation or rotation. *Wikipedia*.
5   *Schund* from German, meaning "trash." A theater without any artistic value, usually light melodrama with a love story, singing and dancing, and with many winks to the audience, most of which do not belong to the play.

Yaniv: You didn't act at the *schund* theater?

Lea: I did a little, like *The Back Street*,[6] but it was a slightly higher level than the *schund* theater, which was really on a very low level.

Yaniv: Your mother wanted you to fulfill her unrealized dream of being in a major theater acting in the main language.

Lea: Very true. She was still alive when I started acting at Habima and when I did *Master Puntila and His Man Matti*, she was very happy because she thought that the role was very suitable for me. She knew about the play *Bereshit* (Genesis), and about the Klausner Prize I received following it. She also heard about the first play in Yiddish that I did with Hirshl, *Hochma Ligt in Keshene* (Wisdom lies in the pocket) and heard me in something on the radio. She passed away soon after.

Yaniv: When you were acting on stage, were there times when you said to yourself, "I am now acting in a role in Hebrew and this fulfills my mother's dream?"

Lea: I never thought about it, but now that you say it, I think you're right. My mother told me, "Start in Hebrew and only after they can recognize you, then you can do whatever you want in Yiddish," and so it was. She died once she knew I had done what she had told me to do. Later, there were people who thought I had started in Yiddish, but it's not true. It was very difficult when we immigrated to Israel. We lived at 3 Reines Street in Tel Aviv with Hirshl's mother and there were many Jews who had emigrated from Romania and knew me. There was a huge crowd that spoke Yiddish and wanted to see me act. Yiddish theater was flourishing at that time, and producers came to me and put 10,000 Israeli pounds on my table, which at that time was the price of an apartment on Dizengoff Street.

Yaniv: And you didn't take it?

Lea: No! We didn't take it!

Yaniv: How did you fight the temptation?

---

6 *The Back Street*, a play by Michael Clayton Hatten based on Fanny Hurst's book. Lea acted in the play in Yiddish with her stepfather, Isak Havis, directed by her husband, Zvi Stolper.

Lea: Because my mother said I should! Parting from my mother was very difficult. We didn't know what would happen, after all. With the communists, it was impossible to know.

Yaniv: And Hirshl didn't want to accept it? Didn't you have arguments about it?

Lea: It's interesting that you ask. He didn't insist. He probably felt it was true. He believed that my mother was smart and knew what she was talking about, and so he went along with it.

Yaniv: You reached the top, the highest point in Hebrew theater. You fulfilled your mother's dream in full, but Hirshl didn't. Did it not bother him?

Lea: Look, I did everything and he did everything. He always knew I was good. He had a very objective view of me as an actress. I always laughed about it. I would say about the different roles, "Me? I can't do it," and he always said, "You can do anything." He believed that my strongest ability was on stage. And hence, he liked to write for me. He had his disappointments because he didn't succeed as much as I did in the Hebrew theater.[7]

Yiddish or Hebrew

Yaniv: When did Hirshl decide he was going back into Yiddish theater to direct small plays in Yiddish like *A Refuah tzum Leybn* (A cure for life)?

Lea: He did it both for financial reasons and because he had a need to be somewhere else because he was not happy at Habima. You know, when you live with a person for many years, after years you say to yourself, "Why didn't I have the sense to say something . . ." Hirshl was a poet, but the attitude towards poetry at the time was not very positive. In fact, the attitude towards him in the theater was also not positive, but only towards the end did he free himself from the desire to succeed in the theater and only then was he able to move forward in other directions.

Yaniv: Did he also want to succeed first in Hebrew?

---

7   The author of this book translated some of Zvi Stolper's writings into Hebrew.

Lea: Only at the beginning. But then he told me, "Whoever didn't learn the language at school, no matter how good he is, will find it difficult to succeed both in acting and in writing." It was obviously easier for him in Yiddish and maybe I made a mistake by not being brave enough to publish everything he wrote. In the sixties, modern theater was very popular; people would talk to things—a bowl, a pan, all kinds of nonsense like that, and he wrote all kinds of excellent modern things for me, but I didn't have the courage to do them. For example, he worked with Ada Ben Nahum,[8] who was very impressed with what he wrote, but I didn't have the courage to perform his work. I was afraid that it wouldn't work. I'm guilty. There's no arguing. I'm guilty. I didn't publish his works in Hebrew.

Yaniv: But he wrote for you in Yiddish?

Lea: Yes, but Ada Ben Nahum helped him translate everything into Hebrew; for example, the monologue *Naches fun Kinder* (Pleasure from the children) about a mother whose children are abandoning her.

Yaniv: When did you do this monologue in Hebrew?

Lea: It happened after a few years. But I didn't agree with the whole show. The first time I did something with him in Hebrew was only in *Kochavim l'lo Shamayim* (Stars without sky) in 1992, and that was good.

Yaniv: But you performed it alone and not together with him on stage. He just directed you.

Lea: He thought it would be better that way. And really, it was a success. They took us abroad to Europe and the United States. There, I acted both in Hebrew and Yiddish. In Germany, I acted only in Yiddish. Listen, when you start remembering things, you blame yourself.

Yaniv: You said that, for him, giving up the language was too great. He felt he could not do it in Hebrew.

---

8   Ada Ben Nahum, playwright and translator, one of the founders of the Be'er Sheva Theater.

Lea: He didn't believe in himself. He knew how to write in Hebrew better than the *sabras* (people born in Israel). Even when I tell a joke, a clever joke, it's better in Yiddish. Telling the same joke in Hebrew won't be as funny or as clever.

Yaniv: It's interesting because you've been acting on the Hebrew stage for more than fifty years.

Lea: The truth? To this day, I'm more used to acting in Hebrew. I speak Hebrew, but my truth is in Yiddish.

Yaniv: When you're on stage, do you translate the monologue from Yiddish into Hebrew in your head? I had a feeling when I saw you doing a monologue once on stage.

Lea: No. Sometimes I feel like sharing wisdom in Yiddish, but from the very beginning, I think of the text in Hebrew. It doesn't turn out well if you translate from language to language.

Yaniv: Do you feel like giving up on Yiddish because you act more in Hebrew?

Lea: Talent exists in every language. I have the Yiddish bubble and the Hebrew bubble. For example, Sholem Aleichem . . . I just can't do his texts in Hebrew, I can't. I tried several translations and none of them touched my soul. Not the English translation, "It's good for me to be an orphan," nor the Hebrew, "*Ashrai yatom ani*" . . . neither is the same as the Yiddish, "*Mir is gut, ikh bin a yosem.*"

Yaniv: What is still not clear to me, in this regard, is whether you are more relaxed on stage when you act in Yiddish or in Hebrew.

Lea: I am more relaxed in Yiddish. That's without a doubt, without a doubt! I don't have the fear that I have in Hebrew.

Yaniv: Fear? To this day? After fifty years?

Lea: It depends on what I'm doing; for example, when I played *King Lear*, fear killed me in the first few performances. The fear also caused me to stop a show in the middle. The fear of this language. I could not and did not have the strength to fight the translator. Now I realize that I am changing the translation into a more understandable language. I suddenly have the courage to change the translation.

I don't understand why I have to use such a high level of language so that people don't understand what I'm saying. In this kind of text, I have a fear that made me tense, made my heart beat faster. Actress Tatiana Canellis Ollier once told me, "Lea, you don't understand . . . the audience loves you with or without mistakes in Hebrew. They forgive you and don't hear your mistakes." I was very tense because I don't have that in Yiddish.

Yaniv: It's a big concession.

Lea: Sure it's a concession, but I got over it. If I had only acted in Yiddish, I would be sitting at home today and not on stage. And what's more, they didn't respect the Yiddish actors in Israel. Here, and this blows my mind, they simply degraded the language, they butchered the language. Performances would be stopped and criminal charges filed against Yiddish theaters. How did my mother sense something like this would happen? I don't know. She didn't know about these cases. She played *Mother Courage and Her Children* in Yiddish. She could have played the same part in the same way in Romanian or Polish, but she chose to play it in Yiddish . . . and it passed, leaving no impression. My luck was that I played Anne in *Anne Frank*. The book was sensational because, at that time, I don't think that anyone from the entire communist bloc spoke about the Holocaust. They didn't want to talk about it. They spoke about the Great Patriotic War, but not in the Jewish context. They spoke about the liberation, about the Red Army liberating the countries from the German occupation, but not about the Holocaust of the Jews. Between 1948 and 1952, they killed Yiddish writers[9] and there was an antisemitic wave, so they did not talk about the Holocaust. But then Khrushchev was elected and things changed. The book was adapted into a play. It made a huge impression. The communists, artistically, did not spare costs. They created a competition between all the theaters in Romania, not only for the Yiddish theaters, but also for all the theaters in all languages. Each theater had to participate

---

9 On August 12 and 13, 1952, thirteen Jewish writers, poets, musicians, actors, and artists who worked in Yiddish, as well as others who were associated with the Jewish Anti-Fascist Committee, a Soviet Jewish organization established during World War II to help the Soviets in the struggle against Nazi Germany, were executed by order of Stalin after being accused of disloyalty to the government. The Committee's good name was reinstated in 1956. Among the murdered were the poets David Hofstein, Peretz Markish, Leib Kvitko, Itzik Feffer, the writer David Bergelson, and the actor Benjamin Zuskin from the Moscow State Jewish Theater (also known by its acronym, the GOSET). The actor Solomon Mikhoels, also from the GOSET, had already been murdered on January 12, 1948, in a staged car accident. In Russian, the night of the murder is called "The Night of the Executed Poets." See *Ma'ariv*, March 16, 1952, 2.

in the competition with all the actors, directors, stage workers, etc., on the condition that all those involved in the play be up to the age of twenty-nine,[10] including the director and stage workers. Even Hanna Rieber, the actress who played Anne Frank's mother, was younger than twenty-nine.[11] The play was such a sensation and I received a national first prize. It made a big difference because antisemitism was always under the surface and suddenly, the Jewish actress who performs in Yiddish wins first place. Then, when the immigration to Israel began, the Yiddish theater in Iași was closed and a whole group from the theater ended up in prison. There was a Jew who paid money to free them and they all made *Aliyah* (immigrated) to Israel with the mass immigration from Romania. There were about 400,000 people. But until the communists closed the theater and the mess began, we all played at the state theaters in Iași and Bucharest. Romanian society knew that there was a Yiddish theater and the Romanian actors liked to come to see us because the Yiddish actors knew how to do drama, comedy, and musicals—everything.

Theatrical Education of Yiddish Actors

Yaniv: Let's focus on this for a moment. What special skills did the Jewish actors in Romania have? When you say both comedy and drama, were they different from those of the Romanian actors?

Lea: Yes. It was definitely different. With the Romanians, a dramatic actor only did dramas, a comical actor only did comedies. They did not use all the disciplines. Studying there was different.

Yaniv: What wasn't the same?

Lea: Today, students study differently. Then, the study was classical, a little Stanislavski, a little Reinhardt, a little French farce. But in the Jewish theater, also because of the language, expression was more round, not square, and actors specialized in different genres. Now that I think about it with you, the language did it

---

10   Lea emphasizes that the maximum age was only twenty-nine, although, in an article about it in the *LaMerhav* newspaper (May 26, 1966, 3), it was written that the competition was open to actors and creators up to the age of thirty-five.
11   The actress Hanna Rieber, born on January 28, 1927, was twenty-nine during rehearsals in 1956, although it is possible that the date of birth listed on her identity card is not accurate.

too. If you make a 'spicy' joke in Yiddish, the timing is different, the music is different. No other languages have it. Yiddish has it and it's hard to spot it in Russian or Polish. Maybe in languages that are developed from Latin, like English or Romanian, you can recognize it; they have the musicality, but it's not like Yiddish. And when an actor speaks Yiddish, the joke comes out better. Better and easier.

Yaniv: I imagine there were Yiddish actors without comedic talent. Is that true? Does the fact that they were acting in Yiddish allow them to learn to be comedians?

Lea: No. No! If he's not funny, then he's not funny. When someone isn't funny, he won't become funny, not in Yiddish, not in Russian, not in Polish, and not in Hebrew. "You can't do comedy with a face of a funeral." (*Mit a levayeh punem ken men nisht makhn komedye.*) In which other language is there such a saying, "The face of a funeral?"

Yaniv: That's exactly the point. It's the culture that is at the base of the language. There is meaning and weight to each and every word. It is interesting that in Hebrew, from which the word *levayeh* (funeral) comes, we do not have such an expression.

Lea: Say "a face of a funeral" in Hebrew and it won't be funny. Hebrew is a difficult language. It is not a language for theater. That's why they say in Yiddish that Hebrew is a good language only for funerals.

What about Talent?

Yaniv: I understand that, in your eyes, Yiddish has an advantage on stage, but what about the actual theater studies? You once told me that Konstantin Stanislavski was one of your teachers, but we mustn't forget that there were other theater teachers with different methods.

Lea: Stanislavski was lucky to have many talented students, especially those who quoted him. They had a talent for acting and he taught them. His method is for those who already have talent. It's the same in all professions; if you have talent, this is a good method.

Yaniv: So, what did the studies give you if you say that what is actually needed is talent and the studies don't add up?

Lea: No, no, studies give you a lot. You study the history of theater, you learn about the theater, not just practical studies. You have to learn about the development of theater, you have to learn how you approach playing a character, how to behave, how to work on a character, but everything also depends on what you have in advance. To walk well on stage, you need good coordination, to say something interesting, you need to have a voice, and, if you have neither a voice nor coordination, it won't work. There has to be something that will work in the first place. Look, you come to the theater, you see so many actors. You see an actor getting off the stage and an actor staying on it. In Yiddish theater, they used to say, "An actor who crosses the ramp" (*iberr der rampeh*), an actor who does what he does crossing the stage into the theater hall and touching the audience. There are actors who do everything well, according to the book, but it still doesn't work. And that's because of talent! There's nothing you can do about it; talent and grace are a must. Grace and radiance are a big thing. There are actors who don't have it. Here in Israel, they don't really know what grace and radiance are. They don't really understand what 'sex appeal' is. Here, they think that someone with sex appeal is someone who weighs fifty-five kilograms and has an hourglass figure. That's not sex appeal!

Yaniv: So, what is sex appeal in your eyes?

Lea: In my eyes, she can be a fat woman, but her face exudes charm, she attracts you. Here, they bring a beautiful girl and that's it. For example, in the show *Behind the Fence*, the two guys who take turns in the main role of Noah, Gal Goldstein and Ala Dakka, are actors who cross that boundary and really reach the audience.

A Mother's Review of the Game

Yaniv: Let's go back to the moment when you decided to become an actress. Were you pushed into becoming an actress when you were at home?

Lea: Definitely not. I was supposed to study philology[12] at the University of Bucharest.

---

12 Philology is derived from the Greek terms φίλος (love) and λόγος (word, reason) and literally means a love of words. It is the study of language in literary sources and is a combination of literary studies, history, and linguistics. *World History Encyclopedia*.

Yaniv: And when you saw the movie *Manasse* in which your father, Yosef Kamien, acts, it didn't do anything to you?

Lea: I was very excited. Very!

Yaniv: Did you see any resemblance between the two of you?

Lea: Yesterday, I happened to look at his picture, which is in my TV room. In recent years, I have seen a resemblance between me and my mother, but sometimes, I can also see the resemblance between me and my father. Yesterday, when I looked at the picture, I don't know what happened, but suddenly I saw it. When I was young, I was very similar to my father and even more similar to his brother, the actor Alex Stein. I met Alex during World War II. He was in Novosibirsk (in the Soviet Union) and I was traveling with my mother. He told me that he had seen me in the theater and said that I looked a lot like my father. I didn't see Dad on stage before his leg was amputated, when he acted in large, complex roles, and when I saw the movie and saw how he acted, I realized that there are many things I have from him. My sense of humor, for example, is similar to his.

Yaniv: And how does it make you feel?

Lea: It makes me miss him and also makes me sad that he was not with me as a child. It makes me even sadder that he didn't know what would become of me. My mother, at least, enjoyed me although she never complimented me. Only once did she compliment me, I must tell you. There were several actors in the theater in Bucharest. Among them was an actor named Fischler and his wife, Sonya Gorman, who was the daughter of a very well-known cantor in Czernowitz. She also had a very beautiful voice, but she couldn't sing. She started acting at the same time I did. I started in the theater in small roles. I loved everything. The desire for the theater only started when I began to act. Before that, I wasn't attracted to it at all.

Yaniv: How could that be?

Lea: I don't know. They didn't raise me into it. They never let me sing or act, even though I sang during the war in the Soviet Union, but mother never said, "The girl is very talented." My mother didn't want to. She was afraid I would be a bad actress.

Yaniv: Didn't she see your talent?

Lea: She only saw my talent when I auditioned in front of her. Maybe she saw my talent first, but she did not encourage it and did not discover it.

Yaniv: During the war, when you were singing, was it professionally?

Lea: No. It was at home and my mother did not encourage this talent of mine.

Yaniv: Let's go back to the compliment your mother gave you.

Lea: I was playing Anne Frank in the theater at the time and in the morning, there was a general rehearsal. My mother was on the artistic committee of the theater, but she didn't say anything to me. And in the evening, we had something to drink together. We had been in different plays and I went into her make-up room—we were in separate rooms—and I asked her how I was when she saw me in the morning. She told me it was fine, you were fine. Sonya Gorman, who played Mrs. Van Daan—yes, she had started to act—said about me, "*Zi is a feyek meidl.*" (She is a talented girl.) So, my mother immediately answered her, "*Sonichka, zi is nisht a feyek meidl, zi is a gitte aktrise!*" (Sonichka, she is not a talented girl, she is a good actress!)

Yaniv: And you remember it to this day.

Lea: Sure, it did me a lot of good. If my mother said I'm a good actress, then that's huge! It was important! My mother was not generous with compliments. Everything was in moderation, so every compliment was very significant. When my mother wanted to describe Sonya, she would say, "Sonya sings and acts like a lady. The man comes home from work, his wife gives him his robe and slippers, he sits down on the armchair next to the lit fireplace, she brings him a cup of coffee and then sits down at the piano and sings him a song. But what does this have to do with the theater or talent . . . ?" She was a very elegant actress though . . .

Criticism of Acting Today

Yaniv: Your mother told you that you are a good actress and it makes you feel good to this day. When you read criticism, how does it affect you?

Lea: At first, every criticism would give me heart palpitations. I have to admit, even today after so many years of work, I still like to have good reviews. But I no longer have palpitations. The fact that they wrote a good review about me in *King Lear* made me very happy. Look, I am nearing the end of my work, I haven't just started so, for example, a challenge as heavy as Lear, at my age, it makes it very pleasant. It brings excitement, but everything is in proportion.

Yaniv: Do you need a review today or do you know better than the reviewer how your performance was?

Lea: Even today, I respect the criticism. I think criticism is a good thing. It's a good thing that you don't become narcissistic because that's a catastrophe, and even at my age, I really consider what they say. Criticism is a good thing, even at my age. And when there is bad criticism, it hurts, but we overcome it. What can we do? It's not pleasant, but at my age, it's no longer a matter of life and death. Thank God, I get so much love from the audience, who love me even with the mistakes that I make in Hebrew. And if the audience still loves me, then I really have nothing to complain about.

Chapter 2

World War II—From Czernowitz (Chernivtsi) to Samarkand

Yaniv: You were born in Poland. When did you move to Czernowitz in Romania?

Lea: We ... look, there was a crisis in the family. My father started to suffer a lot with his leg. I still don't know exactly what happened, but, apparently, he had a problem with his veins and so he stayed. I'm not sure about it, but the Vilna Troupe broke up[1] and our financial situation was very difficult. You have to understand that this was a private theater and there was no one to finance it. I don't remember the details and I never asked. There were also issues between my parents. My father's suffering continued greatly and, at a certain point, his leg had to be amputated, although it was amputated in stages. During this time, my mother had to look after me and my grandmother and then she received an invitation from a theater in Czernowitz because she was very loved there. I don't remember what year it was, but it was between 1935 and 1939. When my father's leg was amputated, he was in Vienna and he blamed my mother for leaving him alone; it created huge problems between them. But she had no choice, she had to support her child and her mother. There were many issues. Traveling was also complicated and visas and work permits were needed. In short, my mother went alone once and came back, and then she went there again and took me and my grandma with her. My parents never officially got divorced. They met in Czernowitz in 1926 and that's where they got married (while my father was

---

1 Since the success of the show *The Dybbuk*, the Vilna Troupe had suffered a crisis. The audience wanted to see *The Dybbuk* again and again and refused to accept other plays. Despite rare successes such as *At Night in the Old Market* by I. L. Peretz; *Kiddush Hashem* by Sholem Asch in 1928 starring Yosef Kamien and Alex Stein in the roles of Mandel and the tailor, Yerman, respectively; and later *Hershel of Ostropol* by Moshe Lifshitz (Livshitz) starring Yosef Kamien in 1930, success did not lighten their mood. The Vilna Troupe disbanded and regrouped again and again. For more, see: Ezra Lahad, "The Vilna Troupe is Seventy" [Hebrew], *Bama* 111 (1988): 5–29. In 1932, Yosef Kamien left the troupe and moved to Romania to act on the Romanian stage. He then returned to Poland and even played in the program *Nadir un Vayin Nischt* (Take it and don't cry) with the duo of Shimon Dzigan and Israel Schumacher.

on tour and filming the movie *Manasse*²). Hirshl saw my father in a show. He was already out of practice, but they said it was an outstanding performance. Hirshl always said he fell in love with me when he saw me riding in a carriage with my father in Czernowitz on the bridge on School Street. (To this day, the street is called School Street, Shkolna in Ukrainian. In Yiddish it was known as Schule Gas.) My mother moved to Czernowitz and started acting. My father came to perform and also to see me and that was the last time we met because right after that, the war broke out. My mother had been invited to performances throughout Romania. When the Soviets came, they built two theaters, one in Chișinău and one in Czernowitz, and my mother went to the theater in Chișinău. Isak Havis was also performing at this theater and he fell in love with my mother, but they got married only after my father died. One day, Havis was invited to Odesa. The Jews were always in favor of the Soviet regime because, with the Soviets, everyone was the same and there was no discrimination against the Jews. Everyone, including my mother, was 'left wing.' They invited Havis to sing at the Odesa Opera. He had a beautiful voice and was always well dressed. He stayed at the London Hotel on the promenade³ and he came to the rehearsal. There was a very good singer on stage. Suddenly, he saw people running and asked where they were all going. It turned out that the production team had brought sandwiches… the singer and all the important people ran to the buffet. They got their food and all the art no longer interested them… He was shocked that the food was more important than the art. Two weeks later, he said he couldn't get used to it and he returned to Chișinău. My mother was also invited to Odesa. She was a very elegant woman and people chased her down the street… She performed at the

---

2 Manasse is a dramatic play written by Ronetti Roman (born Aron Blumenfeld, 1853–1908), which was published in 1900 and was later translated into Yiddish by Jacob Sternberg. It is a four-act drama dealing with religious intolerance against the backdrop of a love story between a Romanian Christian named Matei Frunza and an Orthodox Jewish woman, Lelia, the granddaughter of Manasse Cohanovici (Cohen). In 1925, the play was turned into a film. The screenplay, written by Scarlett Frode and directed by Jean Mihail, was shot as a motion picture in Romania with Romanian actors. Yosef Kamien, who was in Romania as part of the Vilna Troupe, was invited to act in it and played the role of Zelig Sor, a Jewish agent full of folk humor. After the film was released, public controversy erupted regarding its message. "Manasse," IMDB, https://www.imdb.com/title/tt0016084; Tudor 1963; Jean Mihail, Filmul românesc de altădată (Bucharest: Meridiane, 1963); Tudor Caranfil, Fragment din istoria cinematografiei în capodopere, Vîrstele peliculei, vol. 2 (Iași: Polirom, 2009), 456–458.
3 Nikolaevsky Boulevard, today Primorsky Boulevard, near the famous Odesa Steps (Potemkin Stairs).

Opera Theater in Odesa. In Odesa, there was a Jewish theater with very good actors and there she met the actor Jacob Mansdorf, who was with her in the Vilna Troupe. Meanwhile, he had founded the theater in Chișinău.

Yaniv: The Germans were getting closer.

Lea: We had to run away. It wasn't easy. We were living in Belz at the time. The heart of the theater was in Belz and most of the shows were in Chișinău. We ran away when the Nazis started to get close. They had already closed the borders in 1939. My father was in Poland and we lost contact with him. When the Soviets came and the Soviet theater started, it was a great theater and they did wonderful things with wonderful actors. At that time, there was a large audience that liked to come to the theater. During the invasion, the theater was on tour in a city near the border with Romania and they decided to send me alone, without my grandmother, to a sanatorium in the town of Karpacz in Poland.[4]

I was just a girl of nine. The war had started, but no one really understood yet. The parents came to take their children away. I was taken to Chișinău by a woman, I don't remember her name, and she took me along with her daughter, who was with me at the sanatorium. Everyone knew me as Dina Koenig's daughter. My mother walked from Karpacz to Chișinău to look for me. She walked! It's more than 1200 kilometers! Do you understand? There were endless bombings and this lady who took me went to the Ministry of Culture and told them she had taken Dina Koenig's daughter. They told my mother and my mother walked all the way, finally arriving in Chișinău. We were sitting in the basement and, during the bombings, my mother came to the basement and took me. The people were so naive; we drove back to this town instead of running away to the woods because that's where the whole ensemble was. Havis was also with us and he carried me in his arms into the forest. From there, we fled back to Chișinău by freight train, but half of Chișinău was destroyed by bombs, so we fled with everyone from there as well. We arrived in Tiraspol, Moldova. But Tiraspol was black from the bombs and they wouldn't let us stay there. We had to run very fast and they were constantly bombing. The Germans bombed trains in which they knew people were hiding. We arrived in Kharkiv and from there we drove to Samarkand.

---

4 A bathing and recreation town in the district of Jelenia Góra in the province of Lower Silesia in southwestern Poland.

Yaniv: For a girl your age, was it scary?

Lea: Horrible! My mom kept wrapping her arms around me and hugging me. We drove through the bombs. Those bombings were a terrible thing. You don't know what they did; there wasn't a single bomb that wasn't dropped. The Messerschmitt aircraft were very scary when they went on missions and came back. Imagine. I don't remember how long they occupied almost half of the Soviet Union. Do you realize how strong the Germans were? Now, when I hear that the Ukraine is being bombed, it brings back memories. It was terrible! It was a terrible war. The Germans at that time made everything dark! What saved everyone was the Russian winter, which stopped the Germans. They couldn't take it.

Yaniv: And you were already in Samarkand?

Lea: Yes, we were in Samarkand. Jews from Lithuania, from Warsaw, Poland, from all places, arrived there. I remember our first house in Samarkand. People traveled in wagons to get to Samarkand, which was divided into three parts: the part near the train station, the old city, and the new city. Some Romanians lived near the train station, and they gave us a room in which maybe ten people slept. The walls of the room we were in were made of clay and the floor was sand. Mother asked the woman how to clean it and she told her, "Take a pot or a bucket and collect horse excrement from the street, put sand in it and spread it on the floor." You think my mother didn't do it? Damn right, she did it. She and another actress took the excrement and did what they needed to do. An epidemic of typhoid immediately began and lice transmitted the disease. In Samarkand, they immediately started looking to earn a living. There was a park there and there were all kinds of small stages on which they performed. My mother and other actresses went to the Ministry of Culture and got permission to perform and they immediately started putting on plays in Yiddish. And people came to see them! People were dying in the streets and simultaneously, people went to the theater. Do you understand what happened in the war?

Yaniv: How did they feel about performing in the theater under such circumstances?

Lea: They knew they had to survive. They performed to survive. They also formed groups and went to other places. The power to live is so strong that they immediately and instinctively got together and performed in theaters. And people went to watch because they needed it for normality. I really wanted to go back to Samarkand.⁵

From this room, which had ten people in it, people slowly left because they had rented other rooms. We lived with Uzbeks. The Bukharans didn't like us and didn't rent rooms, but the Uzbeks did. My mother fell ill with typhoid. The room we lived in had no closets; there were only alcoves in the wall. My mother was very sick and I had seen that people who were taken to the hospital died and never came back. I promised myself I wouldn't let her be taken to hospital. I was ten, maybe eleven. There was a young doctor in Samarkand named Dr. Kogan and he wanted to hospitalize her. I told him I didn't agree. You don't know what power children have. I said no! So he asked me, "How will you treat her?" I said, "I don't want her to go to hospital." And I took care of her. She was unconscious for a week. I slept in an alcove in the wall and my mother slept in the bed. Dr. Kogan would come by every now and then to check what was going on. In a hospital, they would catch a cold and die of pneumonia, not typhoid. You can recover from typhoid, if you are young. When my mother woke up, she asked who had taken care of me? I said, "Me" and my mother burst into tears. I will not forget that cry. She suddenly realized that if she had gone, I would have remained a child without anyone. Listen, these are memories that can't be explained.⁶

Yaniv: How did you really take care of her? You would've had to bring food for the week.

Lea: My mother couldn't eat. She was unconscious. I stood in line for the distribution of bread and they gave me four hundred grams of bread a day. I was a healthy girl. I still remember the address of the house: 12 Vostochnyi Tupik (Eastern Dead End). I've been told that it still exists. I didn't have a childhood; my childhood was gone. Maybe that's why I have so many toys at home now. Who had time for a birthday? Who even knew what a birthday was? Then my mother recovered. It had taken place in the summer and then I went to school in Samarkand. The Soviets had schools. The Soviets had order. Then Havis

---

5   In October 2019, Lea finally had the chance to go back to Samarkand at the invitation of the Israeli Embassy in Uzbekistan and visited the districts where she had stayed during World War II.
6   Lea says that, after the war, Dr. Kogan came to Israel and opened a clinic near the corner of Rothschild Avenue and Ben Zion Boulevard in Tel Aviv and someone had come in and killed him. She believed that he had probably given someone an abortion or something and had been killed for it.

started courting my mother. He had been exempted from service in the military because the Soviets decided to gather artists from all the occupied territories and form troupes.

Yaniv: During the war, is that what interested them?

Lea: During the war, they did it all! You know, the art didn't stop there for a day inside that horrible place. Havis knew Russian well and the Soviets liked light music and large troupes of folk art. So from Bessarabia they formed a big troupe of singers and dancers, and there was also jazz. There were performances by a band of musicians and there was always a sketch as well as singers and dancers. There were troupes from Latvia, Lithuania, Estonia, Serbia, and more. Isak invited my mother to be in the troupe from Bessarabia and so we joined. The troupe traveled for two years all over the Soviet Union from end to end. We went to Novosibirsk, Ufa (in the Republic of Bashkortostan), Arkhangelsk, Moscow, and more.

Yaniv: What did the repertoire include?

Lea: There were a couple of classical dancers and tap dancers. Havis was the director and also the singer, always doing sketches and telling jokes.

Yaniv: In Yiddish or Russian?

Lea: Everything was in Russian. After two years, my mother said enough is enough, the girl needs to go to school, and we returned to Tashkent. There, my mother joined Yiddish troupes. She was in a troupe with the actor Jacob Mansdorf. Before the war, they were the young actors of the Vilna Troupe. They appeared with the same kind of program: a sketch, jokes, a song, light content. They traveled from city to city, so it was impossible to present complex content with complicated decor. Sometimes, they performed Goldoni's *Mirandolina*. That's how people survived. That was until the Russian army started traveling back. It lasted four years and my mother was already with Havis, who continued with the troupe until Vladivostok. Then his troupe followed the Russian army and he reached Iași. In Iași, the streets were still burning and there were Jews who were baking bagels in the streets. A baker asked if there was anyone who knew Dina Koenig because her mother was in the hospital. My grandmother had survived! They had taken her out of the house in Belz with a bag and a coat and put her on a train. She didn't know

Romanian and they wanted to move her. In Iași, eight elderly people were taken off the train, including my grandmother. The Romanians were not like the Poles. They were a little gentler. They were also confused by the war and they took her to the Jewish hospital. Throughout the war, they had kept her in the hospital and that's how she survived. Havis wrote my mother a letter letting her know that my grandmother was alive.

Yaniv: Why didn't she run away with you?

Lea: She couldn't run away. She was an old woman and it all happened so fast, we didn't have enough time. You can't imagine; there was a *blitzkrieg* (a surprise attack), it was a *blitzkrieg*. We returned to Chișinău via Moscow; it wasn't so fast, don't think it was, and, when we arrived in Chișinău, they brought my grandmother to us.

Bucharest—I'm Becoming an Actress

Yaniv: So, the war was over. What were you and your mother doing?

Lea: Then a new story began. People wanted to escape from the Soviets. Things like this always happen in wars. They said that from Czernowitz you could cross the border into Romania. Many Jews went back to Poland, many through Romania; some stopped there or went to the displaced persons camps in Europe. But since it was difficult to travel with my grandmother, we stayed in Czernowitz. Within a few months, Romania became communist so we decided to leave. We got stuck in Bucharest because we needed documents to cross the border and we didn't have them. In Bucharest, the Jewish actors had this ability to rebuild quickly and they formed acting troupes, good ones, very fast. The communists believed that art was the most powerful type of propaganda, so they encouraged it. They built state theaters. They built two Yiddish theaters. One was in Bucharest in 1948, where the older performers were, and one was in Iași, where the younger performers were. Can you imagine who the actors were? Can you imagine what these people had been through during all these years of war? Sevilla Pastor was an excellent actress and during the war, she was in Transnistria. After the war, she crossed the border to Czernowitz and from there to Bucharest. There were many like her and these people, who came from hell, immediately built a theater. That is the power of art!

Yaniv: So your mother performed in the theater and you went to school in Bucharest?

Lea: I had finished school already in Chisinau. Like all young people, I wanted to work a little. Before the war, when I was brought to Czernowitz as a little girl, it was not acceptable to be housed in a hotel, so we stayed with my mother's acquaintances in Russian Street. I didn't speak German, which was spoken in Czernowitz. I only knew Polish and Yiddish and I was lonely. Then a young girl came to the window and asked me in Yiddish, "*Maidele, du wilst zich mit mir shpillen?*"[7] (Little girl, do you want to play with me?) After the war, when I arrived in Bucharest, someone told me that a friend of mine[8] was working at a branch of The Joint (American Jewish Joint Distribution Committee). I still didn't know what I wanted to do, so I started to work there too. Mother and Havis asked me, "Where do you want to study? The doors are wide open for you." But then Hirshl arrived and started working in the theater. We started traveling together and he convinced me that I had talent. I had nothing to talk to him about; at that time, children didn't chat as they do today. So I recited Pushkin's poems to him. Today, a sixteen- or seventeen-year-old girl is smarter than I was. They know everything.

Hirshl was in the Vapniarka Concentration Camp[9] and later he joined the partisans. He then enlisted in the Russian army and came with them almost to Berlin. He drove me crazy about auditioning to become part of the theater, but my mother told me to do the audition at her place. She wanted to see if I was good enough. She said that my father was a good actor and she is a good actress and, if I am not good enough, it would be a great shame for them. By the way, I'm not sure if I would have been successful at an official audition in the theater. I'm not very good at auditions.

Yaniv: What happened to you at the audition?

Lea: I clammed up. Today, actors are so used to them that they even like to go to them. Back then, I didn't know what an audition even was. Today, I say, "Audition?

---

7   The girl turned out to be Lea's classmate from before the war. Most of their friends had disappeared during the war.
8   The friend lived in Chernivtsi almost all her life until she went to Miami.
9   Vapniarka is a town in the Vinnytsia Oblast region of Ukraine, Northern Transnistria. In October 1941, the Romanians established a concentration camp in Vapniarka under the control of the Nazis and the Romanians.

No big deal." My mother wanted to see if I had something she could discover. Something natural. I didn't know what it meant to prepare for an audition.

Yaniv: So, what did you do? Did you just learn by heart?

Lea: I learned by heart Sholem Aleichem's *"Mir is gut, ikh bin a yosem"* (It's good for me to be an orphan) from *Motl, Peysi the Cantor's Son*. It wasn't difficult for me, so I learned it by heart in one glance. I stood in the living room and recited the passage while my mother sat and rested her head on her palm; that's how she always sat and watched me. And Havis said, "Why does she need it? They will say that she has fat legs, that she has a long nose, they will criticize her, it's a difficult profession." And my mother looked at me and said, "That's right, she has a long nose, she's a little fat, and has big calves." I was a 'healthy' girl then. "But she has something that will reach the end of the auditorium. She has *chain* (charisma), she'll capture the whole auditorium. She is one of the great ones with a good understanding of the theater." You see, today, many actors have it all, but lack the charisma that would make them unforgettable actors. You need talent and you need personality. That's where the charm comes from. Talent and personality are very important. You see actors who do everything, but don't get past the ramp. They go far, but they fail to reach the audience.

Yaniv: How do you explain that?

Lea: I think it's in every profession, not just theater. How do you explain that there is a child who goes to school and is immediately good at math? Where did it come from? A child who quickly learns to read or speak? It's a talent.

Personality and Charisma in Working on a Role

Yaniv: But how is this reflected in your work? When you get a role, how is your grace expressed? Reflected? Do you think about your character? Or your charm, which you know how to use?

Lea: No. I am not aware and do not want to be aware. People come and say to you, "I feel like I know you." There is something in me that I am not aware of, that leaves an impression on people. I don't know what it is, but I feel it. But when I do a play, I don't think about it. In the beginning, I learn how to approach the position. I read the text, what is said there, what is the place, what is the play, what is happening in the play. For example, in the role of Mrs. Shakoripinshchika in the play *Behind the Fence* by Bialik. I kept saying to myself, "It's a small role, I don't have to make an effort." When I started working on it, I said there is a woman here fighting for her existence. She has her truth and her truth is sometimes justified. I didn't put myself in the role, I suddenly remembered that in the war, I saw women like that. For example, during the war when we were in Tashkent, the houses were shared and there were neighbors and there was a wall, which was probably made of plaster, and we heard through the wall the crying of a woman whose son had fallen in the war. A simple gentile woman with a handkerchief tied on her head. I thought, there's something to it, this type of woman. Because of this, when I got to the end, I came to the realization that the woman had a huge transformation. She constantly hides her feelings, her compassion, her sensitivity, she wants to appear strong, she wants to be a Cossack (soldier), but in the end, she reveals her feelings; it turns out that she is not a Cossack in character, she's a mensch, with sorrow and with feelings. But I didn't put myself into the role.

Yaniv: When you finished *Behind the Fence*, in the production in which you participated, your role was not remembered as a small role. The roles of Noah and Marinka, the younger ones, were supposed to be the main roles. This is how the story is structured and this is how the play is structured, yet the feeling is different. I imagine it comes from your acting, which gives the role an intensity that overshadows the other roles.

Lea: I don't know how it happened. I also told you during rehearsals that it wasn't a big role. You asked me if I was working hard and I told you no, it's not a big or hard role. Tatiana[10] came to see the show and told me, "You're crazy, what do you mean it's not a good role; it's a great role." I didn't think so. I really liked Noah's role, his restlessness, the fact that he doesn't find himself until the end; he was giving up his love, he was giving up everything; he doesn't find himself either in religion or in love. It's a role you can bite into. A good actor will stand out in that role, not just act in it. A good actor will show his mental struggles in such a way that will move the audience. The two actors who played the role[11] worked very beautifully and I think they exhausted it. You have to have the personality for it.

---

10 Tatiana Canalis Olier, Habima Theater actress and acting teacher at the kibbutzim seminary.
11 Gal Goldstein and Ala Dakka played the role alternately.

Yaniv: So maybe your role was big because you brought in your personality and experience from your time during and since the war?

Lea: Definitely.

Yaniv: Where does personality come from?

Lea: You're probably born with it.

Yaniv: You are not talking about intelligence and academic studies because the war changed the world for you. You are talking about something internal that was not acquired.

Lea: The war taught me how to survive because we went through things. The war taught me that you don't have to turn everything into a drama . . . even though there were many dramas in the war . . .

Yaniv: Do you feel that the war is constantly in the background in your life?

Lea: I think the war gave me strength to survive, strength to overcome, and strength to understand. To understand life better. To know that things do not come easily. And it annoys me to see spoiled people who think they deserve everything. "I deserve to be happy." "I need . . ." I can't stand it. I've learned to survive. I don't 'deserve' anything. I don't know if this 'survival' affects my acting; it might. For example, in the play *King Lear*, I feel that I survived. I had moments when I told myself I was not normal. And what bothered me the most was that I discovered that I hadn't mastered the language. I learned the text to survive. I got over it very quickly and I'm getting better at it to this day, but it made me feel bad, it made me so nervous. Unhealthy is not good, and that also caused me to feel flat that night.[12]

Yaniv: Does it still bother you?

---

12 On August 27, 2018, Lea felt unwell in the middle of the play, right after the start of the second act of *King Lear* and just before she had to enter the stage, and was unable to act. The CEO of the theater at that time, Odelia Friedman, informed the audience that the show would not continue because of this.

Lea: No, it doesn't bother me anymore because they told me it wasn't bad. It bothered me then; I didn't like that I stopped a show in the middle. And everyone asked me for a few months after, "How do you feel?" It wasn't about feeling. I had just taken on too much. I said to myself, "Hey, Lea, calm down, you've already chosen your career; either you'll succeed or you won't." But the ambition to succeed is very strong.

There Are Small Roles and There Are Big Roles

Yaniv: When you look back today at all your roles in the theater, do you feel that you were fully in character in all of them?

Lea: When I play a role, I don't get as fully into character as you might think. The role is separate and I am separate. Then, if I somehow get into the role, it's because I love it more...

Yaniv: I thought that of all the roles you did—they were all yours and you loved them all equally. Is that not so?

Lea: I don't like to betray my role and say, "I didn't like it." I'm always asked if there are roles I like better... but, let's be honest, there are good roles and there are bad roles. It's not true that there are no small roles, only small actors. There are big roles and there are small roles, and there are also roles that you have anything to do with...

Yaniv: But you took a small role in *Behind the Fence* and turned it into a big role, you turned it into one of the most significant roles in the show, when in fact, she was an old woman and the lead is the girl who lives with her. So maybe you can take a small role and change it into a big role?

Lea: It depends on what's involved in the role. Let's be honest, it depends on what's in it. There are roles where you say, "Hello, what's up?" and that's it. There is no more to them.

Yaniv: Let's take, for example, Machle, the servant in *Mirele Efros*, a role you played alternately with Miriam Zohar. When you read the play, Machle is not an interesting role. Machle carries out Mirele Efros's instructions. She is a little afraid of her, but she also wants to be her friend. She is very loyal to her, but there is nothing very interesting about her. Nevertheless, when you and Miriam played her, you made this role something special. Miriam herself told me that she was not good in the role of Machle compared to Mirele Efros in which, in her opinion, she succeeded. You, on the other hand, created an unforgettable character as the servant, Machle. Just as an example: In the opening scene, you run around on the stage, arranging and moving the props, and, while arranging the stage, you give a long monologue at a fast pace, which begins with the words, "When the wedding is over, I will be eternally grateful . . ." Miriam, on the other hand, did this whole scene more relaxed, at a slower tempo. So how do you build a small role that doesn't have too much to it? What made you run around frantically?[13]

Lea: I think I thought about this role differently from the way Miriam thought about it. This role can be interpreted in many ways and at a different pace. You can do it slowly when Machle is miserable and feels sorry for herself, "I wish everything would be over and we could get rid of this trouble," but I didn't want to do it that way. There are also other types of servants. I had a servant who used to work very fast at home. Today, I have one who does everything slowly. The previous one would wipe in an instant, and the one I have today takes more time; wipes and then puts everything back gently and carefully. Their internal rhythm is different. You decide about the role, what this inner rhythm will be. Machle, in my opinion, ran around. She wanted to help, she wanted to be more efficient, and she is also nervous, and you have to, when you're developing a role, think about how you're going to develop the person. It is also important to remember what I am talking about in the text. How do you want to present the play? It's very important.

Yaniv: When there are two of you playing the same role (double-casting), don't you develop the same role?

Lea: It can never be the same. I once told the doctor that I have a runny nose like hers and he told me there is no such thing, it can never be like hers; everyone

---

13 The play *Mirele Efros* opens with the arrival of Mirele and her family, with all the servants and helpers, to the town of Slutsk, where the family of Yosele and Mirele's daughter-in-law lives with their son. Machle opens the show by arranging all the furniture and tools that Mirele brought from home in the Slutsk hostel room. While arranging the objects, Machle tells the audience the background to what is about to happen when the families, who are very different in character, meet. This difference will, of course, lead to friction and conflict that will drive the plot. Machle's monologue acts as the explanation of the play.

has his own illness. The human being is built like that. It doesn't have to be the same here either because the approach is different and if you do it the same, it's an imitation and it doesn't always turn out well.

Yaniv: When you develop the role, it shouldn't be an imitation, but when you have the same role, the actors have to perform an evening with you and an evening with her. If you are very different, then how can the other actors act? I guess the scenes are the same otherwise the actors wouldn't know where to go and there would be a complete mess on stage.

Lea: The rhythm mustn't be changed either. This is very important. If you play Mirele Efros and the servant says, "Mirele, go to sleep," whether you're begging or commanding strictly, it matters to Mirele. Theater is built on action and reaction. Mirele's reaction will be different in each case. And if you change every night, you can't get used to the different rhythms. And so, the timing needs to be the same. You try to create similarities in the performances of the two actors, but you don't imitate.

Yaniv: But the fact is that it didn't turn out the same like in the example I gave you earlier with the pace of moving the props in the opening scene or, even more prominently, in the role of Mirele Efros herself. In the most significant monologue in the play, where Mirele transfers the property to her children, when you shouted to them, "Out!" this word shocked them, so there was a pause in which everyone froze for a few seconds. It's not an artificial freeze, but it comes from the shock they got from you. But if the other actor doesn't get it, then it looks artificial, so both of you have to be careful about that ability. The actors are the same actors, the scenes are the same scenes, and yet these are two completely different Mirele Efroses. Miriam Zohar's Mirele Efros was more of a lady, while yours was a stronger and more temperamental woman, which therefore also shook my soul more.

Lea: Each one of us comes with her own personality. Miriam Zohar played the role according to her personality. She is very elegant in life and she brought that to the stage. I brought my personality to the stage. You can like or dislike what each of us has done, but this is how you work on a role.

Chapter 3

Father and Stepfather

Yaniv: There is something that I have always noticed, and it is very noticeable to me in our conversations. When you talk about your biological father, Yosef Kamien, you call him 'my father,' and when you talk about Isak Havis, your stepfather, who after all is the one who raised you and lived with you for more years than your biological father, you call him 'Havis' or 'my stepfather,' even though you make sure to say you don't like the word 'stepfather.' Why don't you call Havis 'father'?

Lea: I think it's in honor of my father, even though maybe I should have had complaints against him, but I don't blame him. The outbreak of World War II was a very difficult time and he cannot be blamed for what happened. But somewhere, it pains me that he didn't have time to see me and I didn't have time to see him. There is some feeling inside me, which may be a very deep pain and maybe anger towards him. Sometimes I ask myself, "Why wasn't he interested in me? Why wasn't he as passionate about me as my mother was?" Havis was a beautiful young man and he fell in love with her and she gave him a child during the war, and after the war, in addition to me, he also got her mother. He got both of us and he accepted us.

Yaniv: He treated you like a daughter?

Lea: All the time. He treated me very well.

Yaniv: And at home, what would you call him?

Lea: Yesia.

Yaniv: Not father?

Lea: No.

Yaniv: And your mother?

Lea: Mama ("mother" in Yiddish). My mother has always been Mama. But I called my stepfather Yesia. I don't know why. Sometimes I would make fun and I would call him Dad. When I met people, I would call him Dad and people would say, "You look a lot like him," and we would laugh. But he was always interested in me and made sure I succeeded. He always asked me if I already knew the role. He was still alive when I received the Israel Award. Actually, he came here because of me. He had no reason but me. And he didn't do well here.

Yaniv: And yet, of all the Yiddish actors, Shmulik Atzmon chose Havis when he opened the Yiddishspiel Theater (The Yiddish Theater in Israel) and refused to accept many of the other Yiddish actors who played in Israel.[1]

Lea: Because he was the most interesting and had knowledge of the Yiddish repertoire. He was a good theater actor; watch his filmed segments. There is a segment he did at an EMI (Union of Israeli Artists) event called *Men Khapt* (Kidnappers). He knew Hebrew from home and they wanted him to come to Habima, but he was a man who was always afraid of not having enough money. He always wanted to have spare change in his pocket. He was afraid of a situation where he wouldn't have money, so he went into Yiddish theater because that's where they made money. He had been at Habima Theater for a short time and before that, had acted in *The Back Street*, but then he decided to join the Yiddish theater. He regretted leaving the theater in Romania. He was a lead actor there. A lot of people were disappointed. For example, the actress Hanna Rieber's husband, who always played the lovers in the Yiddish theater in Romania, couldn't find work here as an actor so he had to go through professional retraining and worked in the national phone company. The theater in Israel was not for him. In the end, he was killed in a car accident. Hanna Rieber also suffered from not being cast. She did several films

---

1 When Shmuel (Shmulik) Atzmon-Wircer founded the Yiddishspiel Theater (Yiddish Theater in Israel), he took Yiddish-speaking actors who had acted in the Hebrew theater and refused to take Yiddish actors from the private theaters that were active in Israel at the time, with the exception of Yankele Alperin and Isak Havis (who mainly served as a consultant.) Only later did he begin to take Yiddish actors *ad hoc* for certain plays or for longer periods. The first performance of the Yiddishspiel Theater was *Shver tsu Zayn a Yid* (It's hard to be a Jew) by Sholem Aleichem, starring Yankele Alperin, Israel Becker, Raphael Goldwasser, Yasha Gilinsky, Avraham Horowitz, Isak Havis, Yehudit Yanai, Avraham Naimark, Laura Sahar, and Ethel Kuvenska.

and was constantly working, but was very unhappy. Always with *a levayeh punem* (face for a funeral).

Zvi (Hirshl)

Yaniv: How did your parents accept Zvi? Did they want you to date an actor?

Lea: When they brought Zvi to the theater in Bucharest—he was a handsome guy—I hadn't been to the theater yet and he invited me for a walk. He had recently left the army and had learned to drink and go wild like all twenty-five-, twenty-six-year-olds after the army. When Zvi and I started dating, my mother and Havis were very afraid and they were not happy about the match. Also, in the theater, they didn't like the relationship, and at a certain point, they wouldn't let me go with him. But we were in love. My mother and Havis did not understand that instead of being against him, it was better to accept him, to be nice. They were against him all the way; so was everyone at the theater. So I married him without them. I did a very difficult thing. They thought I was pregnant, but I wasn't. I just went with him and we got married in the town hall. And instead of taking and nurturing him, they were constantly against him. Zvika was sometimes right in his anger towards them. I really don't like to talk about it.

When I married him, Sevilla Pastor said, "I will bless you after two years, if you are still together..." Everyone had some idiotic objection to my marriage with Hirshl instead of cultivating the love of two young people. The fact is that my mother, who was a clever woman, after the first year we were married, saw him on the street with flowers in his hand and a string of onions around his neck and then she said he would be a good husband. A husband who brings his wife food and flowers will be a good husband. But at the beginning, both of them were against him. He suffered because of it and I suffered from it too. Today, I don't blame them because times were different back then. Sometimes I wish I was born several years later... Nowadays, the whole attitude towards young couples is different. For example, I remember the actor Israel Rubinchik... his daughter was in high school and she was sleeping with her boyfriend. Her parents said they would rather they slept at their house so they knew where the two of them were than if they ran away and the parents didn't know where they were. The approach today is different. The approach to children today is very different.

Why I Don't Have Children

Yaniv: If you're already talking about a different approach to children, didn't your mother ever ask you, "What about children?"

Lea: My mother was very scared. I think my mom had the . . . look, the mentality regarding children in Europe was completely different. They didn't have many children; the practical conditions in Romania at that time were difficult. You don't have a child if you don't have wood for heating to keep warm or you don't have milk. I was very young and she didn't push me to have children. I think what she went through during my childhood was very hard. The Vilna Troupe had disbanded and there was no income. There were times when I didn't have a coat for the winter. So she didn't push me to have children. It's difficult to understand this with the Israeli mentality.

Yaniv: It's hard to understand because your mother, after all, came from a Jewish environment where it was important to have children.

Lea: No. she didn't. Her grandparents were from Łódź. My grandfather worked at Adler's Theater, a very advanced theater. Łódź was a big city and had a European mentality and not a *shtetl* (small town) mentality. In the *shtetl*, people used to have many children, but in the big cities, they had one or two children max. Because of the mentality, it was not enough to have children; you also needed to be able to raise them and provide them with good living conditions. My grandmother had three children. My mother and her two brothers.

Yaniv: What happened to the two boys?

Lea: During World War I, my grandmother took her older son to the German border and threw him across the border. She grabbed her head in sorrow, and her hair came out in her hand from the stress. She never saw him again. We have been in correspondence with him all these years. He has two children. He was a communist. When I was already in Israel and I wrote to him that I was in Israel, he wrote to me to ask how I could leave the communist regime. That's when I stopped corresponding with him. I said the man is alive in another world. The second son was killed in Poland and we never knew where.

Yaniv: At a later stage when you were already established, didn't you want a child? And Hirshl's mother? Didn't she ask him, "What about children?"

Lea: Hirshl was also an only child.

Yaniv: So, she still had one son.

Lea: The whole time, we were in survival mode. We came here, we wanted to learn, to survive, then we wanted to travel the world. When we got back, it was already too late. We didn't have the mentality to have a child. One day, we were sitting on the beach and saw a father running after his child, and Hirshl said to me, "Look, I can't run after kids anymore." And then, when he was sick and we were in the hospital, and next to us, there was a big family, Hirshl said to me, "Maybe we made a mistake by not having children." Look, there's a mentality today that people should have a lot of kids. Sometimes, it seems to me that people have children because that's the way it is. But look at the results. You also have to raise the child. In Europe, to this day, they do not give birth to many children.

Yaniv: I thought it was different with Jews?

Lea: Depends on which Jews. The Jews in our area did not have many children.

Yaniv: And you didn't have moments when you wanted a child?

Lea: There were.

Yaniv: Because the stories that are told about you in interviews, and also by friends, say that you had eleven abortions.

Lea: This is true. I had eleven abortions; the last one was in Israel.

Yaniv: Ten in Romania?

Lea: Yes. Only one in Israel.

Yaniv: How does a doctor agree to perform ten abortions?

Lea: Ask the women who came from Romania. They all had abortions. Abortions were done often there! The conditions were such that you didn't want many children. Each person had a different reason. I was very young and we wanted to travel. And with a child, you can't travel so easily. I believe that everyone has their destiny from above. The truth is that sometimes you say, "It's a shame I don't have children," and sometimes you say, "Look at that child. Is this how a child behaves towards its parents?" Recently, I read in the newspaper that a baby was thrown in the trash and had been found. Wouldn't it be better to have an abortion? What is this, throwing away a child? At least my embryos didn't grow. Even the doctors in Romania did not tell women in Romania not to have an abortion. They wanted to make money.

Yaniv: It surprises me that in Israel they are not willing to perform so many abortions on a woman and many fear that the woman would not be able to get pregnant again, and there they did it without blinking, and you say they did it eleven times.

Lea: Right. We were young and healthy. Maybe I really made a mistake. Sometimes I think there is a God in heaven and maybe He decided that Lea would not have children. Maybe He said, "Lea, you're not . . . you will be left alone."

Yaniv: Even without children, you are never alone.

Lea: Sometimes I think, "Who knows what could have been, who knows if my child would've been a good boy?"

Yaniv: And maybe you could have had a talented little girl like her mother?

Lea: Who knows? My mother was so afraid of these inheritances. The fact is that there were many actors who had children and the children did not have the talent of their parents. And besides, there are also actors that had parents who weren't such good actors and their children are not such good actors either . . .

Chapter 4

Playing Anne Frank and Holocaust Remembrance

Yaniv: Let's talk about the role you developed at the beginning of your career to understand how you develop roles. One of the most significant roles of your career in Romania was Anne Frank. When you played Anne Frank, it was in 1957. You were a twenty-seven-year-old woman and you had to play a twelve-year-old girl. The experiences she described, the fear that the Germans would find them... is that the same fear you had during the bombings? Or did you not think about that at all?

Lea: I didn't want to play her because I was already a young, married, 'healthy' woman, and I said, "You guys are crazy. How am I going to play her?" I cried and said I didn't want to do it. But it was a national competition. They said, "We will only do the play with you." There were other sweet little actresses, but they wanted me. When we read the play, Zvika was not in the reading. When I came home, he asked me how the play was and I told him, "Look, the play...," and I couldn't speak. I started crying from excitement about the play. It was a big sensation. I didn't think about my fear. I thought then about the fate of the children at the time of the war. What the children went through.

Yaniv: You were also a child in the war.

Lea: Yes, but then I wasn't as aware as I am today. Apparently, this fear, which I was not aware of, came out on stage as well. Although her fear doesn't come out in the play. She speaks optimistically. She is very optimistic. The role is not structured melodramatically, it is structured as a child sees things.

Yaniv: How did they turn you into a girl?

Lea: The clothing. They made me a child's dress. The sleeves started in the middle of the shoulder to obscure the size of my body. I had a corset around my chest that squashed it. Girly shoes with a button. By the way, at the beginning of the play, there is a section with a cat and I am allergic to cats and I used to sneeze. They brought a lot of cats and nothing helped, so they made me a fake cat. But the most important thing for me in playing the role was working with the director. The director was wonderful, George Teodorescu. He was a gentile and that helped a lot. He taught me many things. Every time we read the play, we started to cry. So he stopped the reading and said, "Everyone, I want to tell you something. I'm not Jewish, I didn't go through these things, but people who go through this do not cry. You need to relax and not play the result, but play the process, play normally as if it is happening now." And it's true! Then I remembered how, when we ran away on the freight train, we didn't cry. We held each other. I held onto my mother's arm; we were afraid that we would be shelled. Mother did not cry, no one did; on the contrary, we were alert. That's what I brought to the role. Hirshl was always angry that on *Yom Hashoah* (Holocaust Remembrance Day) only sad things were read in the ceremonies that made you cry. People laughed in the camps too; there was humor there. Not everything has to be designed to make you cry. It's not true, you don't cry all the time. On the contrary, sometimes you get stronger. And the director worked with us to move away from that need to cry in the play and we spoke normally, beautifully, without crying. As soon as the Hanukkah scene started in the play and they hear the Germans coming, we didn't cry; on the contrary! We held our own. There was silence, there was vigilance on the stage . . . they are coming! Even when the Germans took us from hiding, we didn't cry. The director stopped us and, specifically, Anne Frank. There is a section in the play where she says to Peter, "Look outside, see how beautiful it is. We'll meet again." She didn't cry at all that evening. She woke up at night with nightmares, but not every day. She also had a sense of humor. There are wonderful scenes in the play. Whoever did the adaptation in America did a wonderful job. We played this adaptation. This is the best interpretation. The American setting was also excellent. By the way, there were directors who were afraid to do it with me. They said, "She is a good actress, but she's too old." I remember another thing that Teodorescu did to help me in the role. Anne enters the stage from below, so I was the last to enter, not even Zvi recognized me when I entered. Teodorescu put all the participants on a higher level than the level I was on. We are not the same height. I was on a lower stage to give the illusion that I was smaller and that was his trick. It only had to be in the first scene. After that, it didn't matter anymore because the audience had already accepted me. Speaking of the Holocaust and crying, I remember that they held an evening at the Heichal HaTarbut (Hall of Culture) in Tel Aviv to commemorate the killing of the Yiddish writers by Stalin. It was a very big evening. The actress Hanna Rovina participated in it. The Bundists also came from Australia and Jacob Weisslitz, one of the Bundists who was a friend of my father from the Vilna Troupe, had an amateur theater. I asked Zvi which part I should play and he told me, "You don't have to do a recitation about the killing and how they all went to their deaths; the whole audience will cry." He found me a piece by David Bergelson called *Bei Nacht* (At night), in which he describes traveling by train at night in the Soviet Union. And in it is a description of the rhythm of the train ride and how people talked in the same rhythm. A wonderful piece. There is also a description of how people snore on the train in their sleep. I started reading the passage and did impressions of the pace of snoring according to the pace of the train journey. And I told Hirshl that they would kill me because people would laugh. The audience really did burst out laughing at the imitations. I don't understand why, in Israel, they decided that the writers in Yiddish wrote only tearful words; why didn't they mention that there was also humor? In short, because of this, I was invited to Australia to do plays there. This was also an experience because I was told that we could come and act with the Yiddish theater actors there, and it turned out that they were amateurs who didn't even know what acting was. It was impossible to act with them. I already told you once before that since then, I have no patience for amateurs.

Yaniv: When you received first prize in Romania for the play *Anne Frank*, is that when you became a star in Romania?

Lea: Look, the fact that I won the national first prize caused a stir, but the whole play, everything, the entire theatrical event was very powerful.

Yaniv: Was it different from the plays you usually put on?

Lea: No. This was the version they put on Broadway as well.

Yaniv: I mean in relation to the theater repertoire.

Lea: The repertoire of our theater was similar to the other theaters. Although we didn't play *Hamlet*, we played a lot of Molière and Alexander Ostrovsky. Before *Anne Frank*, I played Katerina in Ostrovsky's *The Storm*, serious stuff. But the fact is that, until the play *Anne Frank*, they didn't talk about the Holocaust. It was a time when the Russians thought they shouldn't talk about it. I said to myself, "Actually, why didn't they talk about it?" And suddenly *Anne Frank* is performed on stage and creates a sensation and they start talking about the Holocaust. It was in 1957, so my departure from Romania was particularly hard. In the Romanian theater, they asked why I was leaving.

Yaniv: Why did you really decide to leave? You had a good time, you did very well in the theater, your mother said you were a successful actress.

Lea: Look, we both saw in World War II and in the Communist regime the failure of reality. People felt the failure of the Soviet regime. It is hard to describe, but if you read Solzhenitsyn, Pasternak, and others, you will see the harsh description of the Soviet failure. The fact that they locked people up, didn't let them travel . . . the longing for freedom was very strong, and the desire for freedom is even stronger among young people. The old have already gotten used to it, but the young want freedom. For example, the director who directed *Anne Frank* with me . . . He wasn't Jewish and he was also one of the guys who was not so accepted by the communists. In Romania, he had been a diplomat and was not very well liked by the regime. So, for example, he got a book of plays by Tennessee Williams and he let me read them. I went crazy when I read *A Streetcar Named Desire*, but it was forbidden to talk about it. The regime's pressure was unbearable. The Communist Party of France invited me and the actor, Yankele Alperin,[1] to some conference. We packed our bags, but, at the last minute, the regime did not let us leave. We didn't get permission and we had to stay.

Yaniv: Was there also intervention by the regime in the repertoire?

Lea: Yes. The repertoire was constantly controlled. For example, the Bucharest municipality had a department that would come to see every premiere. The show was already ready with the music, the sets, the costumes, and all, and if they didn't like it, they would stop the show without even so much as a discussion. When my mother played Mirele Efros, they took the show down after the premiere on the grounds that the play was *bourgeois* (middle class). Nothing we said helped and the play did not run. Only the photos that I had time to take remained.

---

1 Yankele Alperin (1921–2012), an actor at the State Theater in Bucharest, immigrated to Israel. He acted with Shimon Dzigan in a private Yiddish theater. With the establishment of the Yiddishspiel Theater, he was invited to act there, which he did until he died.

Yaniv: Did you want to go to Israel or did you also consider France and America?

Lea: Let's put it this way, I didn't know. Zvika was involved because he was older than me. He was old enough to know about Zionist movements. I knew nothing. At that time, there were Zionist movements in Romania, but during the communist era, no one dared to speak out, even those who were socialists did not dare to raise their heads or they were in prison; for example, Pesach Schechter-Gani, the husband of the set designer Lydia Pincus-Gani, spent seven years in a prison because he was a Zionist, a Beitarist. There was no 'why?' People didn't just leave. You didn't know why. If someone blew the whistle on you and said you had some gold coins, the whole floor was lifted and you had to give the coins to them and you sat in jail. Do you understand? You were in jail because of your property! It's not just that the government failed. It took seventy years, but it failed because people cannot live like that. In Romania, there was a large number who left even before that, both to Israel and to America. Zvika, who also wrote, was more involved in the issue of us leaving. And we thought it was time to go.

Yaniv: What did you do?

Lea: We decided . . . One day a rumor spread throughout the city that the Ministry of Interior had queues of people waiting to register to move to Israel. There were a lot of people who didn't make it on the previous *Aliyah* (immigration to Israel) before the gates were closed. I think the Romanians themselves spread the rumor. But there was a certain Jew, his name was Jacober (Jacobson), and, after we left Romania, we learned that he had paid for every Jew to leave.[2] It cost three or four hundred dollars per person. The Romanians did not have dollars and they needed them, so they allowed the Jews to leave and spread the

---

2 Apparently, it was the intention of the Jewish businessman, Henry Jacober, who immigrated from Hungary to Great Britain and engaged in banking and trade with the countries of the communist bloc. Jacober established contacts with the foreign intelligence organization of the Securitate, the Romanian Intelligence. His contact was George Marko, who officially served as the economic attaché at the Romanian embassy in London and was actually an intelligence officer, later reaching the rank of general. For each Jew who received a visa to leave Romania, Jacober paid large sums of money, hundreds and thousands of dollars. In the case of a Jewish political prisoner or someone who had committed financial crimes, the sum to get him out of prison and get him a visa to Israel could be up to eight thousand dollars. Until 1962, around thirty-one thousand Jews were redeemed in this way. They immigrated to the West and some to Israel. For more information, see an article in the *Mabat Sheini* program, "Jews for Pigs," dir. Eyal Tavor, ed. Roi Ben Ami, Channel 1, December 14, 2011, https://www.youtube.com/watch?v=KeXLic0am2Q.

word that it was possible to go to Israel. Then came the punishments. Zvika and I registered and more followed us because they heard that we registered. A week or two later, the decrees came. They threw us out of the theater overnight. It was a year before we were allowed to board. Then, at a certain moment, we received permission and went to the Ministry of the Interior, but Gamal Abdul Nasser (Egypt's president) made *a groisen gevald* (a big fuss) about giving Jews permission to come to Israel after David Ben-Gurion (Israel's president) also made *a groisen gevald* about allowing the Jews to leave Romania. There was a huge influx of Jews from Romania at that time. Because here, in Israel, they always talk too much, and Nasser said, "Why are so many Jews coming to Israel?" And so, from Moscow, they stopped everything. It was on that same day that Zvika and I received our approval. In the morning, we went to the Ministry of Interior to get the exit form, and, before anyone left, they had to come from the municipality to write a note that you were handing over your house … you had to sign that you were handing over all your property and that you had no claims. We walked from the Ministry of Interior and Zvika told me on the way, "We will not go" because a leading article was published in the party's newspaper, *Scînteia*. Nasser said, "What does it mean, the Jews are leaving?" And there were maybe a hundred of us, and the official opened the porthole and said, "Go home and thank Ben Gurion for eating shit at your expense," pardon the expression. We came home and there was no furniture and there was nowhere to work. There was nothing. It was a terrible time, a time when you didn't know what your fate would be.

Yaniv: So, what did you do? Did you go to your mother?

Lea: No. We stayed at home. We had a basket with things I had packed and they had left the bed. But we didn't know what to do and where to work. Some people have completely forgotten that. When I visited Romania a few years ago and passed by the Ministry of Interior, I felt sick. Meanwhile, the theater had completely changed. The young guys who were in the theater studio were immediately called to act in the plays, except for a few young people in the theater who had signed up to make *Aliyah* and had been fired from the theater. Everyone would cross to the other side of the street when they saw us. With the communists, I always say, everyone has a replacement. They said they would close the theater. My mother said that they won't close! Those who were left went to see how the theater students performed. Besides, there was a group of actors who hadn't registered, like Hanna Rieber. She registered later. Criticism from abroad had probably started, so after that, people were no longer thrown out of the theater. There was one man who had a lumber business. He was a Jewish guy so he took Zvi and Yankele Alperin, who also registered with us and was thrown out of the theater, and gave them jobs in a box factory. One day, I went with my mother to a warehouse to clean strawberries. Bibiana[3] was a dentist's assistant, but she cleaned the floor there. The man who employed Zvika came to him and told him that he could not continue to employ him because he was afraid. I asked the manager of a textile factory to hire Zvika. Zvika worked in the factory making *gatkes* (underwear). Then I went and asked the Minister of Culture in Bucharest for her forgiveness so they would accept me back into the theater. She didn't want to shake my hand, but they took me back and made me a statist (background actor), they punished me. After about a year, they let me act. They didn't allow Zvi back. He was a famous writer and they didn't agree until the end. And when they paid for us again and opened the gates, the massive *Aliyah* to Israel started. My mother was literally a victim of the whole thing. They didn't go with us to the train station to say goodbye because the government was constantly following Zvi. We went at night to the train station. I first said goodbye to my mother who turned around and said to me, "*Geh, geh, geh*." ("Go, go, go.") You couldn't say goodbye to your loved ones in a normal way.

Yaniv: How did you feel when you left? Happy? Nervous?

Lea: We didn't know exactly what to expect from the new country. There is a classic joke that the Soviets used to tell. In Magnitogorsk, they opened a huge factory and started recruiting people. Two Jews decide to travel there to find work, but one went first and the other said to him, "If it's good, write to me in red ink, and if it's bad, write in blue ink." The Jew gets there and sends a letter to his friend. "Joy of joys, what a beautiful apartment we got, what a wonderful workplace. What do you know, it's really quite something here. PS: I didn't have blue ink." That's how it was with them. From Israel, they sent pictures to Romania only of people showing the watches they had bought and a lot of oranges on the table. We didn't know any more than that. No one wrote to us how the theater was. No one wrote to us that the government fought against Yiddish theater and made it difficult for Yiddish actors. But my mother was so smart; she knew it anyway.

Yaniv: How did she know?

---

3 Bibiana Goldenthal, soprano singer at the State Theater in Bucharest. Later, she was a voice coach at the Jerusalem Academy of Music. Today, she lives in Givatayim.

Lea: She was a wise woman. She felt it. My mother used to say to me, "*Ich vel ä tag fällen über dir.*" ("One day I will pounce on you.") She wanted to scare me so that I would act as she wanted.

Yaniv: It's interesting that you remember that sentence. When you came to Israel, your mother told you the same thing.

Lea: If she heard that I didn't do what she thought I should do, then she wouldn't write to me anymore.

Yaniv: Not only did she demand that you not act in Yiddish, but she also warned you that she would give up her relationship with you if you didn't listen to what she said.

Lea: She didn't demand that I not act in Yiddish. She said that first I have to overcome the obstacle called Hebrew. And if I overcame the obstacle, I would be able to do whatever I wanted. And it was just as she said.

Yaniv: What stopped her from acting in Yiddish?

Lea: She was right! It didn't bother her. She said she didn't understand the nature of the independent theater. Today, it's called freelancing. It was very difficult, especially for Yiddish actors. You were always dependent on building a troupe, gathering actors together, finding a manager, finding an impresario to organize it. My mother said that neither I nor Zvi know this world. She said, "You are used to repertory theater and the independents will take advantage of you and you will earn *'sholem aleichem' gelt* ('hello, nice to see you' money)." As long as they want to see you, they say, "Nice to see you" and pay money to see you. As soon as they don't need you, they throw you away without a simple hello and without money. In the first production, they come to see the actor, as if to say to him, "Hello to you," and in the second production, the public no longer comes and the actor remains without a job. And that's what happened. Before we arrived, the actress, Judith (Dita) Kronenfeld, arrived in Israel with her musician husband. Judith was a well-known actress. Because of the large *Aliyah* from Romania, these *olim* (immigrants) needed some entertainment quickly, so they performed a lot plays in Yiddish and immediately took Judith into the Yiddish theater. The impresarios knew her and grabbed her. The first play she performed in was *Di Shikorte* (The drunk), which was a huge success because the audience from Romania came to see it as soon as they could. The impresarios knew that the first show would be full because the audience wanted to see her, but that to the next show in which she would perform fewer people would come because they had already seen her in the previous show. That was how it went. And so it was with her!

Yaniv: But Dita Kronenfeld didn't last on stage either. So maybe it's a matter of the quality of her talent and acting?

Lea: She didn't last in Habima because her Hebrew wasn't fluent and she didn't come to Habima like some starlet. She came as an actress to play a small role they needed her for.[4] She did not last and immediately returned to Yiddish. 'Peace unto you' money! It was very good money to buy a refrigerator and even an apartment, but it destroyed your future . . . and Zvika and I, we didn't do it! As I said, all the impresarios, all of them, a whole line of impresarios, came to Zvi's mother's house on Reines Street in Tel Aviv and offered him ten thousand pounds. In 1961, that was the amount for an apartment on Dizengoff Street. But I said no and Zvi said no! Zvika's mom said, "Buy a refrigerator, buy things," but I said no! And we did well, just like my mother said we would. She understood the nature of the business. She reminded me that Hirshl and I had started in an established repertory theater with great directors and scenery and set designers. That just doesn't exist in the private theater. She also said that we wouldn't fit in with the kind of plays that are put on in the private theater. There, they mainly played *schund*, low level, vulgar plays. My mother knew that I was a good actress, but she also knew that I had never worked in a private theater and the Yiddish theater in Israel was private. There was no financial security there and she was afraid that I wouldn't be able to handle it. In a private theater, there needs to be a star and there are no sets. They would bring a bench from here, a coat from there, and you had to know how to deal with that. You had to be very professional. The actors learn from experience. She was afraid that I wouldn't be able to handle it. Imagine how smart she was. She told me, "You will come to Israel, they will

---

4   Judith Kronenfeld's first role in Habima was in *The Physicists* by Friedrich Dürrenmatt in the role of Martha Ball. After that, in the same year, she played the role of the housekeeper in *The King Tends to Die* by Eugène Ionesco and the role of Mrs. Nanny in *The Whole Man and His Truth* by Luigi Pirandello, all in 1963. In 1964, she played in *A Comedy of Errors* and also replaced the actresses Tamara Robbins and Shoshana Doer in the roles of the sobbing woman and Dreizel the beggar (respectively) in the play *The Dybbuk*, which went on tour in Europe and America in 1964 and 1965. See the Habima Theater archive website (http://archive.habima.co.il). (Recording of the performance of *The Dybbuk* with Judith Kronenfeld preserved by the author.)

offer you everything you want, but if you start acting in the Yiddish theater, you will know that you are lost." And she loved Yiddish. She acted all the years in Yiddish. And as she said, so it was. My mother told me, "Only after you prove yourself in Hebrew will you be able to do anything you want," and only three years after, Zvika and I were accepted by Habima. Zvika wrote a revue, *Hochma Ligt in Keshene* (Wisdom lies in the pocket), about both of us. A musician called Rubinstein performed with us and it was very successful. Only after I had proved myself in *Bereshit* did we do what we wanted. My mother knew that changing your place changes your luck. And there was nothing to talk about—I was lucky.

Creating a Role

Yaniv: What do you mean? What luck did you have?

Lea: I was lucky because I also had a very good theater school in Romania.

Yaniv: In what way?

Lea: In terms of the form of the acting. Romania had a very good theater; we were acting there both in Romanian and in Yiddish. In Yiddish theaters, I do not want to offend, they played a lot of *schund* (inferior plays without artistic and literary value and often quite vulgar.) The State Jewish Theater in Bucharest did not play *schund*. Besides, there were very talented people in the Yiddish theater. It was not one theater; there were many troupes there with many stars. In the end, the Yiddish theaters performed better than the others. My mother also had experience from the Vilna Troupe and the theater in Poland where she had acted, where the type of theater was very different. There they presented literary plays.

Yaniv: Was there a difference in the form of the acting as well?

Lea: Yes, also in the form of the acting. I was taught to act correctly. There is the matter of talent; there are some very good actors, but they are only suitable for an ensemble because they don't have enough talent and they are not able to hold an entire show on their shoulders. I was taught to act from the bottom up. Knowing how to walk on stage, participate, understand, not be in an empty space. As soon as you go on stage, you are in the space of the stage, but you are connected to the environment that is reflected in the writing of the play and that obliges you to be in that environment. You enter a space on which a life is built, a street, a restaurant, a brothel, no matter what; you must learn about that place and feel where you are.

Yaniv: How do you know, if I take your example, how to perform a scene in which you have to walk down a road or go from the kitchen to the living room? It's the same path on stage. How will you show the difference?

Lea: There's a big difference. Your goal, why were you in the kitchen, and what compelled you to enter the living room? Why did you go from the kitchen to the living room. What was the reason? And in addition to everything, what did you do in the kitchen, who were you there, how did you walk, who sent you, who are you that you were in the kitchen to begin with? It starts step by step. Before you enter a space, you need to determine who you are.

Yaniv: And do you do it today in every role and in every scene?

Lea: Almost. It's easier for me because today I don't have to build a role from scratch. I immediately get into the mood of the character, that's the experience. I already have a great deal of experience so when I read the role, I immediately see myself: Who I am, what I am, and everything I already explained to you. All these things, if you are taught correctly, you can act. I learned the basics and obtained a varied repertoire. For example, in the Soviet plays that I started with, we needed to speak normally. You need to know what kind of tone to speak in. So, from the beginning, I acted realistically.

Yaniv: What was the first role you played?

Lea: My first role was in the play *The Foreign Shadow* by Semyonov. I played Lena, a Russian soldier who has returned from the front and volunteers to be given an injection for scientific research purposes. With the recent pandemic, it turns out to be just as relevant because, at the beginning, they were looking for volunteers for the vaccine trial.

Yaniv: But you also did couplets in Yiddish?[5]

---

5   Couplet: A poetic structure of two rhyming lines through which an idea is conveyed, usually in a sarcastic or satirical form. Yiddish actors would sometimes improvise entire songs in this way on stage and, in some cases, it was also done through dialogue with the audience, who used to recite their own verses.

Lea: The couplets are another matter. I learned the basic skills, speaking on stage and how not to exaggerate, and to know what you are saying. For example, I'm talking to you now, but on stage there are moments when two people talk to each other, but you speak in a different tone so that the audience can hear and understand. You also have to sit down so they can see you. But all that, that's the director's job; he's the one looking at you. The one who taught me and led me to artistic theater was the director of *Anne Frank*. When I came here and went on stage for the first time for rehearsals, they immediately saw that I was in the thick of things and that I didn't need to be taught how to act. With the same director, Teodorescu, I also did *The Imaginary Invalid*. I played the servant, Toinette. There were two roles: there was Toinette and there was Argan's wife, an immigrant. Dita Kronenfeld was a very beautiful actress and she wanted to play Toinette, but they let her play the role of the lady. So she acted the role of the lady as if she was Toinette. The director, who was an elegant Romanian bourgeoisie type, told her, "Don't take your role of Argan's wife, the lady, in another direction. Act your role." She didn't really want to, but he cleaned up the overacting, or the *schund* of the Yiddish acting style from the private theaters. I've never been to a theater like that. I started in a state theater and I didn't have that experience or that kind of knowledge, but I had good discipline. Now I can afford to say it, but when I went on stage for the first time in Israel and saw my partners, there was a huge difference between us in terms of the level of acting. I'm not bragging, but they were dilettantes, amateurs. Raphael Klachkin was a good and interesting actor. Finkel had a lot of pathos in his acting, but he was a real theater man. Aharon Meskin was interesting; he had personality. Tamara Robbins was a good actress too. But other actors were really amateurs. They talked a lot about theater, but didn't really know how to act. When I came, I had no problem at all acting with them. The one who immediately felt it was Edna Fliedel. When I played in *Bereshit*, Edna immediately came to congratulate me. Fanny Lubitsch came to see me in Ionesco's *The Chairs*. She didn't say a bad word to me and she liked to give criticism, but she had no reason to. It sounds like I should be strutting around proudly with feathers stuck up my bottom, but I don't feel that way. There were actors back then who walked around like professors. Maybe they were professors, but they weren't my professors. My most significant teacher was Teodorescu. The third show I did with him was *A Million for a Smile*. It's a nice Russian comedy. Teodorescu taught me correct directions in the acting of parlor comedy. It's different from Molière and certainly different from *Anne Frank*. He knew how to put the atmosphere of the place where the play is set into the play. He knew how to sit the actors correctly on the chair. He made sure that the movements were correct, that we would know how to move on stage according to the type of play. That show was the last show I played in Romania. Then we went to Israel.

Yaniv: You told me before that when you came to Israel, you didn't know what would happen to you. What did you feel when you said goodbye to your mother? Did you think you would see her again? Did it bother you at all?

Lea: Those were terribly difficult moments. It was in the time of the communist regime. When people traveled, they didn't know if they would ever see each other again. That was the system. They didn't let you out and they didn't let you in. There were moments when I thought it might not be worth going, but my mother actually wanted me to go out into the big wide world. She thought that my world in Romania was too small and it was getting smaller every day. I didn't think I would move to the Romanian theater and I didn't think they needed me. There were a lot of Romanian actors at the time. I also think that if you are going to make a move, you should move to a place where you feel that you belong and you feel that you should be there.

Yaniv: And you and Hirshl never wanted to go to New York, to act at the Yiddish theater in New York?

Lea: We didn't even think about it. Yiddish theater in New York was never artistically significant. And I also knew from my mother how much they did not accept the actors from Europe and how difficult it was for them and what they did to them. I once heard about Samberg, who was murdered in the ghetto; he was the king of all actors in Poland. He went to New York and said that in America, he was nothing, *gornisht*. But how do you say it? "Schaffhausen watches exist in Europe and Schaffhausen watches exist in America?" That is, a watch remains a watch even in America, but an actor does not. There were a lot of actors who traveled and the American actors were not sympathetic to them. There was no interesting theater there either. I was there in 1976. There was nothing interesting going on there. Mary Soriano was successful there for two or three years and that was it. Mike and the Burstein family have been wandering all these years. They spent a lot of time in South America. In the thirties, they were in Argentina. There were two Yiddish theaters on the same street across from each other. When I was in Argentina in 1967, there was a theater in an alley like a flea market. The set was made of paper and the lighting was with water and there were so many Jews there.

Yaniv: You went to America already in 1967?

Lea: Immediately after the Six Day War. We were invited by an impresario and I came with *Bereshit*, not with the sketches that Zvika had written, and we did a big concert tour. That's how a friend of Zvika came and he invited us to Caracas in Venezuela and from there to Montevideo in Uruguay. Zvi's friend told him, "In order to travel, I have to spend a lot of money; you can travel and earn money, a lot of money. Go to Caracas and perform something." Zvi immediately wrote some material and took parts from *Bereshit* in Hebrew and Yiddish. In Buenos Aires, we played *Bereshit* in Yiddish. Zvika translated it all into Yiddish. They organized an evening for us and we earned two thousand dollars there. It was a fortune at the time. I sent it to Havis who was able to clear the mortgage on the apartment we had in Ma'oz Aviv.[6] This friend called another friend and asked him if his sister was still in Curaçao and she organized a show for us there. That's how we traveled and performed all over South America. In each city, Hirshl had a friend who organized a show for us. One of the sketches that we performed was the sketch, *Di Gest* (The guest), which Hirshl wrote for me, and we sang songs in Yiddish. After I acted in Yiddish, I acted in Fannie Hurst's *The Back Street* and W. Somerset Maugham's *The Silver Wedding*. We also played the rendition, which Hirshl wrote for us, of *A Por fun Gott* (A couple from God). We traveled without an impresario, without anything, just me and him, and everything was based on friendship. When I talk to you now about it, I remember everything. Where we were ... We were in Brazil, in Rio, in São Paulo, in Porto Alegre, in Curitiba. Wherever there were Jews, we performed.

---

6   The apartment was in 206 B'nei Ephraim Street, entrance B, in Tel Aviv.

Chapter 5

The Beginning of a Career in Israel

Learning Hebrew

Yaniv: Let's go back to the moment of your immigration to Israel. You didn't want to act in Yiddish and you didn't know Hebrew. Yours and Zvi's tool for being able to work here was the Hebrew language, which you didn't know yet back then. What did you do?

Lea: We went to *ulpan* (Hebrew class) to study Hebrew.

Yaniv: So, you know Hebrew from the *ulpan* in Israel?

Lea: I don't speak Hebrew, even now, don't you know . . . ? In the show *Behind the Fence*, I say in Russian, "They're knocking, can't you hear?" And the girl answers me, "I have ears, I hear . . ." so I have ears and I hear, but still, I don't know Hebrew well enough.

Yaniv: So where did you live when you arrived in Israel?

Lea: At first, we lived with Zvi's mother. She had already been in Israel for twelve years. We lived with her until we went to the *ulpan*. When we left the *ulpan*, we were renting for a year and then we bought an apartment in Ma'oz Aviv with a mortgage. We had accommodation in the *ulpan*; it was in Petah Tikva. It was called Beit HaPoalot and before that it was called Beit HaHalutzot.[1] There used

---

1   Beit HaHalutzot, the house of the pioneers, which is called Beit HaPoalot as well as Beit HaOlot, is located at 46 Shapira Street in Petach Tikva. It was active from 1939 to 1976 and currently operates as a day-care center for the elderly. Between 1950 and 1961, the building was used on behalf of the Jewish Agency as an absorption center and *ulpan* (an institute or school for the intensive study of Hebrew) for *olim* (immigrants) to study Hebrew. The graduates of the first cohort were Polish *olim* with liberal professions, older people from generally

to be a school there and they turned it into an *ulpan*. We had immigrants from South Africa with us; because of certain events in South Africa, they immigrated to Israel.

Yaniv: Were they Lithuanian descendants?

Lea: Yes, that's right. They also spoke a dialect of Lithuanian Yiddish. They were very rich. They all had cars and they had special kindergartens for their kids. Their luxurious cars were standing outside and Zvika and I were the only two who were like beggars. They knew some Hebrew from South Africa. We had a good teacher. He was the stepfather of the journalist, Ron Ben Yishai. His name was Reuven Bar Sever. We said we were actors and he put us in the third level. I didn't understand a word of what they said. They spoke in English and Hebrew. I understood the English, but I didn't understand a word of the Hebrew.

Yaniv: How long were you in the *ulpan*?

Lea: Four months.

Yaniv: Did you work when you were there?

---

assimilated classes. The rise of the Nazis to power made them realize that they must go to Israel. At that time, there were also immigrants from Latin America studying in this *ulpan*. Each *ulpan* cycle lasted five months. The Jewish Agency took care of the administrative and financial side, while the management of the house and the staff took care of the day-to-day maintenance. The building was large enough to accommodate whole families, which is why it is called a family *ulpan*. Most of the students in the *ulpan* were *olim* from South Africa, whose federation (Telfed) supported this enterprise. These were young families who came to Israel with their small children and, with the help of the agency, an arrangement was made for a kindergarten and school for the children while the parents devoted themselves to studying Hebrew during the day. Once they completed the *ulpan*, most of the *olim* found work and managed to contribute to the Israeli economy. *Olim* from countries beyond the Iron Curtain also came to the *ulpan*, most of them professionals, who yearned to be freed from the communist regime. In total, over a thousand people from twenty different countries around the world studied in the *ulpan*. In 1961, due to economic decisions, the agency decided not to renew the contract and closed the *ulpan*. Vocational training courses for girls were taught there and those who had dropped out of school ended up in financial distress. They learned a profession in a short period of time to help support their families. There, they studied hairdressing, sewing, and more for nine months, and in addition to the professional courses, the girls also studied general studies. See Edna Aridor, *The Story of a House: Beit HaHalutzot–Beit HaOlot 1939–1976* [Hebrew] (Tel Aviv: Naamat Publishing House, Department of Movement Education and the Next Generation, 1982), 28–30.

Lea: We didn't work. There was food in the *ulpan* and we received some pocket money from the agency.

Yaniv: And when you were in the *ulpan*, did you know you were going to make it to the Habima Theater after that?

Lea: Not at all. We didn't know what would happen. In the meantime, we started going out and we got to know people. In the theaters, they heard that two actors were coming. I then met Shmulik Segal and Shimon Finkel, who was the director of the theater with the right of veto. Finkel used to laugh at me for having 'a silver fox,' meaning I had a crown on my head since he knew my mom and dad. He saw my mother in Grodno as a child prodigy in the theater and he had not forgotten her. And besides, they all knew who my father was and who his brother, Alex Stein, was. They were known and appreciated not only in the Vilna Troupe, but also generally in the actors' *milieu* (environment). They were great actors and they were told that I also knew a thing or two.

Yaniv: Hadn't they heard of you?

Lea: Heard of me? Don't forget that at that time, the main immigration was from Romania. I was there after the huge success of *Anne Frank* and people said I was worth something, and then I met Finkel. And there was another Jew whose name I've forgotten. He was an intellectual who admired my father. He worked in the National Worker's Union and he loved me very much on stage. There was Dr. Harel, director of Ichilov Hospital, who saw me in *Anne Frank*. He was ambassador to Romania. How do they say, "His reputation precedes him." They also knew that Zvika wrote and that worked in his favor. One day, even before I entered Habima, a young man with flip flops came over to me; it was Chaim Topol.[2] By then, Yosef Milo (Pepo) had built the Haifa Theater and Topol came to offer me a job in Haifa. It was the period of Orna Porat's success at the time; she did *Joan of Arc*[3] and Brecht with great success, and they thought that a newcomer could also bring some benefit to the theater. In short, Topol

---

2   Chaim Topol was an Israeli actor, singer, and illustrator. He is best known for his portrayal of Tevye, the lead role in the stage musical *Fiddler on the Roof* and the 1971 film adaptation, performing this role more than 3,500 times from 1967 through 2009.
3   Orna Porat played the role of Joan in *Joan of Arc* at the Cameri Theater in 1952, five years after immigrating to Israel.

came to the *ulpan* one day and took us to Haifa to meet Yosef Milo. He was a very nice man. We spoke German, so there was no problem, and he wanted to give me an audition. I wasn't used to auditioning, so I suggested that he work with me on some role and he was very enthusiastic about the idea. Then we met Yaakov Yassoor, the director of the Haifa Theater. The theater was not yet active though. Topol brought us to see what was supposed to happen and Yassoor offered me and Zvi three hundred and fifty pounds a month. It was nothing, pennies. Zvi and I returned home and I told Zvi that I still prefer Habima. Even at home (in Romania), I had heard about Habima. There was an actor here, Nathan Meisler. He was from Poland. He said to me, "Let's build the Haifa Theater, create it, design it." But I still wanted Habima. In Romania, I knew that in Israel there was only Habima. We hadn't heard of any other theater. On the ship on the way to Israel, someone told me that I should see the Cameri Theater. When I came to Israel, I saw Miriam Zohar on stage with Hanna Rovina. It was the play, *Hannah Senesh*. My mother told me to buy a bouquet of flowers for Rovina. After the show, I approached her and gave her the flowers. This is what I knew and that's why I wanted Habima, and indeed, Finkel decided to accept me and Zvi at Habima.

Schund and Intrigue in Israel

Yaniv: So, after the *ulpan*, you started working on stage?

Lea: Yes. But I have to tell you about something else that happened back when we were in *ulpan*. Not far from the studio was the Heichal Cinema where Max Perlman appeared in Yiddish.[4] One day, we went to see him. It was the first time I saw *schund* theater. Until then, I had only heard about it. I realized that my mother had been right; there was nothing for me in that kind of theater.

---

4   The Heichal Cinema at 21 HaHistadrut Street in Petach Tikva was inaugurated on May 9, 1937. It was built by Petach Tikva Municipality and the Workers' Council, and it had 1,200 seats. The cinema had operated on Fridays and Saturdays from the time it opened, which caused protests and an uproar from religious and ultra-Orthodox parties in Petach Tikva. Friday and Saturday performances were then stopped. But in 1984, by order of Mayor Dov Tavori, the activity was again resumed on Saturdays and, once again, demonstrations were held by religious groups against its operation. The demonstrations lasted for three years, but in the end, the cinema continued to operate on Fridays and Saturdays. See Reuven Shapira, "Shabbos in Malabes" [Hebrew], *Davar*, August 1, 1980, 14; Buki Na'eh, "The Religious People Shouted Outside" [Hebrew], *Ma'ariv*, February 26, 1984, 1–2.

Today I can do it, but if I had done it back then, it would have been different. My mother was right, it would have ended up very badly. Perlman was very graceful. He wrote very beautiful songs like *Benzin* (Gasoline), which is sung all over the world. He had another song about his neighbor whose husband is a cantor and she says that upstairs he still has the knack, but downstairs, nothing. I heard it and fell on the floor laughing. In Romania at that time, it was a heavy period, it was forbidden to say such things; every word was censored. And suddenly hearing such things, I laughed and the whole audience was on the floor. They say that *schund* theater is vulgar and low level, but today there are no actors who know how to do such things. There are no actors today who know how to sing couplets. It is also art. It wasn't so rude because he would do it very gracefully.

Yaniv: Mike's father, Pesachke Burstein, was also excellent at couplets.

Lea: Of course. They were great competitors. They all traveled all over the world and they competed in front of the same audiences. After I saw him on stage, I also saw Burstein when he came to Israel.

Yaniv: Hirshl didn't write couplets for you?

Lea: He wrote a lot for me, but not like that. Everything was much more censored. It was natural for me to sing those songs. In Romania, there was Sevilla Pastor, who was an ingenious actress. When she heard I was doing couplets, she said she had to see if I was better than her or not. So, she came to see me sing and said, "She does it well, but I can still live peacefully." She was excellent in that genre. She would do it all so easily and so elegantly. Back then I sang a song called "Men, Men."

Yaniv: Is it easier for men to sing couplets than for women?

Lea: Of course. It's easier to accept a man who talks like that. Another one who was also good at it was Dita Kronenfeld. She was a very beautiful woman; she came to Israel before me and acted in *Di Shikorte* (The drunk) in Yiddish, and there, she sang the song I had already sung in Romania, "Men, Men."

Yaniv: I only saw Dita in the movie *When They Give You, Take,* and I heard a recording of her in *The Dybbuk* on stage; she replaced Tamara Robbins on a trip abroad in 1965.

Lea: They took her because they didn't want to take me. The official claim was that I was acting in *The End of the Race*. It was a complete scandal, that trip. I was so angry that I didn't get to go. I said to Zvika, "We will still travel and I will see all the Habima actors." It was the sixties. I had not been anywhere in the world and they went to America. I so wanted to travel and see the world.

Yaniv: Did they want you for the role of the woman who bursts into the synagogue? I thought they wanted you for the role of Leah.

Lea: They wanted me for the role of Leah, but there was intrigue around the role and they took Eva Leon. But I'm not sorry. I didn't lose out on anything. They wanted me to play the 'bursting woman' and some kind of beggar. It was also a story. I saw "The Dance of the Beggars" and caught the gist of the dance, and then Hanala Handler asked me why I don't come to more rehearsals. I told her that I understood how to move. But they didn't like it and they took me off it. Look, I came from a professional theater, I didn't need that much time to learn a few steps.[5] In the end, they told me that I wouldn't go at all. But it's not important. I'm not sorry about it. In the end, I traveled with Zvika all over the world with the Yiddish performances.

Yaniv: Let's go back to the couplets. Did you do many such couplets in Romania?

Lea: I was a very young star in Bucharest and I was probably good, so they wrote good couplets for me. I had a number for a festival for young actors in Romania. Hirshl wrote a number for me where I start as a young pioneer in Russian, Romanian, French, Spanish, and Yiddish. I would spin and with every spin, I would change outfits. It was called *Checkmate*.

---

5   "The Dance of the Beggars" from the second act of *The Dybbuk* is seen by Habima theater veterans as a theatrical moment that goes beyond just dancing. It was put together by the Russian choreographer Lev Lashchilin from the Bolshoi Theater, who worked with the actors. After the rehearsals, the director, Yevgeny Vakhtangov, told them that they had done a dance, but that the dance should be made into theater. Vakhtangov, who thought up the idea of the beggars' dance with the bride where the bride is freed from the shackles of society, sent the actors to observe nature, and each of the actors chose an animal to imitate. For example, Hanala Handler, who played the role of Babcia, chose the frog; Chayela Gruber, who played Dreisel (later played by Shoshana Doer and Dita Kronenfeld), chose the wolf; etc. Hanala Handler apparently expected Lea to get into the essence of the dance and its depth and not just imitate it outwardly. Each time *The Dybbuk* was staged, the rehearsals before each performance focused generally on technique and less on the depth. For more, see Yaniv Goldberg, "'You are not my groom': A Feminist Reading of the Play *The Dybbuk—Between Two Worlds* by S. An-sky" [Hebrew], *Jerusalem Studies in Hebrew Literature* 27 (2014): 133–153.

Chapter 5

Lea at Habima

Master Puntila and His Man Matti

Yaniv: Let's go back to Israel. After the *ulpan*, you went on stage and started rehearsals for *Master Puntila and His Man Matti* by Bertold Brecht.

Lea: It wasn't so simple. I came from a communist country where Bertold Brecht was very well known. I also did a one-woman play by Brecht in Romania about a Jewish woman who speaks on the phone and everyone is afraid to be in contact with her. In the end, her husband is also scared. The truth is that, even in Bucharest, they did not have much patience for the play. The audience would say, "If she picks up the phone even once, I'll go home." Truthfully speaking, not everything always works out. They would do 'culture mornings' and they did a morning like that with Brecht and that's where I brought it up. But at that time, they were also running *Master Puntila and His Man Matti* and it was a huge success because it is a comedy with a wonderful message. So they wanted to run the show at Habima and Finkel sent for me and Zvika, who was also supposed to act in the play, as well as for the play's director, Shmuel Bonim.

Yaniv: Was it clear that, if they took you, they would also take Zvi?

Lea: No. We were two separate actors, but they accepted both of us into the theater and also put him in the play. He was an actor, not a big guy, but a handsome man, and it was fitting that he acted in the show.

Yaniv: So, did you go to Shmuel Bonim's house?

Lea: Yes, he lives, I think, at 9 Graetz Street in Tel Aviv. We went to his house and he welcomed us barefoot. His son was sitting in the middle of the living room on a potty. Listen, I came from a communist country. It was in no way acceptable to receive a guest barefoot when a child, excuse me, is pooping in the middle of the living room. Bonim was a star at the time. He was directing choruses such as *Green Onions* and directed the play *Little Tel Aviv* in the Hammam Theater in Jaffa. In short, he asked me, "What did you do in Romania?" I answered him, *Anne Frank*. "Was Anne Frank that tall?" he asked. I was a few centimeters taller then and I told him, "Yes, there are some people in Israel who saw me in the role." So, we continued talking and he could see that I spoke Hebrew.

Yaniv: He didn't speak to you in Yiddish?

Lea: No. In Hebrew. After all, they were quite against Yiddish. Then he brought us the play. He told me that the play was a parlor comedy. Hirshl heard this and told me, "He doesn't understand anything. Brecht wrote parlor comedies!" He said to me things like, "Speak quieter, speak louder, speak like this, speak like that." The actress, Edna Flidel, was acting in the theater at the time. Miriam Zohar had just gotten married and was going on a trip, so Edna was brought from the Cameri as a replacement. She had a hard time there because Hanna Maron suited the same type of roles as Edna. In short, Bonim wanted Edna to play the role so he drove me crazy with his "Do this, do that, not like that." He was short and, suddenly, he stood in front of me with his foot on a stool. "Look," he told me, "This will be too difficult of a role for you." But I knew it was a great role for me, I just knew it. When they had just started talking to me about the role, I wrote to my mother and she immediately replied, "It's wonderful! It's a role you have to do." It's a comedic character role that I knew how to carry off well. In short, he told me that Brecht has Finnish stories and this play was also Finnish, and Bonim decided to put them into the play. Brecht wrote about them explicitly that they should not be acted out in the play, but Bonim did put them in. Tamara Robbins and other actresses played them. He didn't understand it. He told me, "Act one of the stories and not the role of Eva Puntila." Hirshl was fuming when we left. We got home and I told Hirshl, "He doesn't want me to act in the play." Hirshl banged on the table and said, "I knew, I knew all along that he didn't want you to act with him, but over my dead body, you'll act with him. He got dressed elegantly with a suit and tie, even though there was a heatwave that day, and he went to the theater. I didn't see it. He called Finkel and said to him, "Mr. Finkel, you brought us here to the theater, thank you very much. But you don't know who you have brought into the theater and you don't understand the value of what you are holding in your hands right now. But Bonim doesn't want Lea to play Eva." Finkel wrote in one of his books that Ada Tal also told him that the best thing he did as a manager was to get me into the theater. Finkel called Bonim and told him, "Either she is playing the role or you are not directing. Bonim came to me and asked me for forgiveness. Tamara Robbins would sit in rehearsals—she didn't know I knew Russian—and she would say to the actors in Russian, "She is the best of all of you here."[6] A few years passed and Orna Porat, who was only at the theater part of the time, wanted to stage *The Old*

---

6 Among the Russian-speaking actors in the play were Aharon Meskin, Raphael Klachkin, Fanny Lubitsch, Niora Shein, Nahum Buchman, Ari Kutai, and more.

Lady's Visit by Friedrich Dürrenmatt.[7] She wanted me and Yossi Yadin, but there was a scandal and she did not agree to have me act in the play. It was the only time in my life that I was paid without acting. They had to pay me compensation. I didn't know it at the time, but Bonim said to Yadin, "You're stupid, you don't know who you're going to act with."

Yaniv: Let's go back to the play about Puntila for a moment. Did it not succeed?

Lea: Not at all.

Yaniv: Why?

Lea: I'll tell you. Bonim got the casting all wrong. Puntila is a young man. It can't be played by an old actor. They built a mountain and they needed to have the strength to climb that mountain. He took Meskin, who was an excellent actor, but he didn't have the strength for it at that point. There should have been a small and bitter person in the role while Meskin was big and warm and he took Klachkin to play the role of servant. They were an unsuccessful pair. In Romania, the play was a hit.

Yaniv: How did Bonim direct you? You said that when you first met, he told you to "speak louder, speak quieter." Was it similar to the stagings they used to do in the military bands and shows? The way he used to direct? Is that how he also worked with you during rehearsals?

Lea: No. After Finkel threatened him, "Either she plays the role or you don't direct," he left me and I built the role myself. I knew exactly how to do the job. After all, I came with twelve years of acting experience in Romania. I had acted in similar roles.

Yaniv: I remember that the review of the play by Dr. Emil Feuerstein, which killed the play, stated that there was a new actress who will undoubtedly enrich theater life in Israel.

---

7   On June 6, 1974, Orna Porat returned to the Cameri Theater after leaving it for some time to manage a theater for children and youth (which was later named after her). The play was directed by Yosef Milo, and Orna played the role of the old lady. See Yaakov Haelyon, "Screen and Mask" [Hebrew], *Ma'ariv*, June 6, 1974, 25.

Lea: Everyone said so. Except for Gamzu, who gave a bad review of the entire show and all the actors. Ben Ami in *Ma'ariv* and Michael Ohad all came out against him and said that there were two actors in total who were brilliant in the show and they were Lea Koenig and Shraga Friedman. Look, Bonim didn't know how to put on a show; he didn't have a clue.

Bereshit—the Great Success

Yaniv: After *Puntila*, you got the role of Eve in *Bereshit*.

Lea: This also wasn't that simple. The Habima actors had a way of interfering in everything. We did Aharon Megged's *Bereshit*. He wrote it first as a sketch in which Zaharira Harifai acted. They gave me the role of Eve, which underwent many changes throughout the play. In the beginning, she has her boyfriend Adam, who wants her all the time. She is young and innocent. After they eat the apple, she immediately wants more. In the second act, she is already a mother, and in the third act she is Ishtar, one of the Nephilim's daughters. It was very modern; the Espresso Generation.[8] I knew how to make changes on stage, but the actors at Habima had a tendency to interfere. "How will she play someone from the Espresso Generation? We need another actress." We had a rehearsal, Finkel arrived, took one look at me and said, "She can act all the roles."

Yaniv: What did you do there?

Lea: Well, by the time I came here, I had had good schooling. I'd already seen a lot of nonsense. I mean it, without all the bullshit. First of all, it's about talent; without that, it's impossible. If there's talent and a good mind, and you have directors who feel that talent and know how to lead you, then it works. I was in a group of people who knew what a theater was and my mother was leading it.

Yaniv: I'm trying to understand about the practicalities of the role you played in *Bereshit*.

---

8   The young people who, after the austerity years of the 1950s, chose to spend time in cafes. They were perceived as egoists, hedonists, and materialists chasing rock and roll stars from abroad. The term 'Espresso Generation' was coined by the writer S. Yizhar (Yizhar Smilansky) in 1960. He used it to accuse the younger generation of chasing entertainment and amusement and pursuing a career, in contrast to the collectivist Palmach generation, which focused on social progress and not on the self.

Lea: I started as a girl. I was in the theater every day. I knew all the parts, both for the men and the women. I studied.

Yaniv: I'm not talking about the history in Romania. I'm asking about *Bereshit*. You start as a young woman and, after the apple, you grow up. How do you do that?

Lea: I understand who I'm playing.

Yaniv: How do you grow up on stage in just a few minutes?

Lea: In a role, the text helps you to understand. I start as a naive girl, then I eat the apple and I realize that I am a woman. This realization penetrates me. I already know what sex is and I want something else. I see that Adam is an idiot and does not understand anything. I know how to talk to the garden's owner (God). In the second act, an elderly Jewish woman sat knitting, *a yiddene* (an elderly Jewish woman). She was heavy set and she had two sons. I immediately felt my whole body change, my look changed, my tone of voice changed. Each role is a different woman who you work on according to the information you have about her. You're just acting the character out as you're supposed to be. Like I said, you need talent and a director who knows how to lead, but you need to know how to work with your talent.

Yaniv: The success was tremendous. You were also well received by the audience, unlike in *Master Puntila and His Man Matti* where you received enthusiastic reviews from the critics, despite the negative reviews about the show. But the show was very difficult for you because it was in the biblical language and you were a new immigrant.

Lea: I was fifty years younger than I am now. My mind and my memory were strong.

Yaniv: Did you understand every word you said?

Lea: Everyone thought I didn't understand what I was saying and that's ridiculous. How can you act without understanding what you're saying? Of course, I understood! I may not have known how to translate every single word on my own, but I learnt it by heart and I knew every word.

Yaniv: Did you write the text in Hebrew or in Latin letters?

Lea: Today, I sometimes write in Latin letters, but then I was afraid. I wrote in Hebrew letters.

Yaniv: And what about the story with the mistake in the word 'trees' in the text? Is it true?

Lea: Yes.

Yaniv: What happened?

Lea: Looking back, it was really nothing. Instead of saying, "He went to cut trees," I said, "He went to cut eggs."

Yaniv: And the audience, how did they react?

Lea: I don't think the audience even understood. Those who caught it were the actors on stage. I wasn't even facing the audience at the time. I shouted it from the wings, "He went to cut eggs at night!" Today, it makes me laugh. In the first year after I finished studying in *ulpan*, I saw IDF soldiers marching and, instead of calling it a march, I called it a parade!

Yaniv: Were you warned by the theater about the mistake with the eggs?

Lea: No. The cast I acted with was very nice. There was Buchman, who was always focused on himself, a nice man. Klachkin was such a gentleman and a real Don Juan. Nissim Azikri was very young, and there was Yehoshua Bertonov, who loved me very much. I have to say that thank God, I cannot complain. They appreciated me right away.

The Klausner Prize

Yaniv: Following the success in *Bereshit* and the success both among the critics and among the audience, you received the Klausner Prize.

Lea: The Klausner Prize was the first award I received in Israel and it was very exciting. The truth is that to this day, I don't know exactly what it is, but it was a very prestigious award. I had also just arrived in Israel. I was 'a newcomer.' In Romania, there were no awards with people's names. It was either an award for successful service or for a specific subject.

Yaniv: In Romania, you received an award for *Anne Frank*. What about when you played Chava in *Tevye the Dairyman*?

Lea: I don't remember exactly what happened then. I have pictures. We got awards. It was all very official from the government and I received an honors certificate. It was a general award for my work in the theater, not specifically about my role as Eve. Regarding the Klausner Prize, I was there twice. I was there once with the critic, Dov Ber Malkin. I received the award and Bertonov congratulated me and said, "I didn't think that a baby I had held in my hands, the daughter of Yosef Oscar Kamien, would steal the show from me." The event was recorded, but unfortunately, I don't have the recording. They asked me to present something and Zvi had written the sketch *Di Gest* (The guest) especially for me. At the time, I didn't fully understand the reluctance towards Yiddish that was here at all. Besides, I could barely cope with the Hebrew text of *Bereshit* and I had no sketches at the time in Hebrew. I started doing this sketch in Yiddish and this gentleman, who was the vice president—I don't want to mention his name here—was bothered that I spoke in Yiddish. It was just unbelievable. He said that I insulted the award and that it was an insult to Klausner because I spoke in Yiddish. I was told to go to his home with Zvika to ask for his forgiveness! From this I understood to what level of humiliation the Yiddish language had reached here in Israel. To this day, it hurts me and I just don't understand it. My parents and so many artists brought joy and happiness to this nation wherever they performed. They appeared in every small village, traveling night and day, in the rain and the heat to bring joy to the people, and he stood there and humiliated this language. Who is this guy? What right did he have to speak to me this way? What a cheek!

Yaniv: And this was when the majority of people in Israel knew both Yiddish and Hebrew.

Lea: What was the excuse? That if they speak Yiddish then they won't learn Hebrew? I studied Polish, Russian, Yiddish, Romanian, and German at home. I knew all five languages from childhood. What's wrong with speaking different languages? But they mainly attacked Yiddish, like barbarians! Not for nothing did my mother tell me to act first in Hebrew and only after they see who and what I am, then I'll be able to go back to acting in Yiddish. Only after I did *Puntila, Bereshit, War and Peace*, and *The Parisian* in Hebrew and had proved myself and received good reviews did I return to acting in Yiddish. Who gave them the permission to issue a death sentence on the language?

Growing Up on Stage

Bereshit

Yaniv: Let's go back to the play *Bereshit*. In the play, you demonstrated your wonderful ability to go through a process of growing up on stage. You explained earlier how you did it. This ability reveals itself in quite a few plays. I want to talk to you about two other roles in which you matured on stage and changed, as Miss Daisy in *Driving Miss Daisy* and Madame Rosa in *The Life before Us*. In both plays, you begin as a dominant woman who knows very well what she wants with two feet planted firmly on the ground, and, as the years pass in the plays, you mature and end them quite broken. How do you do that? How do you know when you need to advance another step, when you need to grow older? In my eyes, the beauty of these plays is that you don't feel it happening, you don't quite understand how it has happened, and you believe that years have passed even though it's less than two hours since the start of the play.

Lea: The truth is that it's also in the material. The material gives you the opportunity to do that, you feel that you need to change.

Yaniv: Do you take it from the text?

Lea: Both from the text and from the fact that I ask myself how I see my character right now. I know it's been years. I see how people change over the years. I see how it happens and I have to feel it. The text also helps you feel that something is changing in you.

Yaniv: There is the scene in *Daisy* where you are looking for your students' notebooks to grade them, even though you have long since retired. Something happens to you there; you start to get confused. A moment earlier, you left the stage a proud woman and now you come on differently.

Lea: When I exited the stage, I already knew I was changing. The text says that several years have passed so you know not to repeat the same thing again. We look at people and observe them. I see how people change. I feel it in myself.

Yaniv: When you acted in the play, at the beginning you were Daisy's age, and at the end you were roughly the age you are today.

Lea: True, but when you read the text and you imagine the personality, you know that years have gone by so you can't act the same way. The years do something to a person. You also think, who is the person I am acting out here, when and where?

Yaniv: Was there a real person who was your inspiration for *Daisy* or *The Life before Us*?

Lea: *The Life before Us* is a completely different thing. With *Daisy*, I knew the style; snobby and stubborn. She is a racist. She says things like "That Negro, he thinks he can tell me . . . ?" The interesting thing about the play was how she came to love him and it kept me busy all the time.

Yaniv: How did you work on that?

Lea: There are conditions for it. He knows how to talk to her, but she doesn't know how to talk to him. He knows how to talk to her, how to convince her with his silence and his wisdom of life.

Yaniv: So, you needed Yaakov Cohen, your partner, who played the driver, to do it for you.

Lea: I think about what I feel, that's what I mainly build on. When I think about the role and what there is in the role, then I look for and find these elements. Suddenly she becomes weaker and each time, she gets back from him the help and compassion she needs. Slowly she realizes that the one who really deserves her love is him and not her son.

Yaniv: And in *The Life before Us*?

Lea: In *The Life before Us*, I imagined that whole period when the Jewish girls were taken to brothels. She is an unusual person and that power to take children that are not hers . . . She couldn't have children of her own, or maybe she did, but it didn't work out well for her. Also, she's a person who knows what it is to be taken advantage of. She had been taken advantage of in life until she reached that state. When I read it, both the book and the play, this was the biggest part of it, it consumed me.

Yaniv: Did you identify with her?

Lea: I really identified with her, a lot! I loved her. She is an interesting woman.

Yaniv: Did you feel that you were taken advantage of in your life?

Lea: Of course, all the time. It made me angry. Also, the love for one child that she loves more than all the other children; the love she had for Momo shows that she was a wise woman. She values Momo more than the other children. There is something in it. And the boy felt that special love, which was reserved only for him. The role of the child in the play is a very special role.

Yaniv: Something is not clear to me. We talk all the time about your successes in Romania and about your successes in Israel, but the thing I don't understand is how and why did you feel you were taken advantage of? Where did you feel that you weren't treated properly?

Lea: I'll tell you. I have heard and also seen how they (the prostitutes) are treated. When I was a little girl in Czernowitz, I would sit on the balcony. Our house was just next to a bridge.[9] Prostitutes used to pass over the bridge and one day, I saw how a pimp beat a prostitute. I never forgot it, till this day. It was a complete shock for me. Grandma told me, "Don't look, don't look." I didn't realize back then that she was a prostitute. But for years, I couldn't forget the scene. Later, we understood to what extent they were exploited, to the point of bloodshed. And I thought about that prostitute too. This was a girl who was probably born into a Jewish family and was carried away to brothels. Who knows where and how. The attitude towards this woman in the play, who suddenly builds herself a house with children and helps prostitutes with their children is an amazing story. They did not understand that this woman had many capabilities. They saw her only as a whore. Even when I came to Israel, they chose to see me in a certain light and did not take advantage of my other abilities. For example, they thought that I could only do light entertainment shows, but actually, there were many other genres in which I could perform.

Yaniv: In Israel, light entertainment is seen as something really common.

---

9 The bridge on Schule Gas, which connects Upper Chernivtsi to Lower Chernivtsi. Lea lived in 5 Schule Gas. This was a Bauhaus-style house, painted antique pink. See the picture of the house and the bridge on page 218.

Lea: The truth is that I was also afraid to do them in Hebrew, so I only did them in Yiddish. There were talk shows on the radio and all kinds of entertainment shows done by entertainers who, today, I can say were far less talented than me. But I didn't do them. But maybe it was my fault after all because I didn't have enough courage. Some people are seen as entertainers and you seem to see them everywhere and not see anyone else. So maybe I'm also to blame, but I don't think they knew how to take full advantage of my skills and abilities because they chose to see me only as a theater actress; comedic, dramatic, a good actress, but nothing more.

The Life before Us

Yaniv: If you're talking about a good actress, then let's go back to Rosa and the scene where she goes crazy and loses touch with reality. She walks in dressed as a prostitute and thinks that Momo is a customer. This is where it happened to me for the first time in the theater that I actually forgot it was you. I believed I was seeing Madame Rosa, so much so that I said to myself, "Wait a minute, this is Lea." It was a tremendous experience.

Lea: Thank you so much.

Yaniv: In the scene, Rosa has moments of madness and moments of sanity and she moves between them. Moments when she doesn't recognize Momo and thinks he is a customer who has come to her, and moments when she recognizes him. How do you act scenes like that?

Lea: It happens.

Yaniv: What do you mean? You don't really feel crazy? Do you remain constantly aware of the role you are playing?

Lea: We do things on stage that we also invent. We try in rehearsals. I'm sitting with you and talking and suddenly I stop and say, "I forgot," and think, "Where did we stop?" Then, "Hey, where were you last night? What are you doing? What are you doing here?" I mean, my train of thought is interrupted and I have to start over.

Yaniv: So, if I understand correctly, this is the text. The text guides you.

Lea: Sure. The text also explains to me what is happening. You see, there is a moment of confusion here and you have to believe it in the moment.

Yaniv: How do you believe it if you are the one playing the role?

Lea: I'm acting, but I believe it because I get into the character of the woman as much as I possibly can.

Yaniv: Do you forget that you are Lea in that moment?

Lea: I don't forget. Actors must never forget who they are. I imagine her very strongly, but I keep my own identity. They always say that if the actor playing Othello forgot that he was an actor, he would strangle Desdemona several times. By the way, Juliano Mer-Khamis, who was a very good actor, played Othello with Maya Maoz, who played Desdemona. She pissed him off so much, he almost strangled the hell out of her. He almost killed her. When you're building the role, the mood is also important. When I create the role, I start it as a healthy woman so I project myself as healthy . . . in the tone of my voice, in my movements, in the way I walk. Then comes the moment when I'm sick so I force myself to feel the pain. I don't literally feel the pain, but I convince myself as I am creating the character to feel as if I'm sick. When I have to play a young woman, I bring in the energy of a young woman, and *vice versa* when I play an old character. Here, too, you change the energy. The text, the situation, you start to carry your body with that energy. You sit more bent, the voice weakens and trembles, the movement weakens. It all goes together.

Yaniv: But you are describing an external expression; with you, is it built from the inside?

Lea: It's not an external expression. The inner feeling produces the outer face. I'm building it from the inner feeling. It's not my decision that I'm old now, but the play takes me there, and the external expression is a result of the mental state in which I am in the same situation. The text, the situation, the emotion obliges you in an external expression as well. You don't leave the feelings outside. It is the emotion that carries you.

Driving Miss Daisy—The Stage as a Reflection of Life

Yaniv: Come to think of it, you've performed in a lot of plays where you age on stage, such as *Daisy*, which we spoke about, and in *Quartet*, in *Mirele Efros*, and also here in *The Life before Us*.

Lea: In *Daisy*, she reaches a state where she is almost gone. The transition in *Daisy* is wonderful. The play also mentally gives you the space to really feel it. There were moments when I really felt that I didn't have any strength left and that I was an old woman. Even now, when I tell you about it, I feel as though I can see myself there, the scene where I try to reach the plate with the cake and I can't because my body betrays me. Of course, there are some technical movements, you are aware that it is technical, but you build it emotionally beforehand. It's not easy. It's a difficult profession, but a beautiful one because it requires you to go through these moments. It's not a technique, you really have to live it! And whoever makes it technical, well then it remains just that, technical and unreliable. Some directors tell me, "When you say this sentence, lower your tone or lower your head." I can't. I need to feel the sentence, and the right movement and the right tone needs to come out. It all stems from my inner feeling in that situation. There are actors who, if they are speaking, can't do another technical action like putting on a shoe or something similar. The stage can't be like that. Life on stage should reflect reality. The emotion needs to lead you to the technical actions. I'll tell you something ... over the years, I have learned to see all kinds of qualities in people. Yesterday evening, a couple of my friends came to the theater. After the show, my friend came over to me and she said, "What a show, how beautiful! How wonderful, I'm telling you ..." And while she's telling me all this, she's eating an apple. Every time she comes to the theater, she always takes an apple with her. I don't know how to explain it to you, but the story with the apple repulses me every time. Not only is it unaesthetic, but, when you come to greet me after the show, do you really have to eat an apple exactly at that moment? Are you really that hungry? All the time with the apple! And she holds the apple in her hand, and when you hold an apple, it has moisture, and her fingers get wet, and then she licks it and then she kisses me and hugs me and it's just really unpleasant. One day, I will have to play a woman just sitting down and talking and all the while just be eating an apple!

Yaniv: It's scary sitting next to you. Everything that happens around you could end up on stage.

Lea: It scares me too. But an actor should always observe. Sometimes you see things like that and you just want to perform them on stage. Theater, in the end, is also an imitation of reality, but this imitation is not just external, it comes from within. The stage should imitate the reality, but not only externally.

Yaniv: I remember that in one of the Yiddish performances of *A Tour Guide to Warsaw* that I attended, during the scene, your earring fell off and you bent down to pick it up, and while you were talking, you continued the scene, and then the second earring fell off and you looked for it and when you found it, you put them both in your pocket and you continued the scene as though life continued on stage.

Lea: Anyone who can't do that can't be an actor. It's a strange profession because people look at and accept the actor as they are, and even say they gave an excellent performance. As soon as you get the applause, everyone thinks they are excellent. So, what is the difference between me and them? We both got the same applause. The audience may feel differences, but not always and there's nothing that can be done about it. I acted in the play *Wedding*. Fanny Lubitsch acted in it in the role of Aunt Yaffa.

Yaniv: Well, she was one of Stanislavski's students in Moscow. How was she as an actress?

Lea: Yes, well, she was an 'acting professor.' Her face was always angry. She would see me on stage and never said I was acting well. She would always come over with a sour face, but you know many people appreciated her. I had a funny story with her.

Yaniv: What happened?

Lea: We performed together in the play *Wedding*, where Shmulik Segal and I acted with her. She was performing with a hat and she came in with the hat on, said one word and left. She had to come on stage and say, "The Rebbe has arrived. Chaim has also arrived." That's all. We were waiting for her to go on stage and we were sitting backstage next to the entrance and suddenly, we see that she takes a chair and walks away from us. I said to her, "Fannichka, where are you going?" So, she told me, "I need to concentrate." In order to say one sentence, she needs to concentrate?! Then she ran onto the stage and said, "The Rebbe has arrived. Moshe has also arrived." The next day, the same thing; she takes a chair and walks away from us. I ask her, "Where are you going, Fannichka?" She answers me, "I need to concentrate." So, I tell her, "You can forget it from here too."

Yaniv: Did you dare tell her that? Everyone was afraid of her, even Shlomo Bar Shavit, who was not afraid of anyone or anything. When I asked him about her, he told me, "She was a horrible woman and I'm not interested in talking about her." No matter what I tried, he wouldn't talk about her.

Lea: I had no issues with her. I will tell you another story about an experience I had with her. I performed with her in the play *The Shadow Box*. It was about a hospice. She played a very beautiful role that suited her very well. She would enter the stage in a wheelchair. One day, she didn't put the brakes on and she almost flew off the stage. It turns out that even a serious actor can get a flat tire every once in a while. At the end, all the actors get a round of applause. I only hope that I will always be remembered favorably.

Chapter 6

King Lear

Yaniv: Let's talk about failures. In 2018, you performed in *King Lear*. Not long after you started, it was announced that the play would only continue for another eighteen performances. How did you feel about that?

Lea: I don't think *King Lear* was a failure. For me, there were several issues here. I had doubts at the beginning whether to take the role or not. I knew I had a lot of hard work ahead of me. The part that scared me the most was the language. There is something that always bothered me, probably in my subconscious—the fact that I learned the language very quickly, but not thoroughly. I wanted to survive and the need to start acting was burning in me. And this issue of the language has been on my mind all these years. I can honestly say that today, if I'm missing a word in a normal text, I can find another word, but when it's written as poetry like Shakespeare, it's more complicated.

Yaniv: When you showed me the text the day you received it, about six months before the rehearsals, I thought it might be worth sitting down with a translator to find alternatives to the words that would be cumbersome for you to say.

Lea: I couldn't say just anything because I didn't have the authority. The truth is that to this day, I know the text perfectly by heart. On stage, if I suddenly get stuck on something, I can get out of it. I don't stop, but it's very stressful because it's poetry and you have to be precise. Also, I wanted to really push myself this once and see if I could actually do it. This is a wonderful play. I really tested myself in terms of my acting. If the director had gotten to know me better, he would've been able to find my strong points and put emphasis on them, but he insisted on the exact text. What I did get from the show was satisfaction from the entire cast. I was surrounded by so much attention and love from all the young guys who were around me, from my colleagues, and from their encouragement all the time. "You are wonderful. You are doing well. Thank you so much for the opportunity to act with you in the play." So, I would say it was worth it. In this respect, I am not sorry. I'm sorry they closed the show so quickly because it was a huge expense. The show was beautiful, in my opinion, and there are those who liked me. *Haaretz* wrote a good review about me. All in all, it was worthwhile for me to make the attempt. I don't regret it and I continued, but I'm just sorry about the way in which I was informed about the cancellation of the show. Neither the actors nor I were informed that the show was being stopped. They should, in my opinion, have come to us and said, "Cast and friends, the theater is in bad shape. It's costing a lot of money. The costs aren't being covered and this is not a show that can be sold outside of Tel Aviv. Thank you very much for what you've done and thank you very much for the investment of your time and effort." Instead, no one announced anything. It's kind of the way things are done here. That's the attitude towards actors here in Israel. I saw it when I first immigrated to Israel. I told you once that when I started acting in Romania and they built the state theaters that everything was supported by the government. The director of the theater, who was the communist of all communists, the really pure type, he said, "Gentlemen, in the theater, the main role is the actor! Everything is based around the actor. We need to help him and the show because the show is based on the actor." Theater people were aware that the actor was the main character. Here in Israel, it's the opposite. The 'lead actors' are the stage workers, followed by the lighting technicians, then the managers, and only at the end come the actors. It's not right. Actors here can be substitute actors without coming to rehearsals. They let them see a video of the play and they wire them up with an earpiece to whisper the lines to them, and that's how you're supposed to act across from them. It's been like this all these years. There is no respect for the profession here, there is no appreciation here. And now, particularly, we live in a time when there is no appreciation for actors and no appreciation for the profession.

The Chairs and the Theater of the Absurd

Yaniv: So, if we're already talking about the attitude towards actors, then even though you received great reviews in both *Puntila* and *Bereshit*, you made *Bereshit* in 1962 and your next success, the most significant one, was only in 1970 with *The Chairs*.[1]

---

1 *The Chairs*, by Eugène Ionesco, is an absurd play that tells the story of an old man and an old woman who imagine that guests are coming to hear the old man's speech about the meaning of his life. The old man invites a speaker to speak in his place, but the speaker is unable to

Lea: That's not exactly accurate. I had other good roles along the way, such as *The End of the Race* in 1963, *The Parisian* in 1964, *Talk to Me in Roses* in 1966; all of them were great successes. They were very different roles from one another, and good roles. The differences between the roles allowed for an appreciation for my talent and my acting range. I think that if people still come to me today and tell me that they remember me from *Bereshit*, it shows that you reap what you sow and I left my mark. The appreciation for me started slowly, but my name became known quite quickly.

Yaniv: It's interesting that even in shows that were less successful, both the reviews and the audience loved you.

Lea: That's true, and I'm happy for that. That came only later in *The Chairs*.

Yaniv: How did you even get the job? Shlomo Bar Shavit told me that the roles were actually intended for Hanna Rovina and Aharon Meskin. The reason was that they were old and would have to rehearse for a long time; they could not take over the role because it was physically difficult. The old woman has to carry dozens of chairs, but as long as they are in rehearsals, they will not nag the management to find them roles. Except that Bar Shavit was enthusiastic about the role and demanded to play it. Is that true?

Lea: Yes. Finkel, who was the director, thought of making *The Chairs* with Rovina and Meskin, and assigned the job of directing to David Levin. Levin told him that two actors who have physical strength should be cast. Sixty chairs had to be brought onto the stage and he couldn't see how Rovina and Meskin, who were already very old, would be able to do it. I don't know what happened, but Finkel gave in to him and told him, "OK, do it with whomever you want." Finkel openly said that he wanted the role for Rovina. Between us, it wasn't material

---

speak. Guests arrive during the show to hear the old man's speech, but they do not exist in reality, only in the imagination of the old man and the old woman. The couple brings a chair for each of the imaginary guests and, at the end of the play, the stage is full of chairs. The play belongs to the genre of absurd plays due to several motifs that exist in it, including the lack of meaning of the text. The couple often contradict themselves; the sets project a sense of both claustrophobia and agoraphobia. The old man's house is surrounded by water on all sides, is in the heart of the ocean, and is far from everything related to civilization in terms of time or place. There is also repetition in the play. The elders talk about actions they take every evening and it seems as if the imagined audience is also an action that repeats itself every evening even though in the end they jump, so to speak, to their death in the water. For more on the analysis of the play, see Eli Rozik, *Basics of Play Analysis* [Hebrew] (Tel Aviv: Or Am, 1992).

for Meskin and Rovina, so Levin took me and Bar Shavit. Levin was worried because it was very different material from what they were used to presenting in Israel. We played in Meskin Hall. Then, it was still called the small hall, and on the day, we did the dress rehearsal, there was a premiere of another show in the big hall, which was later called Rovina Hall. Levin invited several people, among them Michael Ohad, who was highly regarded at the time. I didn't know he had invited him. We performed the play and, the next day, his article came out full of praise for us. Finkel, who was the artistic director and was at the premiere at the Rovina Hall, was furious when he saw the article by Ohad because he didn't know that Ohad had even been invited while he hadn't. It seemed like we bypassed him. We went to Finkel and asked for forgiveness. We told him we didn't know and we apologized. "If you want, we can dress up and do the show for you." We got dressed, made up, the backdrop was on stage, and Finkel sat alone in the hall and saw the play from beginning to end, including lighting, music and everything. After the show, Finkel told us, "I was very offended that I wasn't invited, but it's a beautiful show, you're doing a great job and good luck to you."[2] You know, it was a time when he was laughed at quite a bit, but he was a real man of the theater. He could have said that the play was not good and decided to take it down just because of the insult, but his integrity as a man of the theater forced him to tell the truth and wish us luck. Later on, Finkel had the idea of casting Rovina and Meskin in the role, but they weren't up to it.

Yaniv: How did you come to play the role? You were forty years old at the time and you played an older woman. How did that affect your acting?

Lea: Not at all. She is a childish old woman. She is naive. Everything makes her happy. She is like a small child. She did not lose her youth. When I think back on it, I think it was a great role.

Yaniv: The play is a 'theater of the absurd.' You talk and contradict yourselves. There really aren't any guests. They are invented and imagined by you. The text is there, but it is all imaginary because there are really no people who come.

---

2 This encounter is described from Finkel's point of view in his book *The Margin of Totality: Hesitations of an Artistic Mission* [Hebrew] (Tel Aviv: Akad, 1976), 78–80. Finkel claims that the private show was held for him a week later because Lea had suffered from a sore throat.

Lea: This work in the text in which we talk to imaginary people, together with the direction, was very exciting! We would invent the attitude of the characters in rehearsals. It was a very interesting job.

Yaniv: What was special here about building relationships with the different characters?

Lea: We really created the people. I mean, if I talked to a woman, I really saw her and imagined the way she was dressed, who she was and what she was, and if I liked her. I was shaking with excitement that this fine lady had come to visit the plain old woman. Or when the tall officer came and I could hardly reach him and he was kissing my hand, I felt like I wanted to die of happiness. It's a fascinating work process. The play is wonderful. There was a moment when we were arguing and suddenly, he said to me, "What about Carl?" Can you imagine that suddenly, something is introduced into the conversation that was not there and has not yet been created and it is so real. Suddenly there is something inside of you and you don't know where it came from. I still use lines from the show to this day. For example, when I go to a place or when I watch TV and see some kind of reception, and people arrive that no one knows who they are or where they came from, but everyone behaves as though they know everyone, even though they really don't. I always ask, "Who are all these people?" Just as the old woman asked in the play.

Yaniv: You said something very interesting. You said that you also look for the theater of the absurd in real life, that life sometimes looks like the theater of the absurd.

Lea: That's right. That's how it is sometimes. That's why he wrote it that way. They are in an unspecified time and place and in life, you are in a specified time and place, at home, outside and so on, but the feeling—who you are, what you are, where you are, if you feel lost with no way out and no solution– it's a real feeling, both in life and in the theater.

Yaniv: So, when they jump into the water, what does their suicide mean?

Lea: Their life has no real meaning; they are at a dead end.

Yaniv: If I understand you correctly, you are saying, in fact, that in order to act the theater of the absurd, you need to find the realistic logic in the play.

Lea: Correct. He didn't write absurdity. It's not absurd. Even in madness, there is logic. Think about it, a person opens his mouth and speaks and you hear nothing. How much do we hear every day from politicians and in general on TV and you don't actually hear anything.

Yaniv: Yehoshua (Joshua) Sobol directed *Waiting for Godot* at the Yiddishpiel Theater following research by two French scholars, Valentin and Pierre Temkine, as a realistic play in which two Jews escape from northern France during the Nazi occupation and, near the Spanish border, they wait for Godot to take them across the border.[3] He didn't change a word of the text, but put the realistic logic into it.

Lea: Yes, the same is true in *The Chairs*. It's not absurd, it's life. You have to find the logic behind the text. When I'm acting in a theater-of-the-absurd play, I'm looking for the realistic logic, and that's what I perform.

Yaniv: The show *The Chairs* made history. Israeli television had just been established at that point and they decided to film the show for television.

Lea: Yes, that was our good fortune. A videographer named Paul Salinger came from South Africa and he decided to shoot the show with one camera in one take without cuts. He sat for five days and watched the rehearsals we performed for him two or three times a day. He learned the play by heart and stood with a camera on his shoulder and filmed the play in one take. It's the show exactly as we performed it on stage and it turned out wonderfully.

Yaniv: Shlomo Bar Shavit told me that, after he (Salinger) took the video, he told you that he would come back the next day because there was a section that did not turn out well enough in terms of videography, and you did it again.

Lea: That's right. We worked with him for five days. It was not on stage, but we built the exact setting in his studio in Herzliya. Just so you understand, he was shooting with a shoulder camera, it's not like shooting with five cameras. Although even then it was common to shoot with multiple cameras, but this was

---

3   Pierre Temkine, "Auf den Spuren von Godot: Eine Literarische Ermittlung" [Following the traces of Godot: A literary investigation], in *Warten auf Godot: Das Absurde und die Geschichte* [*Waiting for Godot*: The absurd and history], ed. Pierre Temkine, Denis Thouard, and Tim Trzaskalik, 2nd ed. (Berlin: Matthes & Seitz, 2009), 29–42.

his artistic vision. As if there is only one person seeing the show from beginning to end with a single angle of just that person's vision. The result was very artistic and special. Sadly, he died young.

Yaniv: And Ionesco himself saw your show?

Lea: Yes, we were in Jerusalem and Ionesco came to see us perform. After the show, we met with him; he really liked our production.

Mother Courage and Mother Dina

Yaniv: I want to skip to 1975 to *Mother Courage and Her Children*.

Lea: There were big changes in Habima Theater then. The art director wasn't Finkel. It was the threesome, Yossi Izraeli, Omri Nitzan, and David Levin. They said were doing *Mother Courage* and they offered me the lead role. It didn't go smoothly. Geula Cohen raised a question in the Knesset asking why this anti-war play was being staged in Israel, which was a very young country back then and was fighting for its life. It was a complete mess.[4] But in short, I got the job! I knew Levin from working on *The Chairs* and I knew *Mother Courage* from back home in Romania. In Romania, Brecht was one of the most respected and popular authors so the text wasn't foreign to me. The show was a huge success.

Yaniv: *Mother Courage* was the last role your mother played in Romania. When you were offered to play the role in 1975, your mother had already been gone for several years because she had passed away in 1964. Did this affect you?

---

4   The controversy surrounding the staging of the play in the theater was brought up by Yosef Geva, a member of the theater's board of trustees, who argued against staging the play due to its anti-war nature and due to the fact that it was given to director David Levin, "who has extreme left-wing views and, because of this, the play may take on an anti-war character, which we do not want now." This was in 1975, when the State of Israel was still in the midst of the trauma of the Yom Kippur War. On the eve of the war, the Cameri Theater wanted to stage the play, but, due to the war, and even after it, they chose not to run the play due to its anti-war nature. According to the play, war was not acceptable under any circumstances. With the Yom Kippur War, people understood that this pacifistic stance was not accurate. For more information, see Aliza Wallach, "Lea Courage" [Hebrew], *Dvar HaPoelet*, November 7, 1975, 30; Aryeh Gelblum, "Yossi Courage in Habima" [Hebrew], *Ma'ariv*, July 14, 1975, 5.

Lea: Very much! It affected me a lot! The truth is that I took the play and dedicated it to her. Zvi made a very nice dedication to me. He bought me a gold pendant with *Mother Courage* engraved on it. I told myself that I had to be excellent in the role in her memory and to honor my mother. I didn't see my mother in the role because I was already in Israel, but I imagined how she performed it. She was a great dramatic actress and I know she performed it brilliantly. She was also the right age to play the part.

Yaniv: What did you think of the character, Mother Courage? She can be seen as a woman with no sympathy, a woman who uses the war to make profit.

Lea: That's exactly what she does.

Yaniv: The impression I got from your role is that she is not a cruel woman or someone who takes advantage of the situation.

Lea: No, she's not cruel. Not at all. Mother Courage is, first of all, a smart and sexy woman. She is a woman in every sense of the word. And her strength is that she uses the war to live her life, but what she doesn't realize is that the war takes advantage of her. She thinks the war gives her a chance to live, but she does not see or realize that the war also takes advantage of her mentality as a human being and makes her less moral. Mother Courage is trying to survive and, in the name of survival, she loses her children, but she continues on and continues to live. I think that this momentum of her carrying on, where she says that war is such a terrible thing and it takes advantage of you even after you lose everything, is very important. War means survival in her eyes. In my humble opinion, war is not about survival, it's about moments of survival.

Yaniv: You didn't think she was simply a woman trying to survive so she does it consciously, like doing terrible things not to lose money and, in the process, she takes advantage of everyone around her?

Lea: No, she is a smart woman, but even a smart person doesn't understand everything. She has to lose her children to understand what war is. She didn't do those harsh things on purpose; they happened because of her survival instinct. Brecht wanted the play to be performed without sentiment, but he couldn't do it. He also wanted it to be performed at the same time as the war so that the audience would be indifferent to it, so that they would hate it as much as they hate war. But you can't. It's impossible to remain indifferent to a mother who loses her children. Mother Courage is not cruel. She uses war to survive, but she is not cruel, the war is cruel.

Yaniv: Is it possible that when you played Mother Courage, you thought of the time during the war when your mother was sick with typhus and you had to take care of her instead of her taking care of you?

Lea: Probably. All those things came back to me when I was building the role. All wars have similarities and survival is survival. I remembered how, when we were traveling by train, my mother took me outside the trailer to wash me and I cried because I was a child and I was afraid. I saw my mother's fight for survival. Mother Courage reminded me a lot of my mother, just that my mother was against wars and didn't think it was possible to take advantage of war.

Yaniv: It is possible that through *Mother Courage*, you could, in some way, eliminate the anger of the little girl who was angry with her mother because, instead of her mother taking care of her, she had to take care of her sick mother. And when you play the role of the mother who sacrifices her children and remains silent when her children die, do you feel your mother who was silent when she was sick and could not take care of you?

Lea: Mother Courage's silence is thunderous. When I played Mother Courage, I saw the war and how my mother fought to give me food. Maybe I was also thinking about myself in that period, but in such moments, it was difficult to compare. This play is a great work, it's not a simple piece. Interestingly, I didn't think that I had done anything special at all when I took care of my mother.

Yaniv: When the performance stopped running, how did you feel?

Lea: Honestly, I was at a time in my life when we had gotten used to performing a play and soon after, it would close. It was impossible to travel with the performance outside the city because there was a revolving stage set. We performed in Kfar Saba and in Jerusalem, but nowhere else. It was common to perform and then for the show to stop running. It was an artistic performance, but also a box office success. At that time, I was in three plays: *Mother Courage*, *Kaddish*, and *The Italian Straw Hat*, and after that, I took a vacation and went abroad with Hirshl.

Yaniv: You did *Kaddish* immediately after *Mother Courage*?

Lea: That's right, Yossi Izraeli did a very nice repertoire at that time and right after we came out with *Mother Courage*, he asked me to be in *Kaddish*. Unfortunately, it didn't work well because people weren't used to that kind of show at that time. It's not written as a normal play and there were video clips integrated into the play. It was similar to modern fringe plays, but we did it over forty years ago! For me, it was wonderful, it was a really unique experience. There was a radio commentator who said, "Tonight, a meteor fell from the sky" and I was the meteor! Hanan Snir, who directed, also received good reviews.

Yaniv: *Kaddish* is a long poem. How did Hanan Snir make a play out of it?

Lea: In America, a play was made out of it and also a movie and Habima took the idea, but it didn't go over well with the audience. It wasn't well received, but I really liked it.

Yaniv: After the premiere of the play *Kaddish*, Hirshl wrote you a poem, which you also chose to have engraved on his tombstone.

> When I see a night weeps saying Kaddish after a young day who had died in a work accident,
> I do not cry.
> When I hear a bird saying Kaddish after a felled forest in the jungle of progress,
> I do not cry.
> When I'm standing in a cemetery in the place where Kaddish tears up the graves and cuts a tear in people's hearts,
> I do not cry.
> When I see you on stage when you turn dead words into living monuments, I cry.

What made him write it then?

Lea: Zvika didn't always tell me what he was thinking. I find things out even today. Apparently, the play *Kaddish* had a great influence on him and he decided to dedicate it to me. This poem is very moving for me. You know, on his *yarzheit* (anniversary of his death), when we go to the cemetery, I always ask that they read the poem written on his tombstone. I think it's a wonderful poem. He thought I was a great actress, but he never told me that. He just said it to others. He thought I could do anything. The truth is that sometimes I wonder about what I've done, so many shows . . . I have had a nice repertoire in my career.

Yaniv: But this poem also talks about Hirshl's feelings and sensitivity towards you.

Lea: And his love for me.

Yiddish Concert Tours Abroad

Yaniv: So, after *The Italian Straw Hat*, you take an unpaid vacation and travel to New York for performances in Yiddish?

Lea: Wait, after the Six Day War, we went to Argentina for the first time. We were booked before the war, but the war postponed all plans. The seasons are opposite there; it was summer here and winter there. Then, for the first time, we took unpaid leave and went to Argentina and stayed there for twenty months. That's why you can see that during those years, I have no roles at Habima. This is why there is a break in my activity in the theater from *Tango* to *The Cobbler's Holiday* that was not interesting, and in the same year that I did *The Cobbler's Holiday*, I also acted in *The Chairs*.

Yaniv: And the next time you traveled was in 1977 to New York. Was it an invitation?

Lea: We went to New York, but the intention was to go to Venezuela. In New York, we performed in Yiddish by chance. There was a community from Bukovina (Poland) in New York and there were many people who knew me and Zvi and arranged performances for us. In Venezuela, our friends organized shows for us and, when we returned to New York, we performed there again and then we went to Europe. In Paris and in Berlin, we performed shows. It was our first time in Berlin. After the big trip we did in 1967, we traveled every few years. We also went to Australia twice.

Yaniv: When was the performance of *A Por fun Gott* (A couple from God), which you filmed in Canada?

Lea: It was in 1984, when I made the *Dos Tepel*, Sholem Aleichem's *The Pot*, in honor of the one hundred and twenty-fifth anniversary of Sholem Aleichem's birth. We've been to a lot of places. It's impossible remember everything...

Yaniv: What material did you do in Yiddish?

Lea: Zvika always built an evening that started with nostalgia for yesterday and we would then move onto current events. We would do sketches he wrote. We had a wonderful political sketch of *Mr. Weiss and Madame Schwartz* (Mr. White and Mrs. Black).

Yaniv: These were always evenings of sketches he wrote. You didn't do an entire show in Yiddish?

Lea: We also performed complete plays. We did *Bereshit* in Yiddish. I played the roles of Eve and Ishtar, which I did in Hebrew. Zvika played the snake and local actors played the garden's owner (God) and the other roles. In Argentina, we also performed the play, *Di Zilberne Chaseneh* (The silver wedding). In the shows, in addition to the material that Zvika wrote, we did sketches and segments of the great Yiddish writers: Sholem Aleichem, Eliezer Steinbarg, Yitskhok Leybush Peretz, Itzik Manger, A. Lutzky (Aaron Zucker), and more. In places where there were Hebrew speakers, we also presented in Hebrew, and some of the sketches, like the sketch about the mother, I also did in English. After I did *Stars Without Sky* in 1992, we took it to Manchester. It was a play Zvika put together using excerpts from Yiddish writers he had collected. These are not passages he wrote. Therefore, he says that these writers have no sky. There were some writers he really liked. We did it on the stage in Hebrew and not in Yiddish so that the audience would get to know these writers. The audience wanted to hear some Yiddish, but we did this because we wanted the audience who was not familiar with these materials to get to know the Yiddish writers.

Yaniv: In the show that they filmed, the audience yelled at you, "Yiddish! Do a segment in Yiddish," and you said to them, "Why don't you come to my shows in Yiddish," but you improvised a song *Varnitshkes* (*Gevald, vi nemt men?* / Help, where do you take?) on the spot.

Lea: Is that what I said? Maybe, I don't remember . . . In any case, after we finished presenting it in Hebrew on the stage, we went to perform in Yiddish in Manchester with the same material. There is nothing to be done. In Yiddish, it sounds better . . .

Chapter 7

The Parents

Lea: I would like a significant part of this book to be dedicated to my mother and father and the work they did, which was not for nothing. They left a mark. I have a theory that I'm not sure I'm right about. They managed to introduce a love of theater to the Eastern European audience, which exists to this day, and I would really like to emphasize that.

Yaniv: Here in Israel, there was disdain towards the Yiddish theater of Eastern Europe, but your parents were very important representatives of the theater.

Lea: I don't know how to rank their level of importance; they started to act and perform after the theater was already in existence. Before them, there was Abraham Goldfaden; there was also Sholem Aleichem who wrote *Wandering Stars*, which is such a significant story about Yiddish actors. But, like many Jewish actors, they fought to act and perform.

Yaniv: How did your parents fight? Let's talk about your mother.

Lea: They didn't think they were fighting; they were actors. My mother, well, she was a prodigy! She performed everything in Polish. There were all kinds of troupes she performed in. I have pictures of her on stage as a child, and I know Finkel saw her as a little girl on stage in Grodno and he remembered it. Then she played the grandson Shlomele in *Mirele Efros* with Esther Rachel Kamińska. Kamińska told my mother that she should not change her name, that the name Dina Koenig must remain, and not change it.

Yaniv: I have a Vilna Troupe program and, in it, her name was written as Dina Kamien.

Lea: She changed her name when she got married, but very quickly she returned to using her stage name, Dina Koenig, by which she was known.[1] Unfortunately, I don't know all that much, but I do know that they worked and traveled a lot, and each time they started some new troupe. And forming troupes was not easy. There was always some impresario who would book them and they would travel to do the show. There was no government support back then. They drove with horse-drawn carriages to all the far-flung places where Jews lived at the time. And there were performances in all types of conditions. I think in *Wandering Stars* (*Blondzhende Shtern*) Sholem Aleichem described it really well. I would like for people to really appreciate the lengths they went to.

Yaniv: There is a feeling that the attitude towards these theaters was disparaging because the perception was that they didn't do art theater, just couplets and *schund*.

Lea: You are mistaken. That was the perception that existed in Israel! We are talking about the pre-World War II concept in Warsaw.[2] There were artistic theaters there. Here in Israel, people had the tendency not to speak Yiddish and it created an anti-Yiddish environment in general. There were artistic groups in Eastern Europe such as the Vilna Troupe, the Ida Kamińska Theate, and the Turkov Troupe. They played a serious repertoire and there were serious theaters and not just *schund*. And if you're already talking about them, then take a look at the theaters in Israel these days, only comedies and musicals. You can't blame them and say they only made *schund*. They did good things and had an

---

1   In an advertisement in the *Lodzer Vekker* newspaper dated March 8, 1929, Dina appeared as Dina Koenig Kamien, and in the same newspaper in an ad from July 3, 1931, she is once again called only Dina Koenig, and hence remained Koenig without her married name, Kamien.
2   In Eastern Europe, the intellectual elite did not go to the Yiddish theater as it was considered vulgar and inferior. Yitskhok Leybush Peretz believed in the power of the theater to educate the people and, therefore, tried to make the Yiddish theater more artistic, dealing with higher literary quality, subjects, and culture. Throughout the history of the Yiddish theater, there were lower theaters, but also theaters with a higher artistic level, such as Peretz Hirshbein's theater, the theater of Esther Rachel Kamińska, and of course, the Vilna Troupe. For more, see Michael Steinlauf, "The Jewish Theater in Poland" [Hebrew], in *Existence and Fracture of Polish Jews across Their Generations*, ed. Israel Bartal and Israel Gutman (Jerusalem: Zalman Shazar Center for Jewish History, 2001), vol. 2, 327–349; *Yiddish Theater in Europe Between the Two World Wars: Materialen zu der Histätt von Yiddish Teater* [Yiddish], vol. 1: *Poland*, ed. Itzik Manger, Janas Turkau, Moshe Perenson (New York: Alweltlicher Yiddishcher Kultur Congress, 1968), 13.

interesting repertoire, even if they did operettas and lighter performances. They did it without any financial support. In Israel, they did it and got support.

Yaniv: Did your mother also perform in operettas?

Lea: Of course, she started it.

Yaniv: Like what?

Lea: Many, *Tsipka Fire, Yankele*. They were very beautiful plays with beautiful songs and wonderful music. There was another such play called *The Last Dance* about a girl who is wrongly accused of murder. She sits in a prison and her lawyer falls in love with her. It's *a gantse mayse* (a whole long story). In the prison, she sings a duet. There was a play in which she acted called *Raisel Macht Karriere* (Raisel makes a career), which was adapted from a German play called *The Church Mouse*, also about a poor girl. She had a scene where she sits by the window and has a really lovely monologue. She has nothing to eat, but she imagines what kind of sandwich she's eating. In these operettas, there was always the star with a partner, a young couple who were lovers, they were the *soubrettes*.[3] They danced, sang, and fell in love, and the older couple, the parents, were character actors, and there were one or two comedians. This is how the casts were built and the plays were written for these types of casts. Before I immigrated to Israel, my mother told me I shouldn't act in such things because I'm not used to doing things like that.

Yaniv: But your mother acted in those types of plays and she enjoyed it.

Lea: She did what the troupe wanted at the time.

Yaniv: But it's not just the repertoire in question. In terms of the quality of the acting, the setting, the directing, did the director manage to restrain the actors from making all kinds of unrelated jokes for the audience to give them a good show?

Lea: It always depended on the director. My mother acted in August Strindberg's *The Father* in a private theater. There was a wonderful actor there who came from

---

3   An actress or other female performer playing a lively, flirtatious role in a play or opera. French: *soubrette*.

the Soviet Union. They performed the show in all kinds of conditions. They were performing in some carpeted hangar. In a show like this, they certainly didn't do any tricks and they were still excellent. If you are a good actor, you can perform in any situation. People spoke against the theater, but really, they had no idea.

Yaniv: What were the most interesting roles that you saw your mother in?

Lea: There were many. Frida Trachtenberg in *Hasia, The Orphan*; the stepmother in Abraham Goldfaden's *The Witch*, and in Jacob Gordin's *Kreutzer Sonata*, a wonderful dramatic role. She acted in an endless number of wonderful Russian plays. We both acted in *The Kovacs Family*, hence the picture of me sitting on her lap.[4] It's a Romanian play.

Character Actress

Yaniv: If you had to characterize your mother's acting, how would you define it?

Lea: When she started, she started in operettas. The roles were of beautiful young girls who run, jump, and sing. At the age of forty, she said, "It's over!" She wanted to switch to character roles. She did it and she put it in my head and it saved me. She told me that at the age of forty, the legs no longer look the same as they used to and you have to switch to character roles. And thanks to her, I also moved over to character roles, so I was able to continue my career in acting. There are many actresses who don't know how to make this transition.

Yaniv: Years ago, Bar Shavit told me, "Lea is a tremendous character actress." What does it mean for you to be a character actress; what else do you do?

Lea: Being a character actress depends on understanding the role. You need to really understand the role you're playing. The features of an older person change. You are no longer agile; coordination is no longer as good as it once was. Walking also takes on a different form. When you get a character role, it means you get into that character, an older or a strange character.

---

4   See page 221.

Grocery Store

Yaniv: I can see what you are referring to when I see you on stage, but how do you do it? Let's take for example the play *Grocery Store*. Your voice is lower than your natural voice was at that time. Your body, its heaviness, it's very different from your own.

Lea: I was very young back then. It was in 1982. Our profession is based somewhat on imitation and that's legitimate, but the imitation has to be reliable, not a caricature impersonation. When I worked on *Grocery Store*, I lived in Ma'oz Aviv on the border of Hadar Yosef. There was a grocery store in Hadar Yosef and it was a woman who owned it. I said to myself, "What do I do? How can I build this character?" One day, I passed by and the woman's legs were all swollen and they were wrapped in bandages. I saw her and I said to myself, "This is a woman who went through the Holocaust, who has had such a hard life. I want to be her on stage." So, I wrapped my legs in bandages and became that woman. Of course, I took the features from the text of the play; Hillel Mittelpunkt had described the woman and that was the woman that I had to portray, but I thought about the woman I had seen.

Yaniv: How do you bring out her qualities in the play?

Lea: Firstly, through the text. Secondly, you have to be very careful and curious about what others in the play say about you. What do they say about my character? What am I like as a person? How do people react to me?

Yaniv: Let's take an example, Mr. Shtoch, a man doing his grocery shopping, played by Zvi, arrives in the store and says to Mrs. Laiche, a woman in the grocery store, "What do you want from me? I bought the groceries. You guys can go." And you beg him to leave you at the grocery store. What can you take from this line?

Lea: In this line, there is despair, there is fear, there is worry about what will happen. All these things add up together and then the emotion of all that momentum comes out.

Yaniv: You said you saw the woman with the bandages and you put bandages on your own legs. The bandages are an external prop. How do the bandages touch you inside?

Lea: You imagine that those legs don't know how to carry you and then your walk is affected by it too. You also take a look at the people around you and you see how they walk and you use that a little bit as well. Through the bandage, the gait changes, and it affects your face. You start to feel it. When I played *Behind the Fence,* there is the part with the dog that I have to slaughter. I thought to myself that this passage moves me anew every night because this woman, at that moment, also brings something else out of all the evil and the anger, a kind of compassion emerges from her. She kills the dog so that it won't suffer. Here is a character who seems bad to us, yet suddenly, a moment of kindness comes over her and you say, "How did that come to her?" And it blends in with our own lives and the experiences we go through.

Yaniv: Do you put your life in that scene? Are you thinking about your own dog?

Lea: No, but I always think about that woman.

Yaniv: When you enter the stage for the first time in the play *Behind the Fence* you are a very heavy woman, you even have a lower voice. Is that intentional?

Lea: Yes.

Yaniv: Why?

Lea: Because if I speak in a loud voice, it would not be appropriate. Now my voice is tired, but when I was young, I worked a lot on changing my voice so that it would sound true to the character and not fake. You study people, that's one of the fascinating things. A person's character is always a surprising thing. You know people and suddenly you discover something new and you ask yourself what goes through a person's mind. What makes people suddenly behave completely differently from how they normally do?

Yaniv: I'm asking more than that. You talk about observing the character and I'm talking about technique. When you play someone who is elderly, you don't straighten your fingers, it's a technique.

Lea: I observe people. I have seen old people whose hands do not open all the way; they can't straighten them. You observe. I have acquired these skills over many years. When I sit in the company of others, I see everything. I'm watching. I can feel them.

Yaniv: Did they teach you this in acting studies?

Lea: Yes, but mostly, it's skills that I have accumulated through all the roles I have played over the years. The basis is really the study of people; to see, to feel. At first, I was not so aware of it. But over the years, I started to be aware of the movements of the people around me. There are people you talk to and they seem to sing all the time. There are people who have something that bothers them inside and they talk to you and their voice seems to be acting. It has nothing to do with anything. There was once such an actress in the theater. Her life wasn't easy and she always seemed to be singing, like she was in a good mood, but it wasn't a good mood. It was her inner self. They seem to be with you, but inside, there is something that does not let them rest. There are people that don't notice these things, but I do.

Yaniv: Do you bring all these things with you on to the stage?

Lea: Every time, something different comes out. I wasn't aware of it, but Zvika's cousin told me about my role in *Behind the Fence*. "Only you can play that role," she said. I know why she said that; it's because she saw people like that. She was in Transnistria and she actually saw them. I also saw them in the Soviet Union, in Tashkent when we were nearing the end of the war. The wall between our apartment and the apartment of the gentile next to us was thin and I heard her crying for her son who fell in the war.

Yaniv: How do you create the difference in the roles between a Jewish woman and a gentile woman? In *Behind the Fence*, what makes Mrs. Shkoripinshchika, a gentile, different from when you play *a yiddene* (an old Jewish woman)?

Lea: There is a huge difference—in their education, in their mentality—there is a huge difference! We, my generation and the generation before me, we always grew up with some inner fear. I think possibly because abroad, we were surrounded by gentiles, but we never approached them. In the play, the fact that the child recognizes the gentiles, he perceives the fact that they live a different life, that their ambitions are different.

Yaniv: Is it abstract?

Lea: No, it's not abstract. The gentiles were used to being in nature; the Jews never considered being in nature.[5] The different worldviews make a difference. I always ask where antisemitism comes from and it cannot be silenced. We are in the twenty-first century and it cannot be silenced any longer. I saw it too in the gentiles that were in my life. For example, I can't forget how, when I was just a little girl standing next to my mother, I don't remember where, but there were fields. Gentiles walked in the fields barefoot and sang in two or three melodies. This freedom, the power to sing in a wide range, as they walked with their shovels on their shoulders and sang. It's a whole different world.

Yaniv: So how did you get into the role in *Behind the Fence*?

Lea: The gentile had a problem; she lived there alone for many years. The woman's entire family was buried there and she was not prepared to move.

Yaniv: Was it also the Jews?

Lea: The character is always alone and that's why she's bitter. Jews don't live alone. Judaism is a community religion. There's something inside of her, which she reveals only at the end of the play.

Yaniv: You speak about humanity. The woman in the play clings to the past. She has no children. All she has left are her parents' graves and she clings to them to preserve their memory. This, by the way, is very similar to you.

Lea: Right.

Yaniv: But you acted in the role of a gentile. What do you do so that the gentile does not look like a Jew?

Lea: This is where the technique comes in. First of all, I'm tougher. The technique is to feel one's body is different. She is strong and healthy, she's not melodramatic. Jews sigh and always say, "*Oy vey's mir*" (Oh, woe is me). The gentiles

---

5   This is the case, for example, in *Fishke the Lame* (*The Book of the Beggars*) by Mendele Mocher Sforim. At the beginning of the story, Mendele describes the Jew as someone who does not allow himself to enjoy the beauty of nature, unlike the gentiles. See Mendele Mocher Sforim, *Collected Writings*, vol. 1, *Fishke the Lame* [Hebrew] (Krakow: Va'ad HaYovel, 1909), 1–3.

don't; they cross themselves, but do not sigh as Jews do. The gentiles in the play are Cossacks; they are healthy, strong people. It depends on the education, the mentality, the way they build their lives. There is a scene in the play where I shoot a Jew. I think that a Jewish woman, like the Jewish family in the play, would not have been able to shoot. A few Jewish women were shot during the revolution. The woman who shot Vladimir Lenin was Jewish,[6] but they didn't give Jewish girls handguns.

Yaniv: So, if I understand you correctly, to build a character, you don't just take it from the text, but also from the characters you have known in your life, your observations of their character and behavior?

Lea: When you build a role, you also think about where the person is, where you saw them, and how you met them.

Yaniv: Is it easier for you to play characters that you've actually known in your life?

Lea: No, the point is not whether I actually knew them or not. The point is that every human being, whichever type of person you are, you have to bring that character to the stage, even if you haven't met them. It's interesting ... and you ask yourself, "How can I best shape the role?"

Yaniv: So, let's go back to talking about *King Lear* because that's certainly a character that you haven't met.

Lea: I never met King Lear, but I have met people whose children have left them and mistreated them.

Between *King Lear* and *Mirele Efros*, the Jewish Queen Lear

Yaniv: I will ask it differently. *King Lear* and *Mirele Efros*. *Mirele Efros* is based on *King Lear* and there are monologues in the play taken from *King Lear*. You referred to these two characters in a completely different way. What did you take from her and what did you take from him?

---

6   Fanny Kaplan, a twenty-eight-year-old Jewish woman, shot Lenin (not fatally) three times in the summer of 1918 because she thought that he was no longer loyal to the revolution.

Lea: When I was offered to play *King Lear*, I said I didn't want to play a man. But then together, the director and I agreed that within every person there are male and female elements. Today, we live in a modern world; men live as women and *vice versa*. But that wasn't the point. The idea was that men and women could go through the same things regardless of their gender. I started by getting rid of the fear that I was not a man and all my thoughts were about the desperation of this person. I was not interested in the story of his fascism. I was interested in his endless giving to children and what he got in return for it. His despair for the children was so great that it drove him to insanity. I went with it. The despair begins immediately. Already in the second scene, he gets hit, and again in the third scene, until he is thrown out. His humiliation, his despair interested me. How can you discourage a person in such a way?

Yaniv: So, what does the fact that he is king mean?

Lea: I thought about it. He says that he is not a wise king. He's not stupid, but I asked myself what caused him to give his entire kingdom to children. The director told me it was a historical matter. I don't believe it interested Shakespeare. I just think he wrote melodrama and put the surrounding characters in there to create a story. But the conflict is irrelevant to him being king. He was actually criticizing the environment that was around him. Lear's daughters are not only evil, but also egocentric; they want to take the king's place. If the director hadn't put in the microphones and all the choirs, if he had left it as a simple melodrama, it could have been more successful.

Yaniv: That's what you did when you played in *Mirele Efros*? You acted in a melodrama as you play in a melodrama.

Lea: And those who saw the play *Mirele Efros* will remember it forever!

Yaniv: I will say something that may not be acceptable to you, but, in my opinion, Jacob Gordin improved the play in terms of plot progression and the monologues as well as the development of the characters in his adaptation.

Lea: Without a doubt! And in the production of *King Lear* in which I played, we put so much emphasis on it, but the essence of the play was lost.

Yaniv: There were also complaints against the direction of *Mirele Efros* in the production in which you performed.

Lea: True, but the play *shpilt zikh aleyn* (plays by itself) and it has its success. *Mirele Efros* is a play that stands out. It's a play you can't kill. Even when amateurs perform it, it works. Gordin wrote a play that works in all kinds of situations. At the Yiddish theater, they would always say that when the theater was in trouble, they would take *Mirele Efros* out of the box and save the theater.

Yaniv: Do you think Mirele is different from King Lear?

Lea: Yes, very different from him. She is a woman, and she was a beautiful and feminine woman. She says she was chased a lot after she became a widow. And she's different because she doesn't come from a rich background. She was a housewife and her husband suddenly went bankrupt and died. She makes a change in her life and shows that a woman can succeed in any position and not just be the 'wife of' or a servant. Her desperation is that her children do not understand her. Raising children and trying to protect them from facing difficulties in life is a mistake. I was with my mother during the war and with my parents after it. I saw how they survived. I lived with them. I knew when there was enough and when there wasn't. Why didn't the child know?

Yaniv: You said yourself that you didn't have a childhood.

Lea: No, I didn't have a childhood because there was a war on and I didn't have friends to play with, that's what I meant. But my parents took me to shows all the time and I knew what was playing in the theater. Lear gave endlessly to his daughters while he was still king. He kept only his name for himself. Mirele Efros made a fatal error when she transfers the property; this is a parent's weakness.

Yaniv: When you played Mirele Efros, what was your motivation to give your children the property? You did not show weakness in the role.

Lea: Don't forget, she's in a different position. She proved herself and she proved she could run the business. She transfers the property and she makes a mistake. She has a lot of anger towards her children for asking for the property, so she shouts at them, "Out!" Lear also shouts at his daughters. Mirele is a very strong woman who knows very well what she is doing. She transfers the property from a position of strength, even if I think she made a mistake. When she is beaten (emotionally) by the children again and again, she remains strong, and even when she is forced to live with Shalmon and to work for him, she remains a strong woman!

Yaniv: Did you feel that your mother, as a person, was such a woman?

Lea: My mother was very strong!

Yaniv: Did you bring anything of her into the role when you played Mirele?

Lea: I don't think so, not specifically. I was usually very impressed with what she told me; I also saw her act. She was never weak on stage. She always had some strength, a certain power on stage. In the most difficult moments, she knew how to be strong. When she was on stage, she was an excellent actress.

Yaniv: Is there a role that your mother played that is unforgettable for you?

Lea: There are several roles. For example, in *The Kovacs Family*, she goes through difficult things and she played a very interesting character. In Ostrovsky's *The Storm*, she played the boy's mother and she was very impressive in that role.

Yaniv: Was she unusual in comparison to other actors?

Lea: She was simply a better actress. It's just like here. There are good actors and there are bad actors, that's always how it is. Same story. My mother and Sevilla were good actresses. Sevilla was wonderfully talented and graceful. She was a good comedienne and a good dramatic actress. The theater is not filled with many talented actors. There are all kinds of actors; for example, there are actors who want to be stars, but the question is whether they are able to carry the show on their shoulders. Do they have the power to hold the audience?

Yaniv: When you performed in Bucharest, did you stay only in Bucharest or did you also travel around Romania?

Lea: It was a very well-organized state theater. It was funded by the government. There were directors and sets and all the facilities of the theater. We would only travel once a year. They would take a trailer just for the actors and we traveled all over the country, usually with one show. Then there was a time when we went to Iași and stayed there for two weeks and played a few shows. We were just a small troupe for the smaller cities; they have smaller shows. Havis traveled with my mother, Bibiana, and Dita Kronenfeld's husband, who was a violinist. They would send them to the smaller cities, which were impossible to reach with a larger production.

Yaniv: How long did you rehearse for in Bucharest?

Lea: A lot. We were in rehearsals almost all the time, for three to four months. The theater was an institution. Back then, it was possible to invest a lot in rehearsals. In the private theaters, they would do it very quickly and there were actors who always returned to roles they had already done, so they could speed up the rehearsals. As in any profession, there are always practical constraints in the theater that are not only related to the art or essence of the profession. That's always how it is.

Chapter 8

Mirele Efros and the Israel Prize

Yaniv: Let's talk about honor.

Lea: Honor?

Yaniv: Yes. Let's go back to 1986. You were rehearsing for the play *Mirele Efros* with Israel Prize laureate, Shmuel Rodansky, in the role of Mirele's assistant, Shalmon. While rehearsing for the play, you and Miriam Zohar were informed that both of you would be receiving the Israel Prize,[1] which you received in 1987 while the play was running.

Lea: Do you know that they staged the play to mark seventy years of the Habima Theater?

Yaniv: It is interesting that they chose a Yiddish performance to mark the 70th anniversary of the National Theater, which was established, among other things, to revive the Hebrew language.

Lea: Don't forget though that we performed it in Hebrew.

Yaniv: Not only, but let's start from the beginning because this is a really important show. The production of *Mirele Efros* you participated in was a

---

1 The Israel Prize is awarded annually on *Yom HaAtzmaut* (Israel's Independence Day) in a state ceremony in Jerusalem in the presence of the president, the prime minister, the speaker of the Knesset (Israel's Parliament), the Supreme Court president, and the minister of education. The prize is awarded in four areas: the humanities, social sciences, and Jewish studies; life and exact sciences; culture, arts, communication, and sports; and lifetime achievement and exceptional contribution to the nation. The recipients of the prize are Israeli citizens or organizations who have displayed excellence in their field(s) or have contributed strongly to Israeli culture.

landmark in Israeli theater; it was considered to be groundbreaking theater. Although Hanna Rovina had already played the role in Hebrew in 1939 and they renewed the show with Rovina in 1957, the attitude at the time towards Yiddish was disparaging. Leah Goldberg wrote a review of the play saying, "Although I think she is very good in this role, I would like to see her in another role."[2] And in her review section in the newspaper *Dvar HaPoelet*, she wrote, "It's great to see Hanna Rovina in a big role, but beyond that even better to see her in a big production."[3]

Lea: The attitude here to Yiddish back then was unbearable. It's a wonderful play. In the theater, they would say that every time a theater gets into financial difficulties, they take out *Mirele Efros* from the boxes and it rescues the theater. It always succeeds, no matter who performs it. The play is simply wonderfully written, dramaturgically. There are wonderful monologues and excellent dramatic moments. Only here in Israel, they underestimated it.

Yaniv: So, let's talk for a moment about this character of Mirele Efros. She is one of the most fascinating characters, in my opinion, in plays in general and in your career in particular. When Ida Kamińska played the character, she did a kind of *Yiddishe mama*, a little old and weak woman. Hanna Rovina, on the other hand, played it like a lady. How did you create the character of Mirele?

Lea: When I performed the role, I really worked to build the character. I researched her and the period and how a woman in that period would have reacted to the things that happened to her in the play; her responsibilities, her duties, how people would accept the fact that she is a widow who runs a wood-trading business on her own.[4] It was a time when many didn't understand this type of control by a woman; even today there are many who do not accept it. But then, there were signs of, I don't know if it was feminism, but it was the beginning of self-awareness. Mirele feels that she has the strength to do it on her own. She also says that she proved to the whole world that a woman can run a

---

2   Leah Goldberg, "Hanna Rovina (After Her Appearance in *Mirele Efros*)" [Hebrew], *Dvar HaPoelet*, August 15, 1939, 168–167.
3   Leah Goldberg, "*Mirele Efros* at Habima" [Hebrew], *Davar*, July 26, 1939, 4.
4   The play was written by Jacob Gordin in the United States in 1898. See Jacob Gordin, *Mirele Efros: Di Yiddishe Koenigin Lear* [Yiddish] (New York: n.p., 1898). For more on the historical background of the play, see Yaniv Goldberg and Noga Levine-Keini, *The Yiddish Stage in its Psychological and Juristic Aspects* (Newcastle upon Tyne: Cambridge Scholars Publishing, 2023), 27–50.

business and not just be a wife and a servant. At the same time, things were happening with women in England and America. There was a kind of beginning of resistance to women. I think that, even until this period of the late nineteenth and early twentieth centuries when Gordin wrote this play, women proved themselves in many places and made decisions, but much also depended on the men standing next to them. Apparently, it was also impossible from the male point of view to disprove her abilities. This woman—her mind, her strength, her energy—it was impossible to underestimate her. The very fact that a woman brings a child into the world is also not an easy process. When I started working on the character, all these things built up in me and gave me strength to express the character of this woman.

Yaniv: The woman you played was a very strong woman!

Lea: Because she is a strong woman! She took her husband's debts upon herself; an amount of sixty thousand rubles, which back then was a fortune! She paid off all debts and received credit from all parties involved. She had a lot of strength, a strong will and a lot of intelligence. The people who worked with her also appreciated her. She was no weak woman and being a lady was not one of her significant characteristics. Look how her assistant Shalmon treats her. So, when she asks him if she could live with him, he immediately agrees. She is a powerful woman. When you receive such a blow from your children, when you receive such humiliation from your daughter-in-law, a girl who comes out of nowhere and insults you non-stop . . . Mirele is going through a powerful process in that moment when she decides to transfer the property to her children.

Yaniv: What you are saying is very interesting. If I understand you correctly, you think Mirele could only have reached that moment of transferring the property because Sheindele humiliated her over and over again. Mirele delivers a monologue in which she reveals the whole truth, the truth she hid all those years in order to protect her children, only because she was slowly warming up until she got tired, and like a heater that is boiling and finally explodes, only then does she reveal everything.

Lea: That's right, and it continues until the end of the play. By the way, she appreciates Sheindele. She says to her, "You're right! It's time for me to tell you the truth. Why should I have to hide? You are a grown woman. It's time for you to know. Let's see you. Let's see how you deal with life." It takes strength to say the things she didn't dare to say out loud until that moment. You know, sometimes even on a daily basis, I say to friends who have problems with their children, "Why don't you tell them? You think you are protecting your children, but the truth is that you are ashamed to say it, that's all." Mirele takes this smart decision and says to Sheindele, "You are right." She tells her son, Yosele, "Let her speak. I want to hear what she wants to say, what lies beneath her behavior, what is all that anger and contempt for me?"

Yaniv: So, there's a lot of anger built up in Mirele in this monologue.

Lea: Of course, a lot of anger and also the insult involved in taking the decision to transfer the property to the children. And it doesn't end there. She continues with the insults until Sheindele kicks her out of the house. Her decision to leave and go to work for Shalmon, whom she employed in the past and now he will employ her, is also a decision that hurts Mirele's ego. Mirele is hurt and offended, but she gets over it and leaves. She is not just leaving; she is going to manage Shalmon's accounts and she works for him. She is not just going to live with him as if she were a guest. She goes to work for him, after being his employer. I think this whole process gives her strength. The pain gives her the strength both to get out of there and to shout at them, "Out!" I took all these things when I built the role and everything accumulated into that one moment, in one word, for in the moment I shouted, "Out!"

Yaniv: Your "Out!" was creepy. Your voice was metallic and powerful. It was unforgettable. Where did you get that energy from every night?

Lea: Energy cannot be learned. You either have it or you don't. Sometimes I see such a lack of energy on stage that I can't sit on the chair in the auditorium. You want to just shout at them to move already! You know I'm not hyperactive, but the inner energy, the power to express, it has to do with the talent of the actor. There are actors with lots of energy, but they aren't aware of it and are unable to regulate it. They shout when they shouldn't. You need to know when to raise your voice and when not to. Think about it; when Mirele asks her daughter-in-law to bring her jewelry box so that she can use it as a footstool, she is very angry, but doesn't raise her voice. She says it quietly and calmly despite the internal storm that is raging inside of her. Power is also about self-control. That anger builds up until it erupts, but as an actor, you have to be able to control it, understand it, and pinpoint those moments. After that outburst about the transfer of property, she has no more outbursts. There is one more moment when she demands that Yosele divorce Sheindele and she shouts, "Get a divorce!" but it is much smaller and it no longer works. She feels like she can no longer make an impression. She feels that she has already committed the crime with regards to the property and received another blow because it didn't help and they continued to humiliate her.

Yaniv: When you perform the monologue of the outburst that begins with the words, "What are you saying, Sheindele?" In that moment, do you think about what state she is in or does it just come naturally to you? Do you analyze sentence after sentence or do you feel it naturally?

Lea: As soon as I build a role, a monologue like that just comes out naturally. I'm building it on the go, I construct it, its form, but monologues like that one come out naturally. The monologue is integral to the character, there is no other way to perform the monologue after I have decided what kind of woman she is and what happens to her during the play. This, of course, follows on directly from the text.

Yaniv: Dalia Friedland and Dvora Kedar, who both studied with Zvi Friedland, taught me their work process. They analyze it sentence by sentence and, in each sentence, you ask yourself what state of mind the character is in, why they say what they say. You extract more layers from each word in the text. So, you're saying it's not according to the sentence, but once you have the character, then the sentence will come out correctly?

Lea: That's right. You analyze every sentence as you build the character. You ask yourself why they say that. Besides, not every sentence always means something. Sometimes, a fellow actor can say something that you think sounds really great. It's a process. But when your character is complete, things come out right, if you are sensitive enough to the character and talented enough. During the show, you become the character you are acting. You know, a while ago, I was interviewed and I said that I have come to the conclusion that in this profession, whether you like it or not, when you go on stage, your thoughts go in one direction to the character you are going to act, and sometimes, this frees you from the things that weigh you down in your private life. It helped me a lot after Zvika passed away. On stage, I would momentarily forget my personal tragedy. I continued to miss him, but when I performed on stage, the longing for him stayed behind the scenes while I was busy with the character. I encompass the character. The second I go backstage, I go back to being Lea with all the good things and with all the hard things in my life. The energy and power on stage distracts me for a moment. That's the beauty of this profession. When I play Mirele Efros, it's like, "Hi, I'm Mirele Efros." I live it and behave according to the character. As soon as the show ends, I go back to being Lea.

Yaniv: Let's go back to the event that surrounded the production of *Mirele Efros*. Unlike the production with Hanna Rovina, which was only in Hebrew, this production was the first one in which you performed in Yiddish at the Habima Theater. The theater, part of whose goal was the revival of Hebrew, agreed that after you had successfully performed the play in Hebrew, you would perform it in Yiddish. However, it wasn't performed in Habima's main auditorium, but at Beit HaHayal (the Soldiers' House) in Tel Aviv, with the same actors who had performed it in Hebrew.[5] Hirshl worked with the actors, who did not know a word of Yiddish, on comprehension and pronunciation. This was not about guest performances, but rather about a performance from the Habima repertoire that was performed entirely in Yiddish. What happened that the Habima management wanted you to perform in Yiddish?

Lea: They didn't want it. In 1987, Yiddish was still significant. There was an audience that spoke and knew and loved Yiddish. So the theater made the attempt.

Yaniv: There was resistance all the years in the theater to play Yiddish on stage. When Shmulik Atzmon wanted to put on the play *Di Kleine Mentschelekh* (The little people) by Sholem Aleichem in Yiddish at Habima, they wouldn't let him. In the end, it was an external production and not part of the stage repertoire. *Mirele Efros* was the only play at Habima Theater that was performed in Yiddish. Who asked for it? Who promoted the idea of performing in Yiddish?

Lea: I don't remember. Maybe it was an effect of the time. Those at Habima realized that, if it was performed in Yiddish, it would be possible to fill the theater for more performances of the show because the play was very well known and also very beautiful. We performed the same play in Yiddish with the same set, the same costumes, and the same attitude. The same actors also performed. Some of them did not speak Yiddish and it was a big achievement for Zvika, who worked with them on the language. In Hebrew, we performed the adaptation written by

---

5   The play *Mirele Efros* was performed in Yiddish at Beit HaHayal in Tel Aviv on April 20, 22, 23, 24, 26, and 27, 1989. See the advertisement on behalf of the Habima National Theater, *Ma'ariv*, April 19, 1989, Entertainment section, 4.

Miriam Kainy. Zvi took the adaptation and returned it to Yiddish according to Gordin's text with the additions to the adaptation.

Yaniv: But you didn't perform it at Habima, is that correct?

Lea: That's right, we performed at Beit HaHayal. The mistake was that they didn't address it. The fear of Yiddish and the approach towards Yiddish had an effect in this case as well. It would have been possible to make a huge event out of it, but they didn't advertise it. Just the people who heard about it came. It was not performed much in Yiddish. I think we performed for only two weeks. They didn't even let it warm up and it didn't reach the public enough.

The Israel Prize

Yaniv: The show was a great success. You acted in 300 shows and while performing in *Mirele Efros*, you and Miriam Zohar won the Israel Prize. The third partner for the award was the actor Makram Khoury. It seems as if they chose actors whose mother tongue was foreign, but who had mastered Hebrew and became Israeli actors, to all intents and purposes. When you were informed that you had received the Israel Prize, how did you respond?

Lea: Receiving the Israel Prize, in my humble opinion, is very, very important and very exciting because suddenly, you get the feeling that you belong to a place. That the place recognizes you, that the place respects you and thinks you are important. You did something that deserves an award.

Yaniv: But you were constantly receiving awards, starting with the Klausner Prize for *Bereshit* and many other awards over the years.

Lea: That's true, I received a lot of awards. Some of them I don't even remember. Zvi even made a collection of letters and certificates of appreciation from all kinds of places where we performed. I saw it recently and it reminded me of the places where we had performed, most of which I didn't remember at all.

Yaniv: Would it be correct to say that until the Israel Prize you were considered a valued actress, but since then you've become a star?

Lea: I don't know. I think it was the audience that led me to the Israel Prize. I didn't feel the rewards at work. I think the audience's love is what gave me status and the award committee thought I deserved the Israel Prize.

Yaniv: Did you feel any change in your attitude after the prize? In the audience's attitude towards you after *Mirele Efros* and after the prize?

Lea: I don't think so. I think that in *Mirele Efros* I was honored to play a role that is wonderful. She is a personality, a persona, which dramaturgically demands respect.

Yaniv: Did you feel like a queen in *Mirele Efros*?

Lea: When I performed, yes. Actually, I don't know if I felt like a queen, but I felt very much like a woman. A strong woman. She has a special kind of strength. It's a role that requires energy. Once you feel that strength and power, it's a responsibility that obliges you, makes you feel sure you're responsible for everything, even if you're not. You know, sometimes people, not necessarily in the theater, after some success get some kind of *shtel* (status) with such a position of power. They suddenly feel stronger, more powerful, more beautiful. I didn't get that after playing Mirele Efros. It wasn't like that for me. I wasn't brought up that way and I really don't like it because, at a certain point, it turns into snobbery. Mirele Efros has positive qualities such as strength, responsibility, love. But she also has negative qualities, such as arrogance and snobbery. I didn't like these qualities. I criticized her from the side, but I loved her. She lived in a society where she needed to adopt those qualities to deal with a patriarchal male society. It's probably still necessary today, otherwise women wouldn't use these features. You sometimes see actors who, after one success, change their whole attitude; they speak differently, they walk around differently, answer you differently, their patience is different, and me personally, I just really can't stand that.

Lea Koenig and Miriam Zohar Alternate in the Roles of Mirele Efros and Machle

Yaniv: Each evening in the play *Mirele Efros* you alternated with Miriam Zohar in the roles of Mirele and Machle, the servant. What was it like for you to act in the role of the servant? Did it bother you to play that role?

Lea: I really liked the role of the servant. I loved her very much. She was a poor girl. She worked as a servant and was full of admiration for her *baleboste* (employer). She is a good and warm person. I really liked that she wasn't snobbish. She is a folk figure and she loves because she loves; she isn't very sophisticated. It's a wonderful role.

Yaniv: And from your perspective, when you performed one day as Mirele and one day as the servant, it was . . . ?

Lea: Humiliating? No.

Yaniv: I didn't mean to say humiliating, but rather if it frustrated you. Did you not think to yourself, why should I play the role of the servant when I played Mirele yesterday?

Lea: It's a stupid attitude to have. The play is a beautiful play. You are building a role. It's not the main part, but there are many supporting roles that are very charming. And if you play in a repertory theater where one day you play a big role and the next day you play a small role, then you get it. That's part of it. Besides, it was really just a gimmick that we changed roles every night. There were people who came twice to see the show. Sometimes to see me as Mirele and sometimes to see Miriam in the role.

Yaniv: Wouldn't it have been more interesting to see you alternating the roles of Mirele and her daughter-in-law's mother, Hanna Devorah?

Lea: It could have been done that way as well, but it wasn't. If they had done it that way, it would have been very interesting. The idea of this gimmick was really great, a really beautiful idea.

Yaniv: The idea of the gimmick has been tried in the past.

Lea: What do you mean?

Yaniv: The late actor Yehuda Efroni[6] told me about it. In 1956, he saw Richard Burton and John Neville alternate night after night in the roles of Othello and

---

6 The Actors' Studio with the actor Yehuda Efroni on the occasion of receiving a Lifetime Achievement Award from the Brookdale Program at Bar-Ilan University, held as part of a course under my guidance on March 18, 2013 (YSG).

Iago.⁷ In the seventies, when Shlomo Bar Shavit was the artistic director, he suggested that you and Miriam take turns in the roles of Mirele and Machle, but Shlomo refused to hear about the staging of this play because he thought it was an uninteresting Yiddish play. When Shmulik Omar was appointed manager, he suggested the idea again and this time it was accepted.

Lea: I didn't know that. In any case, unlike Shlomo, I think the play is very good, the story is wonderful, and there are great roles for many different types of actors.

A Tour Guide to Warsaw

Yaniv: I will fast forward a little on the timeline with you and continue with the question of respect, with the recognition of the country, your position as an actress, and the audience who buys tickets to 'Lea's show' without even knowing what you will be performing. Also, almost exclusively without television and cinema performances to bring you fame, you become a star of the theater world. Perhaps it is summed up by the fact that Hillel Mittelpunkt wrote a play especially for you called *A Tour Guide to Warsaw*.⁸ What did it feel like to have a play written especially for you?

Lea: I don't know. Maybe when he came up with the idea, he thought I would be suitable for the role. He didn't tell me while writing it that it was written especially for me. He insisted that I perform it. I was told that he offered the play to several theaters on the condition that they would take me. I didn't even know about it at the time. Luckily, he brought it to Habima as well and then I was able to perform it.⁹

---

7   Melvyn Bragg, *Richard Burton: A Life* (Boston, MA: Little, Brown and Company, 1988), 104, 106.
8   Playwright Hillel Mittelpunkt explained (in a conversation on August 27, 2020) that he wanted to write a play about a mother and son where the mother returns to Poland and to her life before the war. He thought of Lea because she has the rare ability to combine well-tested comedy with tragedy and drama. Lea's strength, talent, and artistry led him to the conclusion that she was the most suitable character for his idea and therefore, he wrote the play especially for her.
9   According to Mittelpunkt, Leah was unaware of what had actually happened. Mittelpunkt immediately offered the play to Habima and did not offer the play to other theaters because he wanted Lea, who was at Habima, for the role. Yaakov Agmon, who was then the general manager of the theater, immediately adopted the idea and the production was launched under Mittelpunkt's direction.

Yaniv: Did you feel that there was something in the play that suited your personality?

Lea: He wrote it for me because he thought my sense of humor would suit the role and the fact that I know those kinds of mothers. I really connected with the play.

Yaniv: Similar to *Mirele Efros*, you also switched to act in Yiddish in *A Tour Guide to Warsaw*, but only years later and in another theater.[10] I was a member of the repertoire committee of the Yiddishspiel Theater and I suggested that we stage the play, and I am proud of the fact that I managed to persuade you to perform in this show.

Lea: Right, that's correct.

Yaniv: Was there a difference in the acting between Yiddish and Hebrew?

Lea: Yes, there was a difference. For me, it's not a very big difference; I'm fluent in Yiddish, I'm stronger in Yiddish. It was a pleasure to act in Yiddish. In terms of directing, it was the same. It's the same woman. I suddenly had the great pleasure of acting in a complete play and a good one in Yiddish and the role is wonderful, I really enjoyed it very much! I also think that you suddenly see an audience that doesn't usually come to Yiddish theater and just really wants to hear Yiddish.

Yaniv: When you performed in Yiddish, did you feel like you were returning to your roots?

Lea: I already said to you that my mother told me that only after I prove myself in Hebrew will I be able to perform in Yiddish and I did it after only three years. When we went on stage in Yiddish for the first time in Israel, naturally, both of us, Zvi and I, got back into it very quickly and easily.

Yaniv: But until *A Tour Guide to Warsaw*, most of your plays in Yiddish were pieces, sketches, and poems. You almost never performed an entire play in Yiddish.

---

10   *A Tour Guide to Warsaw*, the Hebrew version, was staged at Habima Theater in 1999 and then in Yiddish at the Yiddishspiel Theater in 2013.

Lea: I did *The Back Street* with Havis, *The Silver Wedding*, *Doing Wonders* (Helen Keller), and *The Witch*.

Yaniv: When you did them, did you get a vacation at the time?

Lea: At that time, the schedule of performances at Habima was completely different. You knew at the start of the season what you were going to do. They did the show and it ran until a certain date and you knew that after that, you would be free for a month or two. So we would plan to do these shows when I wasn't playing at the Habima.

Hirshl (Zvi)

Yaniv: Was Hirshl a participant in all the plays you did in Yiddish?

Lea: Sure, he directed all the plays except for *A Tour Guide to Warsaw*, which was staged after he had already passed away.

Yaniv: Hirshl died in 1998?

Lea: Yes. He was sick with cancer for eight years.

Yaniv: He was sick for a very long time. You knew he was sick, but did they tell you there was nothing more that you could do for him?

Lea: On the contrary, they said it wouldn't kill him. He had surgery twice. The first operation was a prostate operation and normally, the situation improves within a year, but it didn't improve for him, and then they saw that he had a tumor and did the second operation. The doctor told him, "You won't die from it." He went through all kinds of treatments. There were times when he was better and the disease was dormant. But cancer is cruel; it moved to the bladder and from there, it was another story. It spread immediately and very strongly and it was impossible to stop it. But he carried on with the cancer and we still performed in America and South America.

Yaniv: In the last part of his life, you performed in *Three Tall Women* by Edward Albee where you play a woman whose husband has prostate cancer. What did Hirshl feel when he saw you in it?

Lea: When they gave me the play and I read the monologue, Hirshl was no longer so well and I told him that I would not recite the monologue about the patient's suffering. But Hirshl told me, "You will say it. It belongs to life so say it, it's true." And I said it. It was a description of what happened to him too. You know, normally, if I performed in a play and he wasn't involved in it, he would come to the premiere and that was it. But with this play, he would come very often. The play deals with a person coming to terms with death. And maybe that was his struggle. He would come and sit through the play from beginning to end. Maybe he felt that he was going and wanted to be there more or maybe that section of the play really spoke to him. There is something in the play about facing death. He himself was facing death.

Yaniv: How did you deal with the knowledge that it was the end of his life?

Lea: I didn't believe it at all at the time. What's more, when it came, I thought I couldn't handle it, that I can't be alone. Don't forget, I was with him for fifty years; that's almost the length of a human life. We went through everything together: youth, adulthood, performing in Romania, performing in Israel, immigrating to Israel, which was a period of great struggles, of finding your place and proving to others that you are worth something, and traveling abroad. All this life, going through it all together and then suddenly you're alone. I thought I wouldn't be able to stand it. But if you can't stand it, you say to yourself, "If you can't handle it, then you have to have the strength to walk down to the sea. It's not far. You start walking slowly, no one will stop you. You walk into the sea and there will be no one to stop you. The sea swoops you up nicely and you're done with it." On the other hand, you don't have that kind of power. You are not even aware that you don't have the courage to commit suicide. Zvika always told me that I must go on. He was even sure that I would continue my life with another man. The truth is that that didn't happen for me at all, not at all. You know Zvi. Maybe it's funny to say, but he died as beautiful as he was in life. Cancer sometimes makes you quite terrible. He was lying there when he died, in the bedroom, it was very hard for me to replace the bed because of that. He was lying dressed in beautiful pajamas; friends were standing next to him. Someone came from the hospice. I was next to him on the bed and he was as beautiful as in the pictures, aesthetic and beautiful. And then I didn't even understand what I was going to do with myself; it was very difficult.

Yaniv: What prevented you from walking into the sea and drowning?

Lea: Hirshl left me the will to carry on. I said to myself, "I'll finish like this? Without leaving any memory of anything?" I thought if he said I should continue, maybe I should? I must have had a lot of strength. In the first show after the *shiva* (seven days of mourning), I performed *Three Tall Women* again with the same monologue that I mentioned earlier. The whole audience cried with me. They understood what I was saying better than the previous times, especially in that monologue.

Yaniv: Did the role bring you comfort in any way?

Lea: Yes. The consolation was that I had kept telling him that I wouldn't say the monologue and he told me, "You must say it because this is life and one faces these situations. The audience needs to hear and needs to know that this woman they see on stage has dealt with such a situation, and if there is someone out there that you strengthen because they are also dealing with the same problem, and they hear it and they don't feel alone, that is a great thing! It's really comforting. You have a responsibility to me and to the audience."

Yaniv: So, did you feel that you were fulfilling Zvi's wish?

Lea: Without a doubt. That's why I had the strength to say it. I went to him in the evening to his grave and I told him, "You asked me to say this and I am continuing to fulfill your wish."

Yaniv: Yaakov Agmon, who was the theater manager at the time, told you that he would keep you busy.

Lea: Agmon told me that already at the *shiva*. He said, "You will not sit for one moment without working." And he kept his word. In that respect, he saved me. The theater has power. When you go to work, you have to enter someone else's life, into another realm, and that helped me a lot, working and keeping busy. After Hirshl passed away, I started rehearsals for *A Tour Guide to Warsaw*. Every season, there were a lot of shows. There was a time when I was in five plays at the same time. I even did a one-woman show—*Oscar and the Lady in Pink*.[11] I really liked it.

---

11 *Oscar and the Lady in Pink* is based on a novel by Éric-Emmanuel Schmitt.

Yaniv: The actress Sandra Sade told me that she saw you behind the scenes after *Oscar and the Lady in Pink* and that you looked sad, and when she asked you what happened, you answered that the show wasn't successful enough for you this time. Sandra told me that for her, it was a big thing because if even the great Lea Koenig has less successful shows, then she can let loose a little on feeling guilty about her plays that don't always turn out exactly as she had hoped. But did you really sometimes feel that the show didn't turn out quite the way you had wanted?

Lea: Sure, I felt that many times. Don't you feel it sometimes when you give a lecture and it didn't turn out quite as good as it is usually does? So, you're good and you've got it, but it can always happen that it just doesn't turn out the way you wanted.

Yaniv: Do you need other people to tell you how it was and how it was received by the audience?

Lea: The audience doesn't always feel it. The cast members don't always feel it. They would come to me and say, "What are you talking about, you were wonderful." But deep down, you know very well whether you were good or not and you are not always satisfied. But *Oscar and the Lady in Pink* was a very difficult show. You know, I can't forget that I once went with Zvi for a treatment at Beilinson Hospital and two girls came towards us. One was sick and you could see it, a beautiful girl maybe fifteen years old, and the other girl was accompanying her. Hirshl told me, "Look, look at this girl. I am an old man, but why her?" I never forgot it; it was very powerful and later, I put it in the show *Oscar and the Lady in Pink*.

Yaniv: Life does not always go as planned.

Lea: Not at all. And sometimes I think, "Is it a good thing that I didn't just walk in to the sea?" I think in the end I did the right thing. I don't know how much time I have, but if I die, they would be forgotten too, Hirshl, father, mother, and so on, so I keep them alive a little.

Yaniv: That's what this book is all about.

Lea: That's right. I keep holding onto them. I don't know if they see or not if there is life after death. If they see, they must be happy, and I want to believe that they see me and that they know. I feel like Zvi is at home all the time. Like he's still lying down with his blue dressing gown in bed and always with a book next to him. He loved Yiddish poetry. He was crazy about the poet Itzik Manger. He even once wrote a dedication in which he described how much he loved Manger.

Yaniv: You miss him to this day.

Lea: Very much so!

Chapter 9

Feeling Israeli

Yaniv: In 2012, you received the EMET Prize,[1] an award sponsored by the Israeli prime minister for achievements by pioneers in the field of theater. Among the many awards you have received are the Israel Prize, the Klausner Prize from the Municipality of Tel Aviv, the Theater Award for Lifetime Achievement, honorary doctorates from Bar-Ilan University, Tel Aviv University, Ben Gurion University, and the Weizmann Institute, and a Lifetime Achievement Award from the Brookdale Program at Bar-Ilan University, among many other awards during your career. Did the awards help you feel more Israeli? When did you start to feel Israeli?

Lea: I think I felt the most Israeli when I received the Israel Prize. I felt, "Ma'am, you belong!" It is, after all, a state award and it means that the country cherishes you. Havis was still alive at the time, and it really moved me.

Yaniv: Today, when you look back on your life, most of your professional life you performed in Hebrew. Do you feel more like a Hebrew actress or a Yiddish actress?

Lea: I think I'm an actress and I don't think the language is relevant. Obviously, when I do something in Yiddish, it's technically easier for me. I don't have that fear of making mistakes in the language. But when I perform, the role I play is the same role and it doesn't matter if I perform it in Yiddish or in Hebrew. Only the language changes, nothing else.

---

1   The EMET Prize for Art, Science, and Culture is an Israeli prize awarded annually for excellence in academic and professional achievements that have far-reaching influence and make a significant contribution to society. Prizes are awarded in five categories: the exact sciences, life sciences, social sciences, humanities, and culture and the arts.

Yaniv: Do you feel that by switching to perform in Hebrew, you sacrificed some of your ability? Is it more difficult for you to dive into the role?

Lea: I don't think so. I have to tell you, when I was in the theater in Bucharest, the directors I worked with did not work with me on language. I learned to work on who I was playing and what I was acting in and it didn't matter so much in which language I was performing.

Yaniv: So language was never an issue? A few years ago, we had a conversation and you said something to me that I'll never forget. You said, "I did all the roles, I received all the awards, but I still feel foreign and not fully Israeli." In another conversation we had, you went back a bit on this statement.

Lea: It's not a matter of feeling Israeli. I don't know exactly, it's hard to say. It's not as though I have nostalgia for another place. Maybe over the years, I have become attached to this place. This place is where I feel I should be. How Israeli I am is not that important to me. The place is important to me. The Jewish state is important to me.

Yaniv: If you were made an offer to move to London to perform, would you do it?

Lea: No. I would go for a month or two months, but no more. My place is here in Israel, I would not leave this country. I'm telling it to you straight. I don't know what Israeli is. *Ikh bin a yiddishe tokhter; dos is mayn platz.* (I am a Jewish girl; this is my place.)

Yaniv: I'm talking about the mentality.

Lea: I don't really have the mentality of an Israeli. My behavior, my consideration for others, there's nothing to be done about that. I didn't grow up here. You know, an old woman remembers. I suddenly remember that since I was little, when I would enter the house, I would say hello and sit down. My mother would speak and the little girl would sit quietly. Can you imagine such a thing in Israel, that the children would sit quietly? That's how I grew up. I can't stand it when, for example, I see someone yawning with their mouth open and they don't cover their mouth. Do I need to see all the fillings they have in their mouth? My grandmother wouldn't let me yawn like that. She taught me in two minutes flat to put my hand over my mouth when I would yawn. She told me that once there was a young girl travelling on the train and in front of her sat a woman with a small cat. The girl yawned and did not cover her mouth. "Do you know what happened?" my grandmother asked me. "The cat got scared and jumped into her mouth." Since then, I never dared to yawn without covering my mouth. She also taught me that when I sweep, I should always sweep into the corners because otherwise I will have a husband with sores on his face and she wanted me to have a beautiful husband.

Yaniv: If I understand these stories correctly, you are saying that your mentality is still very much European, but as a Jew, you belong in Israel?

Lea: I really belong here. The past years have tied me to this place. When I came here, there were old people here, but in the meantime, I have grown up and grown old with the country. I am one of the old people today. I can't help myself other than to belong.

Yaniv: And when you went with Hirshl to Romania, did you feel like you were back home?

Lea: Not at all! Maybe it's because I have no nostalgia for the place. I left Poland as a very young woman. I left Romania when I was young too and we didn't settle anywhere permanently until we came to Israel.

Yaniv: But you were in Bucharest for twelve years.[2]

Lea: When we got back there, we had nothing. We didn't feel any nostalgia. It was also right after the revolution and the atmosphere was heavy. Now, when I think back on my career, I was there in some kind of ghetto; it was the theater of the Jews. It's true that I received awards there and my career started there, but I have no sentiments for the place. It's a fact that there are people who, after the borders opened, immediately ran and bought apartments there. I didn't. I became very attached to Israel. The truth is that whenever we traveled abroad in the seventies and eighties, we were enthralled by the landscapes, but little by little, I came to know that this place was home. One day, I returned to Israel, it was already without Zvi, and I felt that I was coming home. The country has also changed a lot. There is construction here just like in Manhattan. I grew up

---

2   Lea and Zvi lived in Bucharest in 3 Rubinai Street. The house does not exist today. Ceaușescu, the President of communist Romania, destroyed entire neighborhoods to build new ones.

with the place and today, I am an old Israeli woman. With all the difficulties that I have had here, all in all, this is my place and I am an Israeli.

Yaniv: What did you do to feel this way or did it just happen over the years?

Lea: It's something that happened over many years, but also something that I worked on and built, certainly in terms of my cultural life. Also, there is something about this place.

Yaniv: There is no doubt that the Habima Theater today is designed in your image; it is no longer a stage with older actors, with their old ways of acting.

Lea: Even when I came, it was no longer the older actors. But when I came to Israel, the style in which they performed was with a lot of despair. I came in with a more natural style and without the tragedy, similar to what was performed at the Cameri, and that was another reason why they accepted me. I brought that style with me. As soon as I started playing the first role in *Puntila*, they realized that it was a style that the audience appreciated. I get very excited when people tell me, even till today, that my performance in *Bereshit* was unforgettable.

Yaniv: You really have left a mark.

Lea: Yes, it does something. That is the ambition of every actor, that you will not be forgotten. And it's a shame if we forget, even though it's the nature of the world; that's how it is. The fact that you travel and guide tours in Eastern Europe following the Jewish theater and remember me and my parents, it's very gratifying for me. I want people to remember.

Chapter 10

Entering the Stage and Performing

Yaniv: You once told me that one of the most important things for an actor is to know how to walk onto the stage, that the first entrance should be significant. What does that mean?

Lea: The truth is that there are things you can't always explain in words. It's a bit of a strange profession. When you enter the stage for the first time, the audience has to be all yours, you need to have their full concentration. It's like you're saying, "I came, I'm here! And I need to introduce myself to you, I need to prove to you that I have arrived."

The Old Lady's Visit

Yaniv: Let's talk about your entrances. In the play, *The Old Lady's Visit*, everyone in the scene is standing and waiting for a lady who was supposed to arrive on a different train. But you took the direct train and made sure that it stopped especially in the town of Güllen.[1] You enter the stage and look at the audience. Your eyes shoot fire and brimstone at them. It was a spectacular entrance and when you said, "It's Güllen!" with that contempt and fire in your eyes, it was unforgettable. How did you build this role?

Lea: That's exactly it. First and foremost, it's the desire to be recognized. It's just as though you knock on a door and someone opens it for you and you say, "Hello, I've arrived." You can say it weakly or insecurely, you can say it quietly, or you can say it strongly! It's like saying, "Do you understand that I have arrived?"

---

1   A town in Switzerland. The name evokes "liquid manure" in German.

Yaniv: When you say, "I'm here," do you mean Lea?

Lea: No. It's me, the old lady. At the same moment that I walk onto the stage, I say my lines in awe, "It's Güllen! Here I am! I have come here to get even. This place is a dung pile and you all humiliated me, but I have come to get my revenge."

Yaniv: All of that goes through your head?

Lea: Yes. I work on it during rehearsals while getting to know the role . . . my desire to prove that I am a lady . . . and, then in the performance, it all comes together.

Yaniv: Let's talk about another entrance in *What are We Going to Do about Jenny?*[2] You first stick your head out and only then do you walk down the stairs.

Lea: This is something else. I wanted to know who came to see me and what they were talking about. I heard what they were saying before I entered. I heard my older daughter saying to her sister that she wants to take me to her home like you take old people. I wanted to convey my curiosity and the joy of life of the character to the audience. So, I peeked out curiously to hear what they were talking about; you can see it reflected in my face and also in my eyes.

Yaniv: Had you simply burst in and descended on the stage, it would've been a more impressive entrance, but a completely different one.

Lea: It really depends on the subject of the play and the character you are playing. Also, why you are entering the stage now, how much you want those who are on stage to see you, who specifically, and what type of impression you want to make on them. There are all kinds of entrances: a hesitant entry; an entry where it's as if you are entering, but you're not; an entrance where you come in peacefully.

Yaniv: In the play, *The Life before Us*, you open the door of the house and go down two stairs with an enormous presence; it's as if you have arrived.

---

2   *What are We Going to Do about Jenny?* by Donald R. Wilde.

Lea: That's right. I open the door. It's my house. I control it. There I am, that's where my life is, it's me, I make the decisions.

Yaniv: So the entry actually depends on the mental state of the character you have to be in that exact moment.

Lea: For sure. Think about you, think about me. Every time you go into your house, it depends on something. Where are you coming from? In what kind of mood are you coming into the house? How do you come into the house? Why do you want to come home now? Are you happy to be coming into the house? You don't know what awaits you at home. There are many reasons, but the main reasons are who you are and where you came from. There are a whole series of questions. An actor entering the stage must always know in any role they play that their entrance should be significant.

Yaniv: I'm thinking about your entrance in the play *Behind the Fence*. You come in bent over, you can barely walk, but you make an entrance.

Lea: And they see me! Because I entered. This is my house and there is someone there that I can't stand. He came and it annoys me. The line goes, "He comes, peeks, but he doesn't give," which means he doesn't help, he's a liar, he left his wife, he left his daughter. When I act, I'm constantly looking for the character I'm going to play. Take, for example, my character of the old *balanit* in the play *Mikveh*.[3] She is not always gentle, but she knows how to treat the women who come to the *mikveh*. I have a line in the play where I say about the new *balanit* that she doesn't perform her duties alone and when she tells me that she knows how to do it, then I respond to her, "Of course you know, who said that you don't, otherwise you wouldn't be here, but let the people get used to your presence first." It's very intimate, the women are all naked. When I start the show, I say, "*Kosher, kosher, kosher.* How many immersions have you done, do one more, do a good deed, immerse yourself once more to ensure success in our next elections." It's part of her character that will affect her style as well as her entrance onto the stage.

---

3   *Mikveh* or *mikvah* is a bath used for the purpose of ritual immersion in Judaism to achieve ritual purity. *Halacha* (Jewish Law) requires that *mikveh* immersion be witnessed by a Jewish woman over the age of twelve to ensure that everything, including her hair, is submerged. This is the primary function of the *mikveh* lady or *balanit*.

Speaking on Stage

Yaniv: What I notice is that your speech also changes—the pronunciation, your tone of voice, your breathing in a given sentence. It changes not only from role to role, but sometimes even in the same role there are different moments of varying styles.

Lea: That's right. It needs to change. Some people talk all the time in the same tone, in the same way and at the same pace with the same intonation. I don't know if you have ever noticed it, but it can be tiring to listen to and, at a certain moment, you just stop listening. There is emotion in our speech, in our intonation. Intonation reveals what we are going through. For example, in the opening scene of *Mikveh*, after I finish checking that the woman has immersed herself, I say to her, "Sorry, I'm alone today, I have to go." In this sentence, I am no longer interested in the woman. So my feeling, the whole situation, my intonation and tone of voice, also change. I know she'll start nagging me and I don't have patience for her. Acting on stage is constantly related to what is happening to me as the character in that moment. Acting is real. You can't think when you are acting. You need to be in character in the moment.

Yaniv: Are there things you can learn or do you feel it intuitively?

Lea: When you study the profession and you work on a play, you learn about it, how to think about it, and how to analyze it. It's like any technical work you implement. Also here, you are constantly connecting the dots you discover through your work that you didn't know before.

Yaniv: It reminds me of when you performed *A Tour Guide to Warsaw* in Yiddish and your son tells you, "I have a headache," and in Yiddish, "*Kop veytik.*" You suggested to Israel Treissman, who played your son, that he should blow up the letter 'p' in the word *kop*, so it will explode like his head. The word and the intonation need to both serve the situation.

Lea: Right.

Yaniv: Is that something you consciously think about or is that just how you speak and when you do it, it sounds better?

Lea: Actors must work on their diction. If there is a 'p,' then you need to hear the 'p.' Syllables must not be swallowed. *Az du host a kop, darf men hern dem kop.* (If you have a head, you need to hear the head.)

Yaniv: So, is it just because of the diction or does it come to serve the situation as well?

Lea: It's both the diction and the word that are significant. The words serve the situation and, if at all possible, we must take advantage of it. It enriches the acting. The expression of the pain needs to be felt.

Yaniv: Do you speak differently on stage from the way you do in real life?

Lea: There is definitely a certain power on stage, but I think I speak the same way.

Yaniv: Do actors who don't work on their diction lose a certain richness that is not necessarily related to the acting?

Lea: Not only do they lose it, it also doesn't come across well. They can't convey what they are going through. They would act better if they paid attention to the diction and used it in their acting.

Yaniv: Is that something you learned when you studied acting?

Lea: When I studied acting, it went together; the diction with the expression and the intonation, which is so important on stage. Little by little, you get used to it and it becomes automatic.

Yaniv: Do you feel that today there is less strictness to do with diction?

Lea: Without a doubt. Many young actors don't pay attention to diction. That's probably the style of the period. The speed of speech, which matches the pace of life, the desire to express yourself quickly, but when you express yourself quickly, half of what you want to say runs away and gets lost. I'm always asked by people why they don't understand what the actors on stage are saying. But it's not just on stage, it's on TV and everywhere.

Yaniv: Isn't it because speaking on stage today is more natural?

Lea: No, natural doesn't mean that you won't be understood? On the contrary, the more natural the better. It's always better to speak naturally. I'm not talking about exaggerated speech; you can speak naturally, but pronounce all the letters. If I'm speaking naturally, can't I say it clearly?

Acting Development and Professionalism

Yaniv: Do you feel that your style has remained the same or have you changed it over the years?

Lea: I don't think I've changed. When I studied, I learned the right style and it has stayed the same until now.

Yaniv: Do you feel that you act today in the same way that you performed Anne Frank in Romania?

Lea: There is no doubt that I have more confidence today. I dig deeper. I search more inside myself and I think that today, I look at things in a slightly more sophisticated way, but basically, that's what I learned. I congratulate myself that I studied well and I thank my teachers, both the directors and acting teachers. Especially for the daily practices they taught me, like observing other actors and seeing how they see things, how they arrive at their characters.

Yaniv: It's interesting what you're saying. The actress Pnina Perach once told me, "The stage is like a lioness." Do you understand why she said this?

Lea: I don't know what she meant. She performed with me in the play *Wedding* and I think she was an understudy in the play *Grocery Store* as well. When I go on stage and I have a task, I work on the task and I don't let go of it. I had a rehearsal a while ago and at a certain moment, I let go because I was tired and then I felt how everything slipped through my fingers. Up to a certain point, I was focused and everything was focused and creative. As soon as I got tired, everything was suddenly not so good, tired, slow, and uninteresting.

Yaniv: Was everything resting only on your shoulders? You once said to me that your mother told you, "Don't always be the best on stage. Sometimes allow one of the other cast members to shine."

Lea: The story was that I had a big role and I complained that I was interrupted during my acting. My mother told me that when playing a big or small role, you don't have to be the best at every moment, you can make small mistakes, but when you get to a moment that is significant in terms of what happens to the character in the play, it has to be excellent. Even when you're acting with another cast member, she said that the moment to shine should also be given to my co-cast members. It's very important. The person in front of you has something to say and you need to respond to what they say so let them say what they want so you can respond.

Yaniv: So, if an actor in a certain play changes his intonation, his emotional state, does that automatically change your reaction as well? If an actor was not focused on the acting and said something completely differently from how they said it in rehearsals, would it affect your acting?

Lea: It depends on how they change it, but you have to stay in character. If he changes suddenly, it disturbs the acting. I'll give you an example. If he says angrily, "You pissed me off," I can answer him angrily, but if he suddenly decides to say it calmly, I can't be upset because of the way he said it. So, after the show, I would tell him to make sure he says it angrily next time so I can be annoyed when I respond. There are good partners and there are bad partners. Sometimes, there are terrible arguments after the show, which can cause a big scandal. This is not an improv evening. There is a show being built and what it will look like needs to be determined during rehearsals.

Yaniv: Does it sometimes happens that an actor can't bring himself to do what is needed?

Lea: Yes, but it's because he can't and you can understand that it's often a once-off occurrence because they don't feel well or had something going on. But serious professional actors, even in such situations, try to do their best.

Yaniv: So, if you have a moment in the show that's designed to take the audience's breath away and you know you don't have the strength that day, you know you won't be able to do it properly, do you give up on it for that day?

Lea: No, I would not give up. I would try to do my best even if it kills me.

Yaniv: Why would you not give up? It won't be good enough.

Lea: Because you have a responsibility. The audience doesn't need to suffer for your weaknesses. If you feel you can't perform, as it happened to me in *King Lear* when I felt ill, I stopped the play. But in a different situation, you can't give up. It might not be the best performance, but you can't give up. The audience won't know it. You know it wasn't good enough, but the audience has nothing to compare it to and won't see anything different. If you're in the role and the role is in you, the audience won't feel it; they will feel that it was good.

Yaniv: Does it affect you in the performances after that?

Lea: You're sorry you didn't do as well as you did yesterday, but you're only human. I can't disconnect myself from myself. The next day is a new day. You start again and you do your best.

Chapter 11

Being Old

Yaniv: You talk about the experience you have gained over the years, but with experience comes age. Does old age annoy you?

Lea: Being an old woman is disappointing, sometimes it's frustrating.

Yaniv: What do you mean disappointing?

Lea: It depends on how you take it. You suddenly see the changes, the physical changes, the strength that disappears, the agility, the flexibility, suddenly you don't hear so well, you don't see so well, but it's not a disease, it's just age, and you're sorry for it. You look in the mirror at your face, your body, your legs, and you think, what is this? How did this happen? When did this happen? But you don't feel it as it's happening. It's a slow and natural process and then it's like, wait, it's almost gone, but let's see what's left of it. But if the mind and memory and the ability to make decisions remains, then you say, "God, thank you very much, you still love me a little."

Yaniv: Do you feel it on stage?

Lea: On stage when I'm acting, I don't think about it at all, and also, since I'm a character actress, I don't have an ego about how I look. My career was never based on my physical appearance, but on character roles. I never hesitated to play characters that were older than me.

Yaniv: At the age of forty-one, you played the old woman in *The Chairs*.

Lea: Yes, and already in *Bereshit* I played the mother of the adult Cain and Abel. I always felt it was important to look like the character. When I performed in *Grocery Store*, I wrapped my legs in rags so they would be swollen. Now, my legs are swollen without the rags, but there you go. I studied theater so when I had to be a beautiful and elegant woman, I acted beautiful and elegant, and when I had to be old and ugly, I acted old and ugly.

Yaniv: But was it nicer for you to play the role of a beautiful woman?

Lea: It never interested me. I was always looking at the character, who I needed to be. I never saw my profession as something I could see in a mirror.

Yaniv: Are there any roles you refused to play?

Lea: I didn't really refuse parts. Thank God, my career went in such a way that I accepted what was offered to me and there weren't really any roles that I specifically didn't want. The roles always interested me. You know, sometimes I think I've gone down a very interesting route. I was old, I was young, I was good, I was bad. I was whatever they wanted me to be.

Yaniv: When you look back on it today with hindsight, do you feel that when you go on stage to perform, you go on with your entire repertoire, or do you have to prove yourself in every performance?

Lea: I need to prove myself again and again in every performance. Especially here in Israel. The Jewish audience is very critical. Abroad, there are actors who have credit. The audience doesn't really comment on whether they were good or bad because they have older performances that they can lean on. Here, you have to prove yourself anew every time.

Yaniv: Do you feel the same when you perform in front of a younger audience? Do you feel sometimes that younger actors lack respect and don't appreciate your experience?

Lea: No, for now, no. And, besides, if they are disrespectful, there comes a moment when they have to surrender and admit a mistake.

Yaniv: Today, with reflection, if you were to meet the young Lea who tells you, "I want to be an actress," what would you say to her?

Lea: I would tell her exactly what my mother told me, "Let's see if you have it. It's very important. Let's see if you've got it. If you don't have it, then forget about it." As Havis told me, "A good seamstress is better than a bad actress."

In any profession, you need to be the best. We are not always geniuses, so you need to look for a profession that you are talented in. And there is something else of course; every profession also needs a bit of luck. You need to be in the right place with the right people. You need good teachers who set good personal examples, and you need to learn to observe wisely. I don't know really. I just know that I've never looked too deep inside myself and I think it helped me. I never held back. Even today, when I am very old, I still hesitate when building a role. I'm still searching.

Yaniv: There is a feeling, when you work on a role, that it seems to come very easily to you. As if something in your instincts directs you to the role and the way you read the text. Without noticing, suddenly there is a character.

Lea: That's probably talent; it comes from within and it comes out.

Yaniv: Do you feel that way?

Lea: No. I don't feel that way at all. Sometimes I do something in rehearsals and I think of a certain direction, and then, in rehearsals, things happen. Sometimes I make a movement because I thought it was right, and the actors laugh without me intending them to laugh. There are things that seem like they come instinctively, but the execution comes from thought and my inner state as well as my personal nuances.

I'm a Comedian

Yaniv: Does the fact that you're a comedian have an effect?

Lea: Of course it has an effect, even though I don't always think that the scene I'm doing is funny. But the humor comes out because it's in me. Drama also has humor. A man walks down the street and falls and sometimes we laugh. It's not a funny situation, but we laugh. He broke his leg; you laugh and then you panic. In general, Yiddish actors were very funny. One actor died and the other cast members came to the funeral. One was asked to give a eulogy, but he didn't know what to say, so he started mumbling and crying with his hands over his face and everyone saw that he was crying, but no one could understand what he was saying. All the actors fell about laughing. I'm telling you, sometimes there are moments of comedy even within the drama, so much so that you can't help but laugh. Even in the theater, in dramas when there are moments of comedy, you don't have to pass on them because it's real, it happens, that's how it is in life. But performing comedy is only possible if you have talent. You can't learn comedy. Being a comedian can't be learned, it's just a talent. You either have it or you don't. You sometimes see people sitting around and someone starts to tell a joke. The same joke told by one person can make everyone sitting around crack up and someone else can tell the same joke and no one will even smile.

Yaniv: Over the years, have you been able to recognize the techniques of comedy and of telling jokes? Where to pause or to change the tone?

Lea: I don't know techniques; for me it's spontaneous.

Yaniv: But in rehearsals, the first time is spontaneous, the second time is already technical.

Lea: But it has to do with my sense of humor. Every time, the feeling of making a joke comes from within. It's not a technique, it's not 'here is a pause of half a second.' It has to come from within. There are people whose humor pours out of them and there are people, and actors too, who don't know how to tell a joke or create a comical situation.

Yaniv: When you play with a comedic partner, does it help you?

Lea: It's not about the comedian. A good cast member lifts you up. It's always good to play with someone good. It's a duet.

Yaniv: When you act with a good comedian, does it bring out things in you that might not have come out if they were not a comedian?

Lea: I don't think so because I still remain in character. I don't think to myself there is a comedian sitting next to me.

Yaniv: I don't necessarily mean the actor's personality, but if you say acting is a duet, then when the person is a good comedian, does that funny scene bring out more things in you that maybe you wouldn't dare do if you weren't with that good actor partner?

Lea: I don't think it happens like that. If you perform with a comedian, it depends on what you're performing, how you accept what the partner tells you, and what you need to respond. Of course, if he's a comedian and it's a comedic scene, then you take that into account, but you don't rely on that, you don't build your character according to how he will react.

Being a Partner on Stage and Dedication to the Profession

Yaniv: Maybe the question should be more general. Shlomo Bar Shavit once told me that he likes to perform with you because you, as a good actress, know how to lift your partner to new heights that he is unable to reach alone. When you perform with a good partner or one who isn't very good, does it affect your acting?

Lea: Like I said, acting is a duet, but I have to do what I need to do. I can't change the role because my partner doesn't know how to act or makes mistakes in rehearsals. If I had to respond to the way a bad partner acts, I would have to deviate from the text and respond differently because he is in a completely different place with the text. But you can't do that. There is a text that leads you to a certain place. When you build a scene with someone, you can't just come up with some other interpretation and put it to the test. That's why we rehearse and determine in advance the relationships and how to act.

Yaniv: Does it ever happen that, after ten, twenty, or thirty performances, you suddenly realize you want to perform it differently?

Lea: Sometimes there are moments like that, when you suddenly realize that you can do it another way or better. If it only affects you, then you can try.

Yaniv: Doesn't it always depend on the cast member you are performing with?

Lea: Not always. Sometimes there is a monologue so it doesn't depend on the person I'm performing with. If it's dialogue though, then I have to work with them and decide in what way the scene will go.

Yaniv: And what about the director?

Lea: Sometimes you also involve the director, of course. You suggest maybe doing it differently and it can happen that there are changes.

Yaniv: Does it bother you? After you come out with a show, do you keep thinking about how it might have been possible to improve it or do you say, "That's how we decided it would be and that's what it is."

Lea: Usually that doesn't happen. If it's not good, you wonder to yourself if it could have been done in another way. But sometimes, it's too complicated to change everything and you just leave it as it is. It might be on my mind for a day or two, but if the show runs, you get the verdict. That's just how it is; there is nothing you can do about it.

Yaniv: If we go back to *King Lear*, were there things in the direction that you didn't like.

Lea: There, it was really difficult to build it or to make changes, even though I didn't like some of the things. The director had a certain concept and it was difficult to make changes.

Yaniv: Did you get the director's permission to make changes?

Lea: It's the director's conception. If I don't want to perform in the show, then I can say I don't want to. The directors are the interpreters of the text and they are the ones who determine how the performance will look.

Yaniv: There is something that still bothers me about this. On the one hand, you are an actress who gives every role her all. Your life is the theater, you strive for perfection in your roles and you always want to perform the role the best you can. On the other hand, you tell me, "Listen, if a show comes out that I'm not satisfied with and I even think that it could be changed and improved, it will bother me for a day or two, but then that's it, it doesn't have to be perfect."

Lea: And? . . .

Yaniv: What "and"? On the one hand, you say that theater is the most important thing to you, but on the other hand, you accept things you don't like very calmly!

Lea: If you are in any profession, as you know, you are not always in a perfect state. There are better shows, there are worse shows. It depends on the material, it depends on the director, and the director has the final say. If he thinks it's good and he thinks it's beautiful, then you give in to him. If you start criticizing him at every show, then you may as well just do it yourself. Don't be tied down to the director, don't be tied down to the theater, perform alone and just do it.

Yaniv: Were you never interested in directing?

Lea: I was always interested in working as an actor, but directing an entire play, not so much. The more years I'm in the business, the more I see that if you don't work with the actors, the show is never good enough, it's not good enough theater.

Yaniv: Isn't that the main role of the director, to work with the actor? When the actor knows the character, the *mise-en-scène* (staging a scene) is easier.

Lea: Not always. To direct an entire play, to construct it, to see it from a broad perspective, I wouldn't want to take that on myself. Working with actors, being a character actor, that interests me, to build the role with them. But not to direct an entire show.

Yaniv: When you see a cast member who is looking and can't find themselves in a role, do you offer to help them?

Lea: Why not? Certainly, if they ask! Sometimes they give me tips too.

Yaniv: I remember, when you performed in *Neither by Day Nor by Night* for the second time, one of your fellow actors who performed with you[1] told me that he used to watch you and learned a lot from your acting. And indeed, his acting was very different between the first play and the last one. Especially his entrances. The more shows there were, the more presence his entrances had. Was that something you taught him to do? Did you talk about it?

---

1 The actor Erez Regev performed with Lea in 2011 in the play *Neither by Day Nor by Night*. He played the role of Tzachik, the blind guy. The old lady, Sokolova, mistakenly thinks he is her long-time boyfriend. The first time Lea played the role of Sokolova was in 1969, alternating with the actress, Miriam Bernstein Cohen, at the Tzavta Theater in Tel Aviv.

Lea: I don't remember anymore, but here and there, I would say all kinds of things to him. You need remember that there is also unique information for each actor. Each actor has a different character and a different temperament.

Yaniv: It reminds me of what your mother once told you . . . that a good actor needs to be able to show many emotions on their face. Is that something that can be learned?

Lea: Can emotions be learned? I don't think so. Temperament cannot be taught. You can't learn strength and power. Napoleon was a small man with a lot of power and there are giants that don't have any.

Yaniv: So, an actor is born?

Lea: Right. Every person who devotes him or herself to a certain profession and succeeds at a high level was probably born to it. You need talent. If you have no talent, no matter how much you dedicate yourself to the profession, it will never be enough. You should pursue what you are good at. That's what my mother always told me. You know, before we came to Israel, my mother felt, I'm quite sure of it, that my acting was going in a more advanced direction. She was performing something at the time and she said to me, "Come and see me in rehearsal." Do you understand? She wanted me to watch her and tell her what I thought. It was the first time she really wanted to know what I thought of her in terms of her acting. She probably felt that I was progressing, that I was more modern, more updated, and my opinion was important to her. That was a huge compliment.

Yaniv: In this request, did she say that she wanted to progress and develop?

Lea: My mother always wanted to progress; she didn't want to be called old-fashioned.

Yaniv: Are you still trying to keep up-to-date and progress?

Lea: Of course. Sometimes I sit and watch TV and observe an actress and say how beautiful, I should do that. For example, when I see Meryl Streep or Glenn Close. I look and I see that there is something special there. Every role that Meryl Streep has ever played has always been different from the one that went before it. I look at her and ask myself, could I do that? Otherwise, you get stuck. Even when I see a play, I ask myself if I could do it. By the way, those two actresses, they don't act in movies, they perform theater in the cinema and it's a pleasure to see them. There is another actress, Carol Burnett, who I also enjoy watching and observing.

Yaniv: Are there times when that happens to you in Israel? When you see an actor or an actress and you say, "Too bad I didn't play that role."

Lea: Yes, sure, and I know how to appreciate their work.

Yaniv: When you see an actor delivering a beautiful monologue, do you sometimes think about using that monologue yourself?

Lea: It's impossible to perform a monologue out of context, and even if there is such a monologue, you can't really say it well without the context of the entire show.

Yaniv: Do you think that performing a monologue properly is only possible within the context of the entire play? That the construction and the process that happens in the rehearsals brings you to the moment of the monologue and the right situation in which to say it?

Lea: Yes, you have to build it from scratch.

Yaniv: If someone were to ask you to do an evening of monologues from plays in which you have never performed, would you be able to act them out as though you were performing in a play?

Lea: I wouldn't be able to do them very well. I was once in Romania at an evening of monologues from plays I had performed in. There was one from *Mirele Efros*, another from *Mother Courage*, and a third one from *The Old Lady's Visit*. I performed monologues from plays that I had performed in and monologues that Zvi had written for me. The monologues that Zvi wrote all stood on their own merits. Each one of them was like a *kleine melodramme* (short melodrama) with a beginning, a middle, and an end. But monologues from plays in which I never performed in . . . I couldn't do that.

Yaniv: I've seen when you sing or do one of Zvi's or another author's Yiddish monologues; you grab the attention of someone in the audience and sing to them or talk to them and look deep into their eyes. Is that not embarrassing for you?

Lea (laughs): It's built differently. I can't perform a monologue in a play and be busy with someone specific in the audience. But a song is something else.

Yaniv: You have a song by Zelig Bardichever that you always sing. The song 'Elle Be'elle', which the poet Natan Yonatan translated for you into Hebrew for the show *Kochavim l'lo Shamayim* (*Stars Without Sky*). In the song, there is a phrase, "From my children, I have *nachas* (pleasure), and from my in-laws, I have *tsoris* (trouble)." You sing it to the people in the audience and look at them, deep into their eyes. How do you this?

Lea: I sing it to the audience, but I don't really see them. It's a different form of acting. Or, for example, in Sholem Aleichem's monologue *The Pot*, there is a phrase that repeats itself, "Why did I tell you this?" I always catch someone in the audience and ask them the question. The sentence is very significant. It is part of the text. Even in the theater at the end of a play when I take my bow, if I see someone in the front row who is not clapping and just sitting, I ask them, "Why are you just sitting there? Do you want me to start the show from the beginning?" It's a different kind of acting. It doesn't embarrass me, it's acting.

Yaniv: Yiddish players were experts at this. It's stand-up. Stand-up wasn't just developed in New York. There was a tradition of Yiddish actors who would do verbal duels with people in the audience.

Lea: This is professionalism. The Yiddish actors were part of a private theater; they had to capture the audience from the first moment. They specialized in it. I studied in such a school with such people; that was their skill. What amazes me is that you perform with actors on stage and it turns out they don't know you at all. I don't understand how actors don't go to see other actors. I think to this day, even after so many years of my career, I still have so much more to see, learn, and develop.

Chapter 12

The Theater Taught Me How to Live

Hanoch Levin

Yaniv: Over the years, eight Hanoch Levin productions have been performed on stage. Of these, you acted in three of them: *Winter Funeral* directed by Levin in 1978; *The Labor of Life* directed by Miki Gurevich in 1989; and *Morris Shimel* directed by Yael Ronen in 2010 after Hanoch's death. What was it like to work with Hanoch Levin?

Lea: You said yourself, *Winter Funeral* was in 1978. It was a long time ago. He changed a lot from then until the end of his life, and I have changed since then too. In fact, it was a time when he was not so accepted yet. There were many objections to him and they didn't know how to take him or understand his meaning and the bottom line of what he wanted to say. But *Winter Funeral* was so full of satire and humor that it was hard not to understand it. There was a lot of grace in the play. If I think about it today, and I have to admit that I didn't think about it at the time, but now that I'm sitting with you, I suddenly realize that there is something in *Winter Funeral*, an idea similar to the writings of the poet Itzik Manger. I played Shratzia, an overly protective mother to her daughter, but notice that she is so overly protective of her that she stifles her and doesn't allow her to grow up and mature.

Yaniv: It's just like in Manger's poem *Oyfn veg shteyt a boym* (On the road there stands a tree), where the mother wraps the child in so many layers of clothing so that he won't get cold, but this actually prevents him from spreading his wings and growing up.

Lea: Exactly, and when I think about it, back then I didn't know how to think like that, so I only thought about the humor and satire, but now I can suddenly see the similarity in the approach to the different characters.

Yaniv: I want to linger on this sentence for a moment, ". . . in the approach to the different characters." There is an approach in theater and in research that says there are 'Hanoch Levin characters.' Do you think that that's true, that there are characters that are unique to Hanoch Levin, or are these characters something that you encountered in Eastern Europe?

Lea: Honestly, I did know those types of characters and I think he was very influenced by Eastern European theater. I never knew how well he knew Yiddish literature, but I have no doubt that he was influenced by it. The characters of the mothers and of the women in general, the snobbery, it was all influenced by Eastern European women.

Yaniv: You played Shratzia in the play. Let's leave for a moment the play on words of Shratzia and *sheretz*, a bug or possibly a blood-sucking leech. But does the mother, who is so protective of her daughter, really think about things in terms of the good of her daughter? Or is it that all that she wants is to be at her daughter's wedding and to show everyone who she is and what she is? In other words, she thinks only about herself and her dignity.

Lea: I think the mentality of those personalities can be seen here in the mentality of the women, something that they themselves were not aware of . . . The role of the mother I played in *Morris Shimel,* Tollebreina, is very different from the role of Shratzia, for example. She sees only herself and doesn't protect her son.

Yaniv: Exactly. Tollebreina and Shratzia are very different women and mothers. Shratzia makes sure that nothing will ruin her daughter's wedding whereas Tollebreina doesn't think too much of her son.

Lea: Definitely, although, to a certain extent, they both think about themselves despite their differences. That's why I'm telling you that there were these snobbish women who would say, "Let them not tell, let them not hear, let the neighbors explode, let them see the wedding and be jealous." I don't know exactly to what extent, but I believe Hanoch was very influenced by these characters.

Yaniv: So, when you played Shratzia in *Winter Funeral,* did you think about Hanoch's character or did you act based on characters that you knew from your own life?

Lea: The truth is that I was very influenced by the idea of Hanoch's characters because, here in Israel, once it has been decided that you are one of Hanoch's characters, that's how you have to play it. I mean, they don't give you a chance to say, "Wait a minute, where did he get the characters from? Am I allowed to go to his source or not?" His sources were the Jewish characters from Eastern Europe who spoke Yiddish. We are talking about a time when it wasn't acceptable to go to the source.

Yaniv: And you didn't just perform the types of characters that you knew from Eastern Europe?

Lea: No, because, like I said, I was also influenced by it. Today, with hindsight, I don't think I followed his direction completely because instinctively, the characters took me back to my theatrical education and my life, the way I am, and I know those types of characters.

Yaniv: And when you acted in *Morris Shimel*, it wasn't many years ago, maybe around ten years ago, and Hanoch was no longer with us by then. Did you allow yourself to do something different or more similar? What do you think?

Lea: At first, I wasn't so sure where I was going with it. But the power of Hanoch's writing was so remarkable that whether you wanted to or not, you drifted towards him.

Yaniv: There was a wonderful scene in *Morris Shimel* where Morris brings his bride to you and informs you that they want to get married. The text is wonderful. You are very happy about the wedding and then, in one second, the sadness overcomes you and you start to mourn the fact that your husband didn't survive and couldn't be at the wedding. You also think about all those loved ones who have also died and couldn't be there. But what caught me in this scene was one non-verbal action. In the scene, you bring your future daughter-in-law drinks and cake and, before she can turn her head, you're already there and you take the plate from her. You don't give her a chance to eat. Where did that come from?

Lea: That's because I grew up in a different theater. I grew up in a theater in Romania, where the typecast of the Jewish mother was not always a very positive character. The characters, as Sholem Aleichem wrote them, like Yente, the poultry seller, and Gnesia, the flower seller in the story *The Pot*, or the woman in *Morris Shimel*, who is like a Gnesia character. She takes care of her children, but she's quite a mean woman, and since I knew characters like Gnesia around me, I saw things like that. To this day in Israel, that type of snobbery is not that well known. It's not major snobbery, it's something you can see even with common people. "My cake is better than your cake." I have a friend, may she live long and be well, who makes dough and she believes no one has ever made it quite like hers. You see cooking shows on TV and they make all kinds of dough, with water and with milk and with who knows what, but she will always say that her dough is better. "Everything you can do, I can do better." I have known types that I cannot forget. One of them was 'Frau Doctor, the doctor's wife.' She's not a doctor. Her husband is supposedly the doctor, and sometimes, her husband was not a doctor, but only a medic.[1] She would not make a cake; it was always a *torte* (a multilayered cake). And she would not open the door wide and say come in; she would only open it a crack and examine the person standing at the door. It's a kind of snobbery that doesn't exist on the ground, but rather a few inches above it. I remember such people like this, mainly from Czernowitz.

Yaniv: You had another scene in the play, a monologue, with your daughter-in-law's mother. She is sitting *shiva* (mourning) for her husband. You come to comfort her. But instead of comforting her, you upset her with your words. At first, you sit alone, just with the children, and you are very critical of her and say that her husband was a nothing. But then, when people come to visit, you turn around and praise the deceased. In the original Hanoch Levin play, these are two different women, but in your adaptation, you perform both roles and actually underwent a transformation—from being critical of the deceased to praising him. How did you move between those two adaptions when you're playing the same woman, but with two extremes?

Lea: It's very acceptable. Tollebreina doesn't have to pretend to be someone she isn't. When you sit alone, you tell the truth and you are critical of the deceased, but when there are guests, you keep the facade. You automatically move over to being nice. It's not fake, it's part of the woman's behavior. You can gossip and talk

---

[1] Lea used the Yiddish expression, *feldsher*, which means a medic or a doctor who heals with herbs. Sometimes, they were seen as 'charlatans.'

dirty, but when people come over, you immediately stop and turn around one hundred and eighty degrees. That's life.

Yaniv: Let's talk about the third character of Hanoch Levin's that you played. Leviva in *The Labor of Life*.

Lea: That's something else entirely, the whole play is very different.

Yaniv: For sure, it's a smaller play, a play for three.

Lea: The fact that it's small is another matter, but it's a play that has a lot of sensitivity and love has been woven into the characters he wrote. These characters require understanding and compassion. He doesn't hate them. He shares in their pain. He understands them. He is a bit forgiving towards them.

Yaniv: Unlike the two previous characters who are mothers, this is a woman who doesn't care if she has children or not.

Lea: That's right, it's a relationship between a husband and wife for good and for bad, with sensitivity and with cynicism, biting and scoldings between them, and in the end, this sensitivity teaches us about life.

Yaniv: Did you identify with her, with Leviva?

Lea: With the character? Very much so!

Yaniv: In what way?

Lea: I really identified with her; she has all the elements: naivety, love, she is ready to sacrifice for her husband . . . This play has everything. The relationship between the two people is shaped wonderfully.

Yaniv: Tiki Dayan, who played this role after you, once told me that in the scene where Jonah, Leviva's husband, dies, she says, "Jonah, don't die! Don't leave me, Jonah! We have to grow old together. Did you forget? All the hard, arduous labor, the work of old age, and wear and tear, the day-to-day work, the despair, illness, waning strength, and fear, oh, fear of death, which creeps up in the long, sleepless nights. It's not fair that you're leaving everything on my shoulders,

I have no strength on my own."[2] In this monologue, she treats life as a hard and arduous job. Tiki claims that Leviva doesn't cry for him. Leviva, in her opinion, is an egocentric woman who needs someone to help her in the hard work of life and she thinks only of herself. That's why Tiki didn't cry in that scene. You did it completely differently.

Lea: Right, completely different and Hanoch saw what I did and really liked it. Although he didn't direct my show. Michael Gurevich directed, but Hanoch saw it and loved it. My approach was not like Tiki's. My approach was that Leviva was losing her life partner: We were together and now he's leaving me. I cried, I hurt at his departure. "Don't leave me alone to carry everything alone." There is pain and pleading there.

Yaniv: Is there love between them, in your opinion?

Lea: Of course. I didn't assume that she didn't like him. I never read what Hanoch Levin said about himself, but I think he had a relationship problem. He had several wives and was constantly looking for the ideal woman. I think in this play, he also wanted to say that eventually, two people make together this labor called life. In my opinion, this is his manifesto.

Yaniv: Basically, you are saying that Leviva's monologue is Hanoch's own monologue. I want a child or a partner who will make this labor called life together with me. Life is not easy, sometimes even hard, and I need someone by my side.

Lea: That's me. This is also my approach to life. And I think Hanoch was also looking for it. Because I played the role with compassion and love and with great pain, Hanoch accepted it. In the other plays, Hanoch is more blunt, more direct. Here, he is very sensitive. Even the obscenities that Hanoch loved are much more subtle in this play.

Yaniv: Speaking of Hanoch's obscenities, did you like the sentence you say to a neighbor who asks, "Why light?" (Why do you have light in the middle of the night in your bedroom?)

---

2   Hanoch Levin, *The Labor of Life and Others* [Hebrew] (Tel Aviv: The United Kibbutz Publishing House, 1991), 195. (My translation, YSG.)

Lea: Sure! Light because light! Because my husband and I do it with the light on! Because we have a rich and well-lit intimate life! Because we tease in the light much more! Because he sees 'me' in the light, what you only dream of in the dark!³ I say, "Let us live and don't pry into our lives." I think this play is Hanoch Levin at his best!

Yaniv: You started the show with Nissim Azikri playing your husband. Azikri died during the performances and he was replaced by Mosko Alkalai. Was it different playing with each of them?

Lea: Of course. It was different because they are different types of actors. Although Mosko joined an existing cast, his personality was completely different and it definitely changed the nature of the play.

Understanding the Stage Space

Yaniv: Israeli television (IBA, the Israel Broadcasting Authority) wanted to film the show *The Labor of Life*.

Lea: Yes, Arye Yas was the director of the IBA drama department and he wanted to film some plays, so they chose ours.

Yaniv: Was it different performing the show for the cameras?

Lea: No, we performed the exact same play.

Yaniv: I mean in terms of directing. For example, when you shout out of the window, "I'm six years old, I've eaten a little from the outside, but it's just the plaster!" In the theater, the window is on the back wall and the audience sees your back, while in the TV studio the camera was placed behind the window and we see your face.

Lea: Because they put the camera in the back, but it didn't matter to me.

---

3   Ibid., 182.

Yaniv: When you're on stage, how do you perform a monologue with so much emotion to convey to the audience and they can't see your face, your eyes, and all they see is your back? It's more than the facial expressions, it's everything you have inside, it's your whole feeling.

Lea: It didn't matter to me at all. If you're in a show and it's staged so that you have your back to the audience and you have to express a feeling, you don't need them to see your face as well. I'm into it. I think my voice and my back give the audience the feeling of what I feel. The audience doesn't even really need to see my face.

Yaniv: You've reminded me of what Omri Nitzan once said about you, that you are an actress with the best understanding of 'stage space.' What did he mean? Let's take the example of Leviva; there is a monologue in the play that you could have performed facing the audience and they would have seen more, but still, it didn't bother you.

Lea: No.

Yaniv: What does 'understanding stage space' mean?

Lea: It means that when you go on stage, the first things that the audience sees are your personality and your power of expression. When you do the job right, then having your back facing the audience can also work; it's not only if you are facing them. If you are in the scene and in character in the right way, then you will project your message even with your back facing them. I once saw a production of Chekhov's *Three Sisters* in Romania. I was very young at the time. The actress who played Irina, in the scene where Solyony tells her that he will kill whoever tries to take her from him because he loves her, she has her back to him. She meets him and he stops her and as soon as she stopped, you saw that she was frightened and disagreed. It was so strong and so expressive, and I only saw her back. If she had turned around, I would have seen the resistance and the fear, but I saw all of this without actually seeing her. It is the power of the actor's personality to do things right. I also saw an actor in Romania who played Othello. He was standing in profile to the audience when Iago told him that Desdemona was cheating on him. I didn't see his face and he fell straight, face forward. You only saw his back and yet it was very strong. Our imagination has great power. I imagined that I knew how he looked. If an actor works correctly, then even when you don't see the actor from the front, you see everything and feel everything.

But in *The Labor of Life*, when it was televised, Leviva's monologue is very long and you can't do a whole long monologue with your back to the audience. The medium is different, so they put a camera in the back as well, and that's how they showed my face.

Yaniv: What else do you understand of the stage space?

Lea: When you go on stage, your personality, the actor's personality, if it is really strong, it fills the stage even if there is no set. The power to convince people that I am here, knowing how to move around on stage, the coordination of your body. There are actors with so much presence, they sometimes don't feel that there are other things around them. I'll give you an example. Let's say I'm sitting on the chair and I need to get to the buffet. I'm talking to my partner and I feel like I've been sitting too long. I feel it in the performance of the role… and then you slowly start to go to the buffet. But how do you go? At what pace are you going? You don't just get up and go. You can get up and go because you got angry or because you want to take something. Your body automatically goes there; you don't even feel it.

Yaniv: Walking on stage depends on the situation. You don't just go to some place; you have a reason why you are going and you have a state of mind that gives you the way in which you walk.

Lea: Always. You also have a reason; you feel like you are in one place for too long.

Yaniv: I once worked with actors who said that they were being upstaged. The other actors were standing behind them and forcing them to speak with their backs to the audience. Is this something that bothers you or something that you think about?

Lea: No, and I'm not terribly afraid of it either. Some actors do this to you on purpose and it is very inelegant and unpleasant. But some actors don't always feel like they're doing it to you. Suddenly, they go off in some direction without feeling that they are pulling you, but you are forced to follow them. There are actors who are terribly afraid of being upstaged. When Omri said that I understand the stage space, it's because I immediately know how to get out of it if someone does it to me. I continue with the text and make a turn with it until I get back to the original *mise-en-scène*. And so, you find a way to get out of the situation.

Yaniv: It reminds me of a scene from a play that we talk about a lot, but it was probably very significant in your career, *Mirele Efros*. In the first act, you sit on a chair and have to go out to the right side, but you get up and turn to the left and walk around the chair and exit from the right side. There is something longer and more dramatic about this exit.

Lea: Very true. Mirele Efros does not run, she walks slowly. Movement helps to shape the character. The movement around the chair gives strength. You don't immediately go out; you leave an impression.

Yaniv: I thought you just wanted to make it more artistic, a more interesting exit, but you're saying, "This is the character."

Lea: This really is the character! The character takes up more space, she is a queen.

Yaniv: Is that something a director would say to you or is it something you do instinctively?

Lea: Usually, the director has to say everything. But an actor who knows how to move around on stage, who understands space, sometimes knows how to do it, and the director accepts it. There are several methods. For example, in Romania, the director would make sketches of all the *mises-en-scène*. Here, in Israel, there are directors with a different method. They say, "Start moving around and we'll make the corrections as we go." The actors start walking around and the director slowly chooses the place for them.

Yaniv: What do you prefer?

Lea: I prefer a good director. The director I liked working with the most was Teodorescu with whom I did Molière's *The Imaginary Invalid*, *Anne Frank*, and other plays. He didn't speak Yiddish and when we did Molière together, he really taught me how to grasp the space. There is a sentence in the play where I tell the patient, "So, you will do this and that," and the director stopped and told me to divide the sentence, so that at the end of the sentence, I was standing next to the patient. For example, let's try it. "Yaniv, you know I wanted to call you, but I had to make some phone calls." You can say the sentence all in one go, but he taught me to break it down and to pause after the words, "I wanted to call you," and then arrange something on the table. Then I approach you and continue with the rest of the sentence, which I say to your face with greater force.

Yaniv: Basically, you took a sentence that could have been very quick and informative and made a whole show out of it.

Lea: Yes, a whole show. I was in my place, I also arranged things, I walked around, I reached you, all of that without losing my rhythm. Teodorescu taught me how to fill the stage and how to extract all the nuances in the sentence and all the words in the subtext, all the non-verbal expressions that are in it. That's the beauty of acting. You don't just talk, you live. Look what happened with Omri Nitzan. Omri directed me in *The Old Lady's Visit*. In my first entrance, I go out on stage with make-up. For twenty minutes, the residents of the town of Güllen stand and talk about my arrival. Everyone is waiting for me and I have to go in and say, "It's Güllen!" Omri said to me, "Lea, talk to the back of the stage, towards the back of the scenes, those are the people who are waiting for you." So I had to go in, turn back around, and then talk. I said to him, "Your Güllen is in the back, mine is in the front towards the audience."

Yaniv: And he accepted it?

Lea: Immediately! Because it was normal. Güllen can be in any direction. This is the city, I'm coming off the train, the whole city is spread out at my feet in all directions. What does it matter which direction I turn. You bring the lady to town, you have to see that she has arrived!

Yaniv: Hang on a minute. First you told me about how a good actor can do a meaningful monologue with their back to the audience because the whole body can do the work for them and now you are saying that it is important to face the audience. What is the difference between the two situations?

Lea: The lady's entrance in *The Old Lady's Visit* is not similar to the monologue in *The Labor of Life*. This is the first entrance onto the stage, so you have to see who enters. Here comes the lady! The audience sees her for the first time. Entering and immediately turning my back spoils things because I have to introduce myself. Besides, the walking around he asked for was not necessary because the city is really there in all directions. In *The Labor of Life*, the window faces from the house towards the outside and I shout to the neighbors. There is no other option of another direction to shout out to. The fourth wall is blocked. The audience does not see the fourth wall, just a window I can talk through. What's more, in *The Labor of Life*, the stage entrance is not a monologue; the audience already knows my character. We have already talked about entering the stage and how significant it is. There is no close-up on stage that will do the job for you. You have to really make an entrance when walking on stage, from the front row all the way back to the last seat in the back row.

What about Television and Cinema?

Yaniv: If you're talking about close-ups and photography, then let's talk about television. You've done some very interesting things on TV. In 1971, you acted in the series *Hedva and Shlomik*, the first feature series filmed in Israel. You played Erika Krakower, Hedva's mother. They were urban parents, not from a kibbutz.[4]

Lea: The snobbish urbanite. They said I was such a snob, people didn't know where the theater ended and life began.

Yaniv: Did the series make you famous? Did it make you a name?

Lea: Very much so! I couldn't walk down the street. Every episode was a sensation!

Yaniv: Was it different for you at that time to act in the theater or on television? It's not as though you had experience in television.

Lea: I had no experience, but not everyone had that much experience back then. This was the first drama series in Israel. But the work was very pleasant. The videographer, Nissim Leon, was very nice; he loved the actors and he always liberated me from my fear of the camera. He told me, "Lea, be calm, don't be afraid, I'm taking care of you," and I think he really filmed me beautifully.

Yaniv: Was there an audience during the filming?

Lea: Not at all. We filmed each take several times until we had a successful shot. It was very successful; it was a hit.

---

4   A kibbutz is a communal settlement where individuals live and work together, sharing resources and responsibilities to create a cooperative and egalitarian society. In a kibbutz, everyone contributes to the community's well-being, with work assignments ranging from agriculture to industry. In traditional kibbutzim, all property and assets are collectively owned. However, many kibbutzim have transitioned to a more privatized model, while still fostering a strong sense of community and collective decision-making.

Yaniv: Did you like the idea of acting in front of a camera at that time?

Lea: I really liked it because it is very tempting.

Yaniv: Why?

Lea: Because it's slightly different acting. For example, you cannot exaggerate because if you exaggerate, it becomes too much. The close-ups are also very strong; suddenly you see the person very close and then you have to be careful how you do the dramatic things, not to exaggerate. The acting needs to be smaller and more understated. But I don't think I've learned that much since then about where the camera is. When I get into a character, I'm not that aware of the cameras. For example, I shot a sketch on the program *This is It!* and when I saw the shot, I noticed that at a certain moment, I didn't notice where the camera was and I had to turn my head a little. I need to think more about the cameras for television.

Yaniv: For many years after *Hedva and Shlomik*, you did almost no television, until 2003, when you did the series, *Ahava BeShalechet* (Love in the fall) with Yehuda Barkan.

Lea: There was *Zimmerim* (B&Bs) before that.

Yaniv: *Zimmerim* was broadcast a few months before *Love in the Fall*. More than thirty years have passed since *Hedva and Shlomik*. Were there no offers? Did you not want to play more TV roles?

Lea: I was not offered any.

Yaniv: Did you want more?

Lea: I wanted to do something interesting. I don't know why they didn't offer me anything. If they asked me, it was for something like one or two days of filming, nothing serious.

Yaniv: Let's talk about *Love in the Fall*. You performed differently from the way you performed in *Hedva and Shlomik*? Did the years do anything to you?

Lea: First of all, I don't remember that much. In *Love in the Fall*, I was very calm. I didn't feel if my acting was different or not. I really never compared it until you asked me just now. I felt very comfortable in *Love in the Fall*, with the story, the cast, the director. Yehuda Barkan was an excellent partner. He really appreciated me in the role. He said I am an excellent film actor. After all, he was the film expert between the two of us.

Yaniv: So, let's stay with your TV roles. One of your last roles on television was the grandmother, Bubbe Malka, in the series *Shtisel*. In New York, I was contacted by the newspaper *Forverts* (*The Jewish Forward*). They asked me to write an article about Lea Koenig from *Shtisel*. On a Zoom call with a radio station in Argentina, you were introduced as the grandmother from *Shtisel*. This role came to you in a little bit of a strange way. In the first season, the role was played by the late actress Hanna Rieber, your friend from Romania. She passed away during the series and they contacted you. I will ask a slightly cheeky question. Was it insulting that you were approached only after her and not offered the position to begin with?

Lea: No, it wasn't insulting. I debated whether or not to do the role not because I wasn't offered it in the beginning. The role was originally intended for Dvora Kedar who gave it up, and so they approached Rieber. When they approached me after Rieber passed away, I agreed because I thought Hanna would have been happy if I played her part in her honor and her memory and I loved the role.

Yaniv: You once told me that this is the type of role you could pull out of your sleeve. What did you mean?

Lea: For me to play a Yiddish Jew, a *Yiddene*, is not something new. I like to play those types of characters. I like the style. There are those who don't like it. I love it and I don't care if there are those who don't like it. In Yiddish literature, such women are the ones who dominate and are the leaders, and I know these types and love them, so it's not complicated for me to play them. In *Shtisel*, there is a lot of *Yiddishkeit* (Jewishness, the Jewish way of life or its customs and practices) and a lot of warmth for the Jews of that time, so it wasn't hard for me to get into character, and I loved it.

Yaniv: In the series, you played in Yiddish and Hebrew. Did they write it for you in Yiddish or did you translate it on the spot?

Lea: They wrote it in Yiddish. There was a religious guy hanging around there, a tall handsome guy, and he was correcting our mistakes. He had a sense of humor and I asked him what kind of garbled Yiddish he spoke. He said, "You're right, but this is how the ultra-Orthodox speak. I'm telling you, you can't understand anything they say." So he would hang out there and, one time, I sang Mordechai Gebirtig's song *Kinder Yoren* (Childhood years). Suddenly, he came over and I asked him if I could sing, after all, he's ultra-Orthodox and maybe he doesn't listen to women singing. But he's a smart guy. He asked me to continue singing so that he could listen. I asked him if he would come to my show in Yiddish and he was very excited about it and asked me to tell him when the show would be.

Yaniv: Was there a difference in the pace of the acting when you acted in Yiddish or Hebrew?

Lea: No, it was the same. The language didn't affect the acting at all.

Yaniv: I'll tell you why I'm asking. Here in Israel, there is a perception that, when you act in Yiddish, you are playing a more vulgar role, that it's not good acting… I'm afraid to continue because I see you're already getting angry.

Lea: Who says that?

Yaniv: All kinds of Hebrew theater researchers and also Hebrew actors.

Lea: They are stupid, forgive me. There are very good actors who perform very well in Yiddish. Don't be confused. There are vulgar actors in every language. Vulgar acting in Yiddish? Yiddish was never performed in a vulgar style. There are good actors and there are bad actors. There are actors who know how to speak and some actors who don't. What nonsense is it to say that performing in Yiddish is vulgar?

Yaniv: Is there a scene you particularly remember from the series?

Lea: There was one scene that made me laugh so hard I couldn't speak. It's the scene where the grandmother makes the mistake of thinking that an old Moroccan man is her husband and she brings him into her room. I speak Yiddish, and he speaks Moroccan, and we seem to understand each other. He is not an actor, they just took someone to read the text, and I'm talking to him, and it was just so funny. I couldn't control myself and they had to stop filming several times because of my laughter.

Yaniv: One of the most beautiful scenes I loved was your scene with Hana Laszlo, who is your son's fiancé, and she comes to visit you and she starts to congratulate you and you get worked up till you explode and shout at her, "*Shvayg shoyn, klafte!*" (Shut up already, bitch!) When you yell at her, you see on her face the panic and insult. With no words, only through her facial expressions.

Lea: She was really excellent.

Yaniv: When she starts blessing you, you get more and more agitated until you explode. When you are in a scene like this, do you really get angry or is it technical and you know that at this moment, you need to step up and get angry?

Lea: We rehearse first. Even before filming, the characters are built, but they remain similar throughout the series, in the same tone and the same rhythm. When I played the grandmother, I built her from scratch. She is an older woman, a bit senile, but she knows who her son is and it annoys her that he brings his new fiancé. She is annoyed from the start. She sits quietly, but she is annoyed. As an actress, I build it inside me, it's annoying me, she's annoying, until enough is enough! And you explode. You do it inside yourself. You have to really live this momentum.

Yaniv: You joined the cast in the second season, so did you have to adjust yourself to what Hanna Rieber did?

Lea: No, and they didn't talk to me about it either. I haven't seen any of her clips. Hanna and I, we were very different, both in terms of personality and in terms of our acting. I, as an actress, have different ways from what she had. Also, she was a completely different genre.

Yaniv: If it hadn't been Hanna Rieber who played in the first season and you had been approached to replace another actress in the second season, would you have agreed to do it?

Lea: Yes, because it's a good role. Why not? Possibly because it might have been insulting?

Yaniv: An insult or the attitude towards the actress who has been removed from the position.

Lea: It very much depends on what your relationship is with that person. Right now, there is a series on Netflix, *The Crown*. The actresses who play the queen and the queen mother change and it doesn't matter.[5] I don't think it would have mattered to me. There isn't the opportunity to play really good roles every day.

Yaniv: If you're already saying that there isn't the opportunity for really great roles every day, then let's go back to roles in cinema. You had a few cinematic roles: *Lupo, Lupo Goes to New York, Katz and Carrasso, The Highway Queen, Kadosh, The Testament, Madam Yankelova's Fine Literature Club*. There were a few more, but those were all pretty small roles.

Lea: They didn't offer me other roles.

Yaniv: Did you want any? Did you try?

Lea: Did I fight for it? No! Cinema in Israel is very different from the theater. People in the film industry do not know theater and do not appreciate theater actors. They almost don't know each other.

Yaniv: But Menahem Golan, for example, he did know you.

Lea: Yes, he did offer me roles. He offered me *Lupo, Katz and Carrasso,* and *The Highway Queen*. Then he started doing action movies and he didn't have roles for me here in Israel. The main film actors were Assi Dayan and Gila Almagor.

Yaniv: Do you feel you missed out?

Lea: Not at all.

Yaniv: So, if you were offered a movie or a play in the theater today, which would you choose?

Lea: It depends on the movie and, now I'm also being practical, it depends on how much they pay. In the cinema, there is huge publicity, it goes without

---

5   In the role of Queen Elizabeth, Claire Foy acted in seasons 1 and 2; Olivia Colman in season 3; and Imelda Staunton in seasons 4 and 5. In the role of the Queen Mother, the actresses change from Victoria Hamilton in seasons 1 and 2 to Marion Bailey in season 3.

saying. If you succeed, many people see you, but thank God, people know me from the theater.

Yaniv: It's really interesting. When Hanna Maron was a guest at my Actors' Studio at Bar-Ilan University, she said, "I played all the biggest roles, but people only remember my shouting 'Open' as Hanna from *Krovim Krovim* (Near ones, dear ones)."[6] Dvora Kedar also told me that she played really beautiful roles in the theater such as *Metamorphosis* and *The Beauty Queen of Leenane*, but what she is most remembered for was her role as Benzi's mother in *Lemon Popsicle*.[7]

Lea: And Lea is remembered only as Shemesh's mother in *Shemesh* with Zvika Hadar.

Yaniv: That's not true; you are perhaps the only theater actress, almost, who is known even by those who don't go to the theater.

Lea: Maybe because of the interviews on TV. I did lots of TV series such as *Parpar Nechmad* (Nice butterfly), *Sesame Street*, *The Beilis Trial*, *The Table*, *Zimmerim*, *Love in the Fall*, *Shemesh*, *Hedva and Shlomik*.

Yaniv: On the one hand, it seems like a very respectable list, but on the other hand, with hindsight, it seems like you made only a few appearances. Perhaps because they were spread over many years. It may be that what you did on television and in the cinema was still enough to establish you in the public consciousness, and yet, when they say "Lea Koenig," they're talking about theater. Even for me... I followed your career very closely and I remember every moment of what you did in film and on television. It's not that you didn't succeed or didn't perform well, you did. But maybe because in the theater, you always had bigger roles or roles that were more interesting.

Lea: In the theater, the fact that there is a direct connection with the audience is a very powerful thing. If you take actors like Hanna Maron, for example, who did

---

6 Hanna Maron starred in the first Hebrew sitcom, *Krovim Krovim*, which aired on educational television in the mid-1980s. Each episode of the series opens with Maron calling, "Open!" Hanna would answer this way every time the doorbell rang and this call became the main hallmark of the series in general and with regards to Maron in particular.

7 The Actors' Studio with actress Dvora Kedar on the occasion of her receiving an honorary doctorate from Bar-Ilan University, which was held as part of a course under my guidance on April 23, 2017 and more (YSG).

Krovim Krovim, the ratings were very high, but she is still mainly remembered from the theater.

Yaniv: I'm not sure. We know she was in the theater, but apart from theater people and some old theaters goers, the general public doesn't really remember what she did.

Lea: Maybe because she retired from the Cameri even before her official retirement. She acted a bit in Be'er Sheva and a little at the Habima Theater. We did *Desire* together and Miriam Zohar did *Mary Stewart* with her. But all in all, many years passed without her performing. Maybe that's why they forgot. She didn't perform enough.

Yaniv: You were supposed to replace her in *Hello, Dolly*, right?

Lea: Yes, but I didn't want to. They wanted me to be an understudy only if she couldn't perform, so I passed up on it. I also gave up on Golda in *Fiddler on the Roof*.

Yaniv: Were you supposed to replace Lia Dultzkaya?

Lea: No, I was originally supposed to play Golda. But I didn't want to because in the musical, the role is not interesting at all. What is she doing in this musical? She has nothing going for her.

Yaniv: In the musical, she really doesn't have any interesting moments, but in the play, she has some wonderful parts.

Lea: In the play, of course. To this day, I can't forget when my mother acted in the play. The night before she died, she said to Tevye, "Tevye, who will prepare dinner for you?" It was heartbreaking! In the musical, she has nothing, she has no role. Anyway, going back to what we were talking about; if you've done a lot of shows and you've done something on TV, the audience connects with that and they remember you for it. It's not like I was only on TV. I was much stronger in the theater and only a little on TV, so they remember me better for it.

Yaniv: You said earlier that, in cinema and television, there are very few rehearsals and the character remains quite similar during filming.

Lea: Almost.

Yaniv: And in the theater, do you feel that the characters develop more?

Lea: Of course. There are TV series where you build a role and in every series the texts change, but the character remains the same, speaks the same, looks the same; you don't have that kind of power on stage. On stage, you have to convey the difference. If you have to change on stage, you have to convey it from the guts. Maybe from season to season on TV, the character can change. On stage, you have to make it louder and clearer because it's for that moment in that place. On television, you can do another take and another take until it comes out the way the director wants or so that it doesn't interfere with filming or a fly hasn't just flown past or I don't know what. On stage, you have just one minute and you must succeed.

Yaniv: But isn't this because you rehearse for three months in the theater.

Lea: It's not from that. It comes down to how you approach the character you're playing. Even in the cinema, when there is a strong drama, you have to do a lot of repetition and take it seriously.

Yaniv: So, let's take an example of a role where you haven't played many similar roles. When I saw you in the role of Alexandra in *The Velocity of Autumn*, I was very surprised. A lot of your characters are women with two feet firmly planted on the ground, down-to-earth, strong women. Suddenly, you are playing a very spiritual character, a painter who, when she talks about her tour of the Guggenheim, is literally floating on her experience. Your clothes were also softer and the long braid made you a completely different person. When you build a role like that, is it something that you can only do in the theater?

Lea: No, you could play a role like that in the cinema as well, but with a role of that length, you need enough rehearsals until the character comes out. With television, it also takes time.

Yaniv: For *Shtisel*, did you have two months of rehearsals?

Lea: No. But don't forget that *Shtisel* was already built. I joined the series in the second season. Everything was already built and ready. I came into an environment where I had to adapt myself to them.

Yaniv: So, let's take *Love in the Fall*, which is a role you built from the beginning. Did you have long rehearsals?

Lea: There were rehearsals. It wasn't a month, but there were long rehearsals. Don't forget, in the theater you build a role and you have to perform it for an hour and a half on stage. On TV, it is divided into short takes that you manage to build as you work. You don't need to know how to do the whole job in one go.

Yaniv: What about the fact that a film is not shot in order and it's possible to shoot the final scene on the first day of filming; does that bother you?

Lea: At first, when I started acting in movies, it really bothered me. Now I am used to it. It really depends on where you shoot, who the director is, and how well the production team knows what it wants, among other things.

Each Role Left Its Mark

Yaniv: Let's go back for a moment to the play *The Velocity of Autumn*. Itzik Weingarten directed you. In fact, he directed you in many beautiful roles such as *The Life before Us, Driving Miss Daisy, Oscar and the Lady in Pink, Autumn Sonata,* and *A Time for Love (Et Dodim)*. He knows you well. Is he the one who knew how to get the character out of you or is it something you brought?

Lea: When I read the play, I realized that I was going to do something that I hadn't done in a long time. This is a woman who knows she has dementia; she is aware of it. Weingarten was very involved, we talked about every scene we did.

Yaniv: Dementia is on the sidelines in the play.

Lea: It's always in the background. She knows she has it. I'm acting it all the time, I know something is 'wrong' with me, I know why they want to kick me out of the house, but Alexandra, of course, wants a little more control over her life and is therefore not ready to leave the house.

Yaniv: This thing, this desire to be in control, the fear of losing one's memory is really common for everyone and certainly for actors who need their memory. But there is something else in this character, her spirituality, and I don't remember you doing anything like that anywhere else in your career.

Lea: If I didn't then maybe that's why I liked this role.

Yaniv: It's not just that. This character is different from you. You are a strong and stable woman with two feet on the ground. You don't get confused between the stage and life. You know very well how to create the separation between the stage and life. You know very well where you want to go and where you come from, who you are, and what you are. Here is a character that is very far from you, spiritual, fleeting, even sentimental. Did you feel it?

Lea: What do you mean, did I feel it? I knew who I was playing and I certainly felt it. But in an actor's career, if the actor is more or less good, he should know who he is going to play. I knew it wasn't me. This is Alexandra, and this spirituality, I know those characters, plenty of them! One of the conditions of being an actor is to know how to look around and not just at yourself. You have to observe, and I met many spiritual people and also those who were not spiritual, but wanted to be spiritual. I know this community of painters. When I went to play the role, I remembered a whole series of people who lived in a similar way. They were not such great painters, but they lived the life of artists. When I made the character, I remembered my friend who was a painter and how she saw life and how her life unfolded. And she was kind of spiritual, and, in her old age, her spirituality bordered on dementia. This life of the painters, they behave quite strangely.

Yaniv: Throughout our conversations, you have told me that you are an observant person, that in every role you tried to think of people you knew during your life, who were similar to the people you were going to play.

Lea: Right.

Yaniv: But you didn't imitate them. You built the character according to the personality of these people that you knew.

Lea: Right.

Yaniv: What interests me is how well these characters you study stay with you after you finish with them. How much does it filter into your private life? One association that comes to mind at the moment is that since *The Labor of Life*, you have been using Leviva's sentence, "I am an old, sick, and weak woman." How much does the stage penetrate into Lea Koenig's life as you, the person?

Lea: Honestly, maybe I don't adopt new ideas and I'm not even aware, but the things remain inside me. They stay because I learned from all of those characters. I think my character was slowly built from all the characters I played and from all the things I learned. I always took these characters from wherever. These characters taught me about life and if I talk to you about the characters, then I realize now that I'm not aware of it every day, but without awareness, I took something from every one of them and it stayed. For example, the matter of painting. This friend I had was a painter, and she was a very interesting girl, and there was beauty in the way she knew how to see the beautiful things in life and I think I took that trait from her. I also took a lot from my mother. I already told you that, when I made *Mother Courage*, I remembered that during the war, when we arrived in Samarkand, the room we lived in had a dirt floor and my mother asked how this floor was cleaned. The neighbor gave her a bucket and told her, "Go to the street and collect horse excrement and then spread it on the floor, that way lice won't come from the sand and you won't get typhoid." And my mother, the blonde beauty, with the suitcase of silk dresses and furs, took heavy shoes and the bucket, smiled and returned with a bucket of excrement and spread the excrement on the ground so that it would be clean! I constantly use this strength to carry on and survive. It helped her to survive the war while there were people who fell in the streets. So, when I made *Mother Courage*, I thought about my mother and how she survived the war. And why did I remember this moment? I don't know, but it was a powerful moment! Her personality, her strength, the will to survive was probably so strong that I saw the same thing when I played the woman who survives the war.

Yaniv: Could it be that Lea Koenig, the woman, and Lea Koenig, the wife of Zvi Stolper, are both a couple of actors who leave the theater in Romania where they were very successful, come to Israel to a country where they don't know the language and where the locals ridicule the language they spoke (Yiddish), and Lea has to prove to herself and to her mother that she can be an actress in a language she doesn't know well, and Lea Koenig feels she has to survive. Just as your mother did not shy away from taking the horse excrement and smearing it so that you could have a house and be able to live, Lea also needed to take control of Hebrew and show everyone in Israel that she is a good actress and a survivor?

Lea: Exactly!

Yaniv: So, it's not just *Mother Courage*, it's your whole life.

Lea: True, but all these characters in my career, the good and the not so good, each personality probably left something in me. I chose a good profession. I chose an interesting profession. I chose life and the theater teaches you to live! The theater taught me to live.

Survival

Yaniv: In an interview in July 1962, after you made *Bereshit*, you said that you and Hirshl were making private shows in Yiddish and easy Hebrew to make a living. You told me in our conversations that only after you had proven yourself in Hebrew, only in 1965, did you do your first play in Yiddish, *Hochma Ligt in Keshene* (Wisdom lies in the pocket). So, what was the article about?

Lea: First of all, it was after *Bereshit*. Secondly, it was a side job. We would travel with an accordionist to the places that the Histadrut (the labor union) would send us, Hirshl would tell jokes, we would sing a little, and that was it. It wasn't a show and we didn't sell tickets. It had no publicity. It was through the Histadrut.

Yaniv: This is also survival. Sometimes you just need to make a living.

Lea: Right. Hirshl also immediately went to teach theater at a school in Herzliya. It was, by the way, a lovely thing to do and he liked it very much. To this day, I am stopped by people who studied with him and haven't forgotten him. Don't forget how little we earned at Habima; it was impossible to live on the salary of a stage actor in this theater.

Yaniv: In Romania, was it possible to live on an actor's salary?

Lea: Yes. The gap was not that big, but the cost of living in Romania was much lower and no one there had the pretensions of wealth like here.

Yaniv: It's the same line. If we have to live, then the theater gives us a salary. But if it's not enough, we do what is necessary to survive.

Lea: Don't forget, we needed a home. It was impossible to buy a house and furniture with the Habima salary. We started from scratch. We had brought nothing with us and Zvika earned less than I did from Habima.

Yaniv: In a later article, when you did *The Back Street*, they wrote in the newspaper that you were doing it for the money—because what you earned at Habima in a month, you could earn in Yiddish in a week.

Lea: That was true, by the way. Everyone had work on the side. I also had some side jobs, even in the Hammam Theater in Jaffa.

Yaniv: When did you appear in the Hammam?

Lea: When I came to Israel. Dan Ben-Amotz invited me to sing songs in Yiddish at cultural evenings. The composer, Nurit Hirsh, accompanied me on the piano. This was even before *The Megillah*[8] with the Burstein family. I performed in Hammam in Yiddish before that.

Yaniv: It's interesting that it's eighty years after the Holocaust, eighty years after you left Samarkand, and still, survival is what drives you in your career.

Lea: We grew up all the time in survival mode. After all, Hirshl had nothing left either after the war.

Yaniv: Do you remember life before the war in Czernowitz or Łódź?

Lea: Besides what I already told you, I remember pictures. I remember the school in Czernowitz. I remember myself with a ribbon in my hair. No more than that. I don't remember anything from Poland at all. Don't forget that there was a big disaster in our house. My father lost his leg and he went to Austria and my mother was busy surviving. There was no money and I needed a coat for the winter. My mother went to work and then they invited her to Czernowitz. So my mother and I went with my grandmother to Czernowitz. My grandfather was no longer alive. I didn't really know my grandparents from Vilna. I only know that they had a legal firm.

Yaniv: For a child, usually their formative years are until around the age of seven. For you, the Holocaust is the defining event of your life, but you were already a ten- or eleven-year-old girl. It's strange that you don't remember.

---

8   *The Megillah* was a very successful show in Yiddish by the poet Itzik Manger, composed by Dov Seltzer and performed by the Burstein family. After the success in Israel, they performed it on Broadway and around the world.

Lea: I think that, during my childhood in Poland, I moved around. I was with my grandmother a lot because my father was in Austria and my mother was working. I started traveling with the Vilna Troupe only in 1931 when they went to Vienna. The other times I stayed with my grandmother in Łódź. We lived in 12 School Street, Szkolna in Polish. It is interesting that, in Czernowitz, we also lived in School Street, but there it was number 5, and the street was called Schule Gas in Yiddish. In any case, there were probably very difficult years in Poland and I don't remember.

Yaniv: Do you remember your father in Czernowitz?

Lea: I only remember that he performed at the Scala Theater in Czernowitz, I think I remember that he sat alone on the stage and was wonderful. Zvika remembered him from the performance there. Anyone who saw him couldn't forget him.

Yaniv: Did you think that the Holocaust was very significant in your life?

Lea: I told you before that we didn't really know about the Holocaust. We were not in the camps. We lacked bread, but we were not with the Germans. We only heard about the Holocaust when we returned to Romania. The Russians did not talk about the Holocaust at all. They talked about 'The Great Patriotic War' and about the fact that they were liberated, but they did not mention the Jews.

Yaniv: Even without the camps, the trauma is huge. The difficulty, the poverty, the fact that you don't have a home. It's a difficult thing, but on the other hand, you are a very optimistic, happy person. You don't let the difficulty you had in life affect your daily conduct and yet, in our conversations, it turns out that World War II was a defining event in your life that had a great impact on you.

Lea: That's very true, to this day.

Yaniv: You came full circle in a very exciting way when you were chosen to light a torch on Israel's seventieth Independence Day. The girl who went through the horrors of World War II as a refugee, who knew scarcity, who observed the people who gave up their dignity for survival, who chose to live, the woman who, night after night, performed on stage, shows that it really is possible to overcome all difficulties, to be alive and to live. And the torch says, "I'm here! I made it." Did you feel all of that?

Lea: The lighting of the torch was a very impressive event and when I lit it, I thought of all those who made me who I am. My mother, my father, and Hirshl, who did not get to see this exciting moment. When you go out on stage there and you see three thousand people and you say, "I'm appreciated; so maybe three thousand people don't know me, but one thousand do." It's very exciting. In general, at events such as the university awards and the Israel Prize, you feel that you are appreciated beyond the show and they are saying bravo to you. My personality created something that a group of people sat and chose to give me credit for. People's appreciation is very exciting.

Yaniv: Is appreciation from the public important to you?

Lea: I think so; that's the most important thing. For me, when I didn't act because of the pandemic, I don't miss the stage, but I did miss the audience.

Yaniv: But you don't get the appreciation through television and the movies?

Lea: Why not? On stage, you get it right away, and in film and television, you have to wait for the audience to see you. It's just a little later, but then people tell me they saw me. It's very exciting when they call me to say they saw me and they really enjoyed it.

Yaniv: Was it hard for you, when you didn't perform during the pandemic?

Lea: I did some television and I was filmed for a movie. It's true that I missed the theater, but let's get things into proportion. During the pandemic, I was constantly asked in every interview, how do you survive, how you manage? But how can you compare it when you have a house, food, air conditioning, a television, and a telephone, and people call and are interested in you? So, of course, it hurt me when I wasn't acting and running around, but negative talk is no good and we need to say thank God for what we have.

Yaniv: This is exactly your choice in life. You could choose to see the glass as half empty, sink into the difficulties of the new immigrants, perform in Yiddish because that's where they make money, but you said . . .

Lea: I said "No!"

Yaniv: Exactly, you chose to say, "I will make an effort and I choose to see the good points. Here, I succeeded in *Bereshit*, and also in *Puntila* I received good reviews, and here I received the Klausner Prize. I choose to ignore the hard points and choose to see the good."

Lea: Very true. What will it help me to sit at home and cry? I had a beautiful career of seventy years. I think God wants us to see the good in the world.

Yaniv: This is a really important life lesson.

Lea: So you got it. This is the stage of my life.

Chapter 13

Four Years Later: Reflections

Yaniv: Today, it's four years since our previous conversations, four not-so-easy years. Our past discussions took place during the COVID-19 epidemic and, while the world has returned to normality, we are now in a time of war. In retrospect, is there anything else you would like to add?

Lea: The truth is that everything you wrote in the book and everything that can be in the book is important to me. I'm already an 'old girl,' and, at my age, you don't know how long it will last. If, thank God, I've reached this age, then I'm happy that I can add a little more to the book.

Yaniv: What have you done that makes you happy?

Lea: I ask myself if I did everything I wanted and if I did it well. I wanted to be an actress and I succeeded. I think overall I was lucky. Talent is important, but you also need luck. And I think that I've had good luck since the beginning of my career.

Yaniv: Is there anything you would do differently?

Lea: I don't think so. Maybe I would have done things better than I did, but not differently. The most important aspect that guided me in this profession is my love of the audience. And I remained loyal to them from the beginning... To the audiences in Romania, the audiences in Israel, and to the audiences around the world in the places where I performed. Zvi and I were always very honest and wherever we went, we brought our whole hearts, with everything we knew and how to do it the best way possible.

Yaniv: Do you feel you have unfinished business?

Lea: The fact that Zvi left too soon upsets me. With his potential, he could have contributed a lot more. He had a feeling for time, for people, for the changes in the world. We live in a time in which you need to be up to date, to know how to react to every change in all aspects of life. I still feel sorry that I didn't encourage him to write more, direct more, do more artistic things in his life.

Yaniv: Do you ever think about what Zvi would say about the current situation in Israel?

Lea: I feel Zvi is very present in everything I do. I feel him and my parents and my grandmother, and they are present with me. I haven't played a single role in which I didn't feel that Zvi was with me, so of course, I always think about what he would say about everything that happens here.

Yaniv: Not long ago, you acted in a film about ultra-Orthodox women and afterwards you were very excited about the technique and technology. The story focused on an older woman giving her younger self life advice. But you told me it wasn't the story that left an impression, it was the technology. Does it still excite you?

Lea: Of course. I wish there were more things that did this. Both in the theater and in the cinema every day, there are exciting things, and that's good. As long as it continues to be exciting, it's good.

Yaniv: If you still manage to get excited in the theater, then I would like to talk to you about a special theater role of yours. Although we talked about it in previous chapters, something is still new. I am referring to the play, *A Tour Guide to Warsaw*. You performed in it in 1998 for the first time right after Zvi passed away, and the performance was a great success. The second time, in 2013, you performed in Yiddish. And most recently, for the third time in 2023, you did the role in Hebrew again. The audience received you in each of the productions with great enthusiasm and love. Was performing it a third time different? Was it still exciting?

Lea: Yes, it was very exciting. The play is very well written. The type of role I play was of a woman who really moved me. This is a woman who has been through things in her life. She thinks she has solved the trauma of World War II in her life, she thinks she has solved all her problems in life, and all her son's problems past, present and future, and in the end, she sees that things are not exactly what she thought. This play depicts a very authentic life that exists in almost every Jewish home. There was something like this or something similar to it in all Jewish families after World War II. As far as I'm concerned, I have changed, personally and as an actress. Some things in the way I act are more developed. Physically, I also changed. This time, I couldn't move freely like the previous times.

Yaniv: May I talk about this openly?

Lea: Yes.

Yaniv: One of the funniest scenes in the first production was the scene where you got on the bed on which your son is sitting and drawing and you start dancing and singing. He has to tear up the sketch of the drawing each time because your dancing is shaking him. In the second production, you didn't get on the bed, you danced all over the stage. This time, you are walking with a rollator (walker with only wheels) and it has a price; it greatly limits your movement. How do you deal with performing with a rollator?

Lea: I didn't deal with the rollator, I dealt with myself. I wanted to dance. There are people who walk with a rollator and cannot dance, so they move their legs a little, but the energy in the content and the desire to dance was there, so instead of standing on the bed, I sat on it and did the movements while sitting, and in the end I lay down on the bed and lifted my legs up in dance movements. And I think I managed to convey the feeling that the woman wants to dance so much even while sitting.

Yaniv: If I understand you correctly, you are saying that you have physical limitations that you didn't have before, but you have a choice; you either say you can't do it exactly like you used to do it so you don't do it, or you can learn to live with the limitation and take advantage of it to convey the feeling that you need to convey. It was so clever of you that people asked why they had put the rollator on the stage; people thought it was part of the show. Whose idea was it?

Lea: Mine. It's my thing with myself. The director didn't interfere and gave me a free hand because he knows me. He needed that moment and the energy of that moment; the energy was inside me and I transferred it, so instead of standing, I was sitting. You know, your comments remind me of my late father. As you know, he lost a leg at a young age and he started to perform recitations in a chair. He did these readings so well that people didn't notice that he was sitting and not running back and forth on the stage. I'm telling you honestly that today in all my shows, I bring my energies with me. I hold on to the rollator because of the fear of falling, but I use this energy maybe even more strongly to transfer my feelings to the audience and if I am convincing, no one asks why the rollator is with me.

Yaniv: And offstage, how significant is the rollator?

Lea: The same. It's very annoying, but I hold onto it because my stability is not good enough without it.

Yaniv: I hear something very optimistic here.

Lea: What?

Yaniv: You say, "I hold onto it because my stability is not good enough, but I don't let it limit me."

Lea: I don't know what people around me feel. The rollator annoys me and I would like to be without it, and with all the medical and scientific progress, they still haven't found a solution to the matter—why the leg doesn't obey as it should—so I'm holding on to it. It helps, so I have to be optimistic and go that way.

Yaniv: You treat your medical problems with vigor and positive energy; you say that's how it is and I have to make the best of it.

Lea: Optimism, thank God, I have. This is my character; the way I learned to survive over the years, and the desire to know that as I'm still here, I won't be a nuisance and I won't be *nebech* (a poor person that is pitied). And if I'm here alive and I can, then I won't limit myself.

Yaniv: What values are important to you?

Lea: I believe that as long as I am here and as long as I have the opportunity to move forward, I must not surrender to myself; on the contrary, I must move forward and carry myself without giving up.

Yaniv: Do you have any advice for new actors starting out on what they should do to make this dream come true?

Lea: They have to be in love with this profession. If you love it and if you have found the goals you want in it, it is a profession that teaches you to love the world. Even though there may be those who say there is nothing to love, I think there is so much to love. There are many wonderful things in the world. Look at the green in nature, look at the animals that they have so much love for life and for humans. The world is so beautiful that simply not loving and enjoying the world is a shame.

Yaniv: Do you have any advice for directors?

Lea: Directing is a difficult thing. A director should have a vision of how he sees theater, what he wants from the theater, and what he wants from any play he wants to direct. A director must love the play and the characters. If he doesn't and isn't sure he can give the audience the performance they deserve, it's better not to make the play. If you direct a play that you like and you ask yourself what you want from it, then you know what you want from the actor. The director must make sure the actors understand what they are doing, who they are portraying. Not only about themselves, but also about their partners . . . They have to know how the characters and actors fit together. The director should also be able to see the stage in general and see the big picture, the overall play.

Yaniv: And what would you say to the playwright?

Lea: The playwright has to write his soul. Every play should have a piece of the writer's soul. You can't write a play that isn't related to you in some way. The playwright should also love what he writes.

Yaniv: Do you think that today the theater is run the way you would like to see a theater being run?

Lea: It's a bit difficult because there are many constraints relating to the times, the social atmosphere, consideration of the audience, and whether it is time to present a certain play. There are many reasons for putting on plays. During the times in history when Brecht lived, when S. An-sky lived, their plays related to what was happening in the world at that time. The theater reflects the transformations and changes that happened in the world.

Yaniv: So, let's talk about what's happening in Israel now. The war has been going on for almost a year. What does this war do to you? How do you see this war? How does it make you feel?

Lea: Personally, it takes me back almost eighty years to the days of World War II. It was a terrible war that gripped the whole world. The results were terrible. People lost homes, families, and this is even before talking about the Jewish people and the six million who were murdered. And if you will allow me to return to the theater; the theater was also present during the war all the time, in the refugee camps, the ghettos, and concentration camps. There was music, poetry, theater; it never ended. And now, every night, when I go to the show and before the curtain opens, I ask if there is an audience and they tell me there is. This is the great power of the people who come and sit and listen, clap, and sing. I think art has an unusual power; people are not even aware of how much power art has.

Yaniv: Would you like to do something related to the war on stage?

Lea: Everything has to do with the war. Even before I start performing, the announcer announces what to do in case of an alarm during the performance. This means we don't let you forget that we are performing and watching a show during a war. This war is not easy not only because of the situation between us and our enemies on all fronts. It is also not simple even among our people.

Yaniv: What do you mean?

Lea: I was in Romania. I had a good job. I was very successful as an actress and had won awards. I acted in my mother tongue. I was near my mother, grandmother, and stepfather. We had a home. If you think about it objectively, I would not have had to leave everything I had and immigrate to Israel. But I did. You know why? Because of antisemitism. When we went to South America for a concert tour, I saw them, those who left together with me from Romania. They did not flee to Israel, but to Venezuela, Colombia, and all those countries. And how did they settle down? My people lived there, but sent their money to the United States because they were afraid to invest in South America. They bought houses in those countries, but left everything and ran away to Miami because of the antisemitism. And here in Israel, people do the same. They live here, but invest in America. I came here to Israel because I didn't want to hear one more time with hatred, "You are Jewish!" I hear young people in Israel who say it is impossible to live here. I ask them, "Did you live there? The fact that you went on a trip to Europe is not called living. Have you ever lived in a country that has antisemitism?" I experienced antisemitism at the age of six, and at the age of seven, and at the age of eight, and at the ages of nine and ten. And even among the communists, who supposedly were forbidden to show antisemitism, it was there, and that's why I came here to Israel. So the young people who were born here tell me that they have to leave, they can't live here. How can they say it? They don't what antisemitism is. For me, these are my people. And I think that these youngsters should decide whether they want to be here or somewhere else.

Yaniv: And what is your conclusion?

Lea: My conclusion is that we have to think seriously about whether or not we want to be here. Let me explain. We are unstable. We have a problem besides the situation with the Palestinians. We have to sit down and solve this problem first. I have a friend in Israel who has four sons; one lives in Australia, one lives in America, one in London, one lives on the line between Israel and America. Every time we talk, she tells me that doctors, engineers, high-tech professionals, and others say it's impossible to live here, that they're leaving, and my friend agrees with them. I asked her, "Why are you saying that? You were here in the army when the State of Israel was established. I wasn't, so why do you say that we should go away? To where?"

Yaniv: What bothers you is that people give up everything they have established here and leave?

Lea: Yes. I think we have to fight for what's here because it's called patriotism. Why are we here? People like my friend say we conquered the land. I didn't know we had done this. Others say to me, "No! We have always been here." Those who leave say, "Yes, we did conquer the land." The Arabs also say that we conquered it, so we have to decide whether we did or didn't. This debate should be ended; we were here or we weren't here.

Yaniv: But it's not a debate that can be ended. It's a different look at history because each camp sees it differently. The only fact that is not disputed is that we are all here now.

Lea: That's not enough. We need smart people to rise from among us and say, "This is us here, this is our place!" But instead, we have people all the time who say we shouldn't be here. They say we need go somewhere else because it's not ours.

Yaniv: If I understand you correctly, you expect our people to say loudly that this is our land and when we finally all believe in our right to be here, then we can also face our enemies?

Lea: Exactly. The Arabs believe in something and that's why they fight so hard. Many of us don't believe enough in our right to be here. You can see it. Look what is happening here in Israel. I keep seeing the quote on the signs and advertisements, "Together we will win." "We are all together." How are we together? How can we say 'together' if not everyone believes that we really should be here and nowhere else? First we have to believe it. Finally, we have a country, finally there is construction and development all over the country, but because of our enemies, we can't reach a state of peace and plenty. I always look optimistically at life, the land . . . it is flourishing, it is progressing in all aspects! Do we know how to appreciate it? We look and think that it happens on its own, but it is not true. We're the ones who help it flourish, we do it, this is where we are together! Only if we are all in it together can we build the country and make it a good place. We must know how to keep this togetherness, appreciate it, and love it. Unfortunately, there are also those who have fallen in the war. These soldiers are from all ethnic groups and from all social strata in Israel, and we are all here together. We need to make sure that, with this togetherness, we will prosper, the country will prosper. We have a beautiful land. We must all protect it. This is the peace and plenty.

Yaniv: So, talking about peace and plenty, do you feel that after so many years of acting in the theater and all the roles you've portrayed in your career—classics and modern, realistic, epic, and the absurd—you have reached the peace and plenty in your career?

Lea: Yes, I already told you yes.

Yaniv: Does it hurt you that the younger generation and even young people who deal with Yiddish culture and language around the world, only know you because of your role as Bubbe Malka in *Shtisel*, and they don't know how much you've traveled around the world with your husband and your performances in Yiddish?

Lea: I always knew, and heard at home, that a Jewish actor never had the fame and recognition that an English or American actor had. Yiddish was the language of a limited number of people and publicity was also limited. An English actor spoke in English and was heard all over the world. Yiddish was heard only by those who knew Yiddish. Also, regarding *Shtisel*, I don't know how many people who don't know Hebrew or Yiddish have seen the series. This is the fate of an actor. For example, in Russia, there were wonderful and great actors and no one remembers them. Hollywood actors who acted in films are well-known, but theater actors throughout the non-English speaking world remain unknown. So it doesn't bother me. I've accepted it.

Yaniv: If you look back at your career, which role do you believe is closest to Lea Koenig herself?

Lea: I have played many roles and I love them all, but I think the role that was closest to me, my character and my life, was Anne Frank, whom I played in Romania. Because, as a child, I was very much like Anne Frank. I think I was a curious girl like her with a similar character. I think that's why I was able to play a thirteen-year-old girl even though I was in my twenties . . . because I felt her inside me. She reminded me of myself.

Yaniv: And one last question. How would you like to be remembered?

Lea: If they remember me, then let them remember that I was a good actress who really liked her audience and her people and gave them great respect because they loved her. They made me who I am and they still embrace me to this day at the age of ninety-four, and I am thankful for it.

Epilogue

Lea Koenig—The First Lady of the Theater and Always Dina's Daughter

Between the Two Languages

"When you arrive in Israel, prove yourself first in Hebrew and only after everyone knows you are a good actress, then you will be able to go back to performing in Yiddish, in your mother tongue." This is how Yiddish actress Dina Koenig warned her daughter, Lea, before her immigration to Israel. And she added a threatening warning . . . if she heard that her daughter had chosen the easy way out by performing in Yiddish and not in Hebrew, she would cut off her relationship with her. This warning, which her daughter made sure not to ignore despite all the temptations, shaped the artistic path of the actress, Lea Koenig, and made her a leading Israeli actress.

Lea, who was born in Poland (on November 30, 1929, in Łódź, according to her identity card),[1] survived World War II as a child in the Soviet Union with her mother. Later, she began acting in Yiddish at the Jewish State Theater in Bucharest, Romania. She speaks eight languages: Yiddish, Russian, Polish, German, Romanian, English, Spanish, and Hebrew, but the language in which she dreams, thinks, and expresses herself when she wants to be precise is Yiddish, her mother tongue. Even during the conversations between us, Lea switched many times to Yiddish, whenever accuracy and clarity of thought were important to her. The fact that she began to perform in Hebrew on immigrating to Israel was for her a very significant relinquishment of an actor's first instrument—language. But Lea didn't let the language barrier stop her. She mastered Hebrew within four months and almost miraculously, certainly in relation to other actors, was immediately hired by the Habima Theater. From

---

1   Dr. Brizma, "Theater" [Yiddish], *Grodner Moment Express*, November 28, 1929, 8.

the very first moment, her talent stood out and she won the love of the audience and critics alike.

For four years, from the moment she immigrated to Israel until her great success in the play *Bereshit*, Lea refused offers to play in Yiddish. She turned her back on the language she was born into and in which she began her stage career. How is it possible that an actress chooses to give up her first form of expression? How is it possible that an actress is willing to give up her most familiar, rewarding, and effective way of connecting with her audience? How is it possible that an actress deletes from her lexicon a language with which she is so comfortable and finds it so easy to express herself? Why would an actress choose to struggle night after night in fear of forgetting a word and not knowing how to replace it with another one because she doesn't have mother-tongue level in the language in which she is performing?

When the Yiddish actor Shimon Dzigan was asked why he does not switch to perform in Hebrew and if he is not embarrassed about the fact that he doesn't speak Hebrew, he answered jokingly that it is easier for him to be ashamed than to learn Hebrew. Dzigan later explained, in all seriousness, that in Yiddish he has a range of emotions and expressions that simply do not exist for him when speaking in Hebrew and, therefore, acting in Hebrew is not possible for him. "A large part of the humor in Yiddish is found in the music, the intonations, the *krechtzim* and *knaitschim* of the language. I don't know how to translate *krechtzim* and *knaitschim* into Hebrew."[2]

The linguistic and cultural richness of Yiddish allows for a wider range of emotions, content, satire, ambiguities, direct criticism, which is very difficult to reproduce in Hebrew, even more so for those who do not speak it at mother-tongue level. Lea chose otherwise. She insisted on mastering Hebrew, pronouncing words correctly in this new language for the sake of her art. Lea recites a poem that her husband, Zvi, wrote for her, at almost every performance in Yiddish, correctly expressing her feelings in relation to both languages.

---

2 *Krechtzim* ("to sigh," for example, when someone says "oy") and *knaitschim* (literally, "a fold," but in this context it means "innuendos"). From an interview with the Israel Broadcasting Authority in 1972. Also included in the documentary series *In the State of the Jews* [Hebrew], by Anat Zeltzer and Modi Bar-On, episode 3: "It Sounds Better in Yiddish," Channel 1, Matar Productions, 2003–2004, https://vimeo.com/155535096.

Mayn Yiddish lid, mayn Yiddish vort,
Dos zennen mayne alte fraynd.
Mayn Yiddish lid, mayn Yiddish vort,
Ich hob zey beide lib noch haynt.
Ich kon zey nischt farggesn vi lang mayn otem gleet,
In mir zey zingen beide chotch haynt ich red Ivrit.
Ich red Ivrit, ich spiel Ivrit, oon dos is nischt kayn chiddish,
Nor tut amol mir epes vey—dan zog ich "oy vey" oyf Yiddish.

My Yiddish song, my Yiddish word,
Old friends they are to me.
My Yiddish song, my Yiddish word,
I love them both till today, you see.
I can't forget them as long as I live, it's true,
They both sing in me even though today I speak Hebrew.
I speak Hebrew, I act in Hebrew, and it's not something to
                                        diminish,
But when I am in real pain, then I say "Oy vey" in Yiddish.[3]

Lea sings in Hebrew, performs in Hebrew, expresses herself in Hebrew even though her home language is Yiddish. When she hurts, she hurts in Yiddish, when she's happy, she's happy in Yiddish, and yet, she does not agree to surrender to the comfort of the language. She insisted and insists to this day on proving herself in Hebrew, the language of the majority, the official language of the country she now calls home.

But Lea is a multilingual actress. She has performed on stage in Yiddish, Hebrew, Romanian, Russian, Polish, and English. In whichever language she performs, it always serves to enrich her acting style. The linguistic and cultural richness within which she lives also enriches her acting. Lea does not differentiate nor limit herself to one language, she lives in many languages. She performs in any language that is requested of her and does not give in to the limitations of language or different cultural connotations. She doesn't let this stop her.

When she acted as Eduardo De Filippo's Italian Filumena, she was Italian. When she played Jacob Gordin's Mirele Efros, she was a Yiddish-speaking Jew. When she played Mrs. Shakoripinshchika in Russian in Bialik's *Behind the Fence*, she was a Russian Cossack. When she played the French Clotilde in *The Parisian* by Henry Becque, she was French. And when she played Leviva in *The Labor*

---

3   My translation (YSG).

of Life by Hanoch Levin, she was Israeli. Despite the uniqueness associated with her, Lea is a chameleon on stage. She adapts to the point of completely stripping the character of Lea Koenig and literally wearing the character she plays. This is how she knew how to be both a carnal woman with two feet on the ground in *Grocery Store* and an American spiritual painter in *The Velocity of Autumn*, a Holocaust survivor prostitute in *The Life before Us*, an ultra-Orthodox woman in *Mikveh*, the surrealist old woman in *The Chairs*, Eve in *Bereshit*, Olga in Chekhov's *Three Sisters*, and Shakespeare's *King Lear*.

She played an old woman at a young age and a young woman when she was older. She has acted crazy and intellectual. In every role, she tries and succeeds to not fall into the realms of caricature. Each character she plays is different from the previous one and she tries not to recycle, but rather to reinvent herself in every new role. To this day, Lea is not ready to stay in her familiar comfort zone. She is not interested in resting on her laurels and playing only the roles she can pull off easily 'off the cuff,' but strives to prove herself anew. Lea puts her artistic talents and abilities to the test again and again.

She performs with young people and with adults, with old actors and with new ones. She gives everyone an unforgettable lesson in acting on stage and proves to them again and again what a great actress is. The reason for this is the engine that has driven her throughout her life from birth until today—survival!

The Defining Childhood

Lea Koenig's formative years were not easy. Her actor parents struggled to make ends meet. Her father fell ill and had to have his leg amputated, then her parents got divorced and her father remarried. Her mother remained the sole breadwinner and had to support her daughter and her mother who lived with them. While her mother worked, her grandmother raised her. When her mother could no longer make a living in the Polish theater, she moved to Czernowitz, first alone and, after being accepted into the Czernowitz Folk Theater, sending for her mother and daughter. They lived there until the outbreak of World War II. She and her mother had to flee to the Soviet Union for fear of the German occupation while her grandmother remained in a Romanian hospital throughout the war. During the war, Lea's mother fell ill with typhus and little Lea had to take care of her. She fought hard to keep her mother out of hospital as, in most cases, not many made it out alive. World War II shaped Lea's world. The shelling, the need to survive, the daily struggle of a little girl to find food and medicine for herself and her mother, and especially the realization, 'if I am not for myself, who will be for me,' all left a mark on the young child.

During the war, Lea was sent to study at a school together with all the Jewish refugee children. Her mother and other theater actors set up a theater and presented plays in it. The message Lea received was clear and unequivocal: even in war, we must continue to live! Lea understood that she did not have the privilege to break, that she had to be strong. She must strive every step of the way in her life, she must always achieve her goals and be the best she can be. Weakness meant death and she did not allow herself that. This insight is so significant in her eyes and inherent in her personality. It's what keeps her alive after the death of her husband; she has been left alone, outliving her entire family. Suicide and death are rejected because of the awareness that has been instilled in her since childhood––the duty to live, to survive! And her way to survive is the theater.

Passing the Baton from Mother to Daughter

Lea was an only child. Her mother, Dina, played a significant role in her life and continues to do so to this day. Lea needed to get permission to be an actress from her mother; she auditioned for her mother, who confirmed her ability to be an actress in the most significant statement in the theater, "The girl has the charisma that will cross the ramp and reach the end of the theater hall." Over the years, her mother continued to compliment Lea, sometimes directly, but mainly indirectly, when Lea would hear her mother bragging about her in front of other actors. Her mother shared the difficulties of life with her, making sure to reflect reality as it was, not trying to beautify things for her for fear of hurting her tender soul. Her mother believed in her mental strength and did not overprotect her. When Lea deserved a compliment, she received it, and when criticism was needed, she received it as well. Along with the compliments, her mother did not spare criticism, both in terms of her daughter's acting and about Lea's conduct in her private life. However, the significant event in the mother-daughter relationship occurred shortly before Lea left Romania to make *Aliyah* (immigrate) to Israel. Her mother asked Lea for her opinion on a role she had performed as a mother and, in asking, gave her daughter the ultimate approval: her opinion counted in her mother's eyes; she could stand on her own.

With her sharp senses, Dina felt that Lea performing in Yiddish would ruin her career. Once she'd moved to Israel in the 1960s, Lea noticed the lack of status of Yiddish actors in Israel. Even though it was no longer a question of the establishment persecuting Yiddish theaters as it had been in the 1950s, Lea realized that this time too, her mother was right. She had to perform in the language of the majority, in the language of the cultural 'tone setters' in the country, and that she couldn't be in the theater of the minority. Lea also remembers the sense of sacrifice her mother experienced when acting in the State Jewish Theater and not the Romanian Theater because of the language barrier. She understood that in Yiddish, she would not be able to develop artistically as she could in Hebrew. Lea came to this conclusion even before she had to ask for forgiveness from the Klausner Prize committee, which was given to her for her performance in the play *Bereshit*, for 'daring' to appear at the award ceremony with a Yiddish sketch. However, Lea does not apologize for her theatrical education, which was in Yiddish, or her acting style, which was acquired in the Yiddish theater. On the contrary, she believes that her theatrical education was excellent. This was a European theatrical education and she is doubtful to this day that Israeli actors received the same level of education.

Yiddish theater is considered among the Hebrew cultural *milieu* to be inferior compared to Hebrew theater. "Lea is very talented, but she is part of the Yiddish theater." I heard this sentence from the mouths of quite a few theater people in Israel whom I interviewed. They ignored the fact that the Hebrew theater in general and the Habima Theater in particular have been relying on Lea's talent for many years. The fact that the theatrical training in Bucharest consisted of various modern methods, including the methods of Stanislavski, Meyerhold, Reinhardt, and others, theater teachers from whom the pioneers of the Hebrew stage learned and performed according to their teachings. Teachers who laid the foundations for modern theater.

The Choice—Hebrew

Lea refused all the tempting offers to perform in Yiddish, which were offered to her before her success on the Hebrew stage. She allowed herself to return to the Yiddish stage only after her great success in the play *Bereshit*, her second performance in Israel. Her first performance in Israel in *Master Puntila and His Man Matti*, albeit a commercial failure, was good for her. The reviews praised Lea in her role, praised her saying "a pleasant surprise," "deserving of praise," "no doubt she will enrich the life of the theater in Israel," and other such superlatives. Everyone who saw her, without exception, recognized that this was an actress who everyone would be hearing a lot more about.[4] Lea's return to the Yiddish stage was accompanied by harsh tones. Along with the love of the

---

4   Nachman Ben Ami, "*Master Puntila and His Man Matti*" [Hebrew], *Ma'ariv*, January 18, 1962, 8; Yosef Yambor, "Behind the Scenes—*Master Puntila*, Habima" [Hebrew], *Al HaMishmar*,

audience who was just waiting to hear her in Yiddish, *mame-loshn* (mother-tongue), the reviews were ambivalent. On the one hand, they could not ignore the fact that Lea was an excellent actress in both Hebrew and Yiddish, and on the other hand, they were furious that the actress, who had been embraced by the Hebrew theater and thought of as a Hebrew actress, could betray Hebrew by acting in Yiddish!

Dr. Emil Feuerstein said at the time, "Lea Koenig's talent is beyond doubt. She received an excellent professional education and was gifted with excellent natural talent such as sensitivity and intelligence, but for this reason, her importance on the Hebrew stage is enormous and we do not take kindly to her wasting her talent on the Yiddish stage. An actress must maintain her level; it is doubtful that the Cameri Theater would have allowed one of its important actresses to appear on the Yiddish stage in such a musical comedy. The name 'National Theater' obligates you to speak Hebrew, even if it is economically meaningless. It should not be told stories about the actress having 'commitments' to her Yiddish audience. If they want to see her and enjoy her talent, they will trouble themselves to go to Habima. Koenig performs so that they will understand and enjoy her, even if they don't understand every word that comes out of her mouth."⁵

The patronizing and condescending statement, "We do not approve of her wasting her talent on the Yiddish stage," was infuriating, insulting, and outrageous. From the point of view of the Hebrew establishment or the Hebrew theatrical *milieu*, the actress should rather starve than perform in Yiddish. Performing in Yiddish is seen as a betrayal of the Hebrew language and unforgivable! That's why Lea was forced to apologize to the Klausner Prize committee for appearing in a Yiddish sketch at the award ceremony; according to them, she had dishonored the prize by doing so. Lea had to apologize even though the award committee specifically asked her to present a sketch at the ceremony and they all knew very well that she came from the Yiddish theater and that she did not present sketches in Hebrew. Yiddish was seen by the Hebrew cultural *milieu* as inferior, even though, for most of them, it was their mother tongue, and they tried to warn Lea about being tempted to perform in Yiddish lest it damage her career. Allegedly, Lea did not accept this assumption and continued to perform

---

January 19, 1962, 7; Dr. Emil Feuerstein, "*Master Puntila and His Man Matti* at the Habima" [Hebrew], *HaTzofe*, January 26, 1961, 8.

5   Dr. Emil Feuerstein, "Lea Koenig in Tragedy and Comedy" [Hebrew], *HaTzofe*, February 26, 1965, 12 (courtesy of Historical Press Archive, the National Library, in partnership with Tel Aviv University).

in Yiddish. She appeared all over the world and in Israel in Yiddish plays with her husband. But the truth is more complex.

Relative to her extensive career, since she started acting in Hebrew, Lea appeared relatively little in Yiddish and usually only in sketches and short performances or a few comedies; she hardly ever appeared in dramatic plays. Most of her performances in Yiddish were abroad, away from the prying eyes of the cultural establishment. Her husband, Zvi Stolper, who did not find his place in the Hebrew theater and turned to directing small plays at the Yiddish theater, was usually unable to convince Lea to participate in the plays he directed. Lea used to occasionally come to rehearsals and make directing comments, but she did not take a very active part in his theater,[6] despite the enormous love they had for one another, a love that filled them both and perhaps also alleviated the need for children. Zvi's death broke her heart, but she found her purpose in the theater, which brought her back to life. During the conversations between us, Lea blamed herself in retrospect and said that maybe she should have helped her husband more and should have participated more in his Yiddish plays. Lea added honestly that she was afraid and perhaps didn't trust him enough. "I didn't have the courage to grow with the roles. I was afraid that he wrote it and perhaps it wouldn't work. I'm guilty. There's nothing to argue about. I'm guilty."[7] Only in 1987, when she acted in *Mirele Efros*, did Lea perform in Yiddish for the first time in the repertory theater and not in a private theater.[8] The only other full play in which Lea performed in Yiddish was at Yiddishspiel, the Yiddish repertory theater, in *A Tour Guide to Warsaw* in 2013. She decided to take on the role and perform in Yiddish after I persuaded her to do it and connected her to the director of the theater. At the time, I was a member of the repertory committee.

As mentioned, Lea felt that the royal road to artistic success in Israel and to survival in the world of institutionalized Israeli theater was in Hebrew and not in Yiddish. Yiddish, the language in which Lea feels like a fish in water, could have failed her in her theatrical life and defined her as a marginal actress. If she wanted to survive in the theater in Israel, she knew she had to act in Hebrew. That's why Lea refused requests to perform in Yiddish by her husband who directed in Yiddish, by her stepfather who performed in Yiddish, and by different producers and Yiddish theaters.

---

6   This was said by the actor, Natan Hecht, who performed in, among other things, the play *A Refuah tzum Leybn* (A cure for life). Directed by Zvi Stolper, during my interview with him (YSG).
7   See Chapter 1, the section "Yiddish or Hebrew."
8   In her husband's private theater, Lea acted in additional plays in Yiddish.

The Pursuit of Truth

The need for survival, which motivates Lea, does not stop her when she goes on stage. She does not come up with emotional defense mechanisms and masks. Lea is a person who strives for the truth. She survives. She overcame tremendous obstacles in her life: her circumstances, the difficulties of making a living, the period of World War II, the mother who prepared her for life and did not overprotect her, the communist regime that abused her; all these things strengthened her greatly. All the drama of the European world at the beginning of the twentieth century is woven into the history of Lea's life, and this complexity is reflected in the way she portrays the characters on stage. Lea brings to the stage characters she has known throughout her life. She is an observant person. She immediately recognizes small nuances that people don't notice and manages to give volume, weight, and, above all, truth, to the characters she plays. Lea does not hesitate to expose herself and face all the emotional and physical difficulties when she has to play a character. Her characters are not flat. They are full of mountains and valleys, ridges, and depths that life's experiences cultivate.

All her life, Lea was connected to the truth, to private truth and universal truth. This fact should be attributed, in my opinion, to the merit of her mother, who did not seclude her from the world, but forged and strengthened her, and helped her reach artistic heights, even if there were usually kernels of criticism in her compliments. Her mother who, as mentioned, raised her alone as a single parent, is the most significant other for her to this day. The style of education chosen by her mother is what shaped the creative and ambitious person who is Lea Koenig.[9] Lea's mother, Dina, was, in the eyes of little Lea, the most wonderful actress and it was impossible to compete with her. During her career, Lea played many maternal characters, including the American Jenny, who refuses to give in to old age (*What are We Going to Do about Jenny?*); the Italian prostitute Filumena, who asks for a father for her children (*Filumena*); the Yiddish Mirele Efros (*Mirele Efros*); Hanoch Levin's Shratzia and Tollebreina (*Winter Funeral* and *Morris Shimel*, respectively); mothers of various Holocaust survivors such as Mrs. Laiche (*Grocery Store*) or Marga (*A Tour Guide to Warsaw*); queens such as Gertrude (*Hamlet*); the mother, the elegant painter (*Butterflies are Free*); the teacher Daisy (*Driving Miss Daisy*); Alexandra, the painter (*The Velocity of Autumn*); and perhaps the highlight is Brecht's *Mother Courage*. This role was

---

9 For more on a mother who is rewarding, frustrating, and not overly protective, see Heinz Hartmann, *Ego Psychology and the Problem of Adaptation* (New York: International Universities Press, Inc., 1958).

also the last role Lea's mother played. On reflection, you can clearly recognize that each mother figure is different from the previous one. Lea manages to revive different characters from different people and cultures and is completely believable in each and every one of them.

Some of the characters, as mentioned, were also played by her mother, who cast a big shadow on Lea due to her great talent. But Lea was able to meet the artistic challenges and created unforgettable characters even in the roles previously performed by her mother. Perhaps it is so because, in every role that Lea plays, she observes and asks herself what her mother would say and whether she, her daughter, brings her pride, because if she is not good enough, "It will be a very big shame for her."[10] Shaming her mother through mediocrity in acting is unforgivable, not to mention impossible, in the eyes of Lea; she is always Dina's daughter.

Lea is aware of her power and personal strength on stage and off, but even so, somewhat contrary to that, she still needs an external confirmation that will find solace in the difficult and painful places in her life. For example, she needed words of reassurance from the director of the theater that it was okay to stop the performance of *King Lear* in the middle because of overwhelming heart palpitations that she experienced that night. She could live with the hard feeling that she had to stop a show in the middle, even though, as they say, 'The show must go on.' In the end, even the review that praised her acting[11] eased that sore spot, similar to her need for approval from her mother when she performed and when she commented on her performance.

---

10 See Chapter 2, the section, "Bucharest—I am Becoming an Actress."
11 Nano Shabtai, "King Lear, a Timeless and Relevant Shakespeare, as well as the Talent of Lea Koenig" [Hebrew], *Haaretz*, January 20, 2019, https://www.haaretz.co.il/gallery/theater/theater-review/2019-01-20/ty-article-magazine/.premium/0000017f-e6d4-dea7-adff-f7ffba090000. The review referred to Lea not only in the acting aspect relevant to the play, *King Lear*, but in relation to the entirety of her many years of work. "And finally, last and dearest, Lea Koenig, who takes on this huge role. Koenig is a great actress, that's known. It is impossible not to watch the show without being aware of her age and the certain parallel between the present shown and the present behind the scenes. Despite the difficulty of performing such a demanding role at such an age, she copes with it bravely, gracefully, and with talent. Here, she presents Lear, who is not an English nobleman as usual, but she is also, according to her gender (which is not the character's gender), a kind of simple queen mother, who actually shows the banal and universal face of a man in his old age. The blind side and heartbreak of anger, at first, the heart-wrenching element of helplessness, and finally, the grace of a man who has lost his material possessions, but gained spiritual and emotional freedom. Despite some shortcomings in the emotional and poetic aspect, *King Lear* is a well-made, original, and fascinating production. Koenig shows us how timeless and relevant Shakespeare is as well as how talented she is and that she is a stage queen or rather, a king."

At the same time, Lea herself knows very well how each of her performances went. As she demands of herself to seek the truth on stage and in life, she is not afraid to face the truth, even when it's unpleasant. Life has forged her and she no longer has fear. The actress Pnina Perach told me that, on stage, Lea is like a lioness. I didn't quite understand what she meant until I sat next to Lea while she performed and sang.[12] The warmth that emanated from her, the transformation she went through when she entered the character and when she left it immediately at the end of the segments she performed, the energy that emanated from her capturing the entire audience were unforgettable. Lea took hold of the roles and the crowd just like a lioness who holds onto her prey without letting go. Her need to make the character precise, to give her the inner and outer truth, not only inspires, but also creates unforgettable moments, and she does not rest until the entire audience is captivated by her magic. It seems that when Lea goes on stage, the spotlight that shines on her also turns on and does not go off, just as her mother told her at the audition, "You have charisma that will reach the end of the theater hall."

The Yiddish Actress Is Making a Comeback

Lea doesn't just have grace. She is perhaps the last Yiddish actress who carries on her back the hundreds of years of history of Jewish theater. Yiddish theater originated from the Jewish jesters who traveled the road with the German jesters, through the amateur actors in the Purim *shpiel* (play) and the wedding guests whose role was to make the bride and the other women cry in the hope that if they cry before the wedding, then they will be happy afterwards.[13] Among them were the Brody singers, Velvel Zbarjer and others, who wandered from place to place with their folk songs and connected with Abraham Goldfaden's initiative to establish a modern Yiddish theater in Iași in Romania.[14] Yiddish theater used to present sketches and songs, operettas and melodramas, and, over time, also tackled more serious plays: tragedies,

---

12   The Actors' Studio with actress Lea Koenig, held at Bar-Ilan University as part of a course under my direction, January 31, 2012; the Actors' Studio with actress Dvora Kedar on the occasion of her receiving an honorary doctorate from Bar-Ilan University, which was held as part of a course under my guidance on April 23, 2017, and more (YSG).
13   For more about the jesters, see Ariela Krasney, *The Jester* [Hebrew] (Ramat Gan: Bar-Ilan University Press, 1998).
14   Israil Bercovici, *A Hundred Years of Yiddish Theater in Romania* (Bucharest: Criterion, 1975), 74–135.

realistic plays, and expressionist and *avant-garde* theater. Its peak was perhaps the play *The Dybbuk* by S. An-sky, which was performed for the first time in 1920 by the Vilna Troupe. Lea's father and uncle participated in the premiere.[15]

Unlike the European repertory theater, and even the Israeli one today, the Yiddish theater before World War II was mostly a private theater that was not funded by the government (except for the GOSET, which was state-owned and budgeted by the Soviet government). The actors, whose livelihood depended on the number of tickets sold, had to develop a skill to 'capture the audience' immediately, otherwise they might starve. Therefore, on the basis of *commedia dell'arte*,[16] they opened the genre that would later be called stand-up in New York (a genre developed by Jewish comedians who continued the tradition of American Yiddish actors from the old homeland, Eastern Europe.) Yiddish actors would argue with the audience by joking with them and would improvise making fun of each other. They became professional in song and dance and perfected the ability to excite and laugh at the same time. The nature of this performance by the Yiddish actors naturally created a phenomenon of 'stardom'—a star actor loved by the audience, an actor who likes to argue with the audience and throw jokes and witty remarks at them. The phenomenon of stardom was in complete contrast to the ensemble theater developed by Stanislavski in Moscow,[17] or to other theaters that saw themselves as artistic theater. Later, and after seeing their experiences in Lviv (Lemberg) with Yiddish players, Sholem Aleichem wrote his famous novel *Wandering Stars* (*Blondzhende Shtern*) about the Yiddish actors.[18]

Lea grew with the Yiddish actors and absorbed these traditions of Yiddish theater. Since she was blessed with comedic talent and dramatic talent, she knew very well how to use these techniques to capture the audience with her magic. But this was not the end of Lea's talents. At the State Theater in Bucharest, Lea was educated in the modern and classical art of acting according to the Russian

---

15 Another peak of Yiddish theater in Eastern Europe was the performance of *King Lear* at the GOSET. King Lear was played by Shlomo Mikhoels and Benjamin Zuskin. For further information, see Mordechai Altshuler, ed., *The Soviet Union: Diplomatic Studies* [Hebrew] (Jerusalem: Hebrew University, 1996).

16 *Commedia dell'arte* was a form of popular theater that emerged in northern Italy in the fifteenth century, featuring improvised dialogue, stock characters, and a strong emphasis on ensemble acting within a structured framework of masks and stock situations. (Encyclopedia Britannica.)

17 Konstantin Stanislavski, *My Life in Art* [Hebrew] (Tel Aviv: Masada, 1942).

18 Sholem Aleichem, *Blondzhende Shtern* (serialized in Warsaw newspapers from 1909 to 1911; Warsaw: Vilner Falag fun B. Kletskin, 1922).

and German schools. Afterwards, she studied with the one who became her most significant theater teacher, the director George Teodorescu, who polished her acting and made it more modern, more realistic, refined, professional, and richer. Even in Israel, Lea continued to perfect her acting and adapted it to the rhythm of the times, the changing dynamism, and the cultural atmosphere in which she performed. In other words, Lea Koenig carries on her back the traditional Yiddish theater school as well as the European and Israeli theater school, while making sure to refresh, renew, and change over the years to remain relevant. This is perhaps one of the reasons why she acts with young actors. They could be her grandchildren or even great-grandchildren, yet she is not seen as outdated. Unlike past actresses, Lea does not come on stage as a monument, but as a performing actress. The applause she receives at the end of the show is not based on her past roles, but is given to her on her current role, even if her age, past successes, and immense love from the audience increase the intensity of the applause.

The Ghosts Echoing in the Theater

One of the ways to look at Lea's work is through the concept of 'ghosting,' a term coined by comparative literature scholar, Marvin Carlson.[19] It refers to the ghost of a previous production, a shadow from the past, a shadow cast by a previous production of the current one. Each production echoes a past production, each actress echoes an actress who preceded her in the same or a similar role, and even the previous roles of the same actor echo in his new role. As a character actress, Lea manages to change in almost every role she plays. The change is expressed in the tone of her voice, how she holds her body, the tempo of her breathing and speech, all of which stem from the inner nature of the character as Lea perceived it. And yet, a closer look reveals a ghost, the most significant of all for Lea, the one who observes her in every performance—her mother's spirit, of course. This was especially noticeable when Lea played Mother Courage, the last role her mother ever played. Lea consciously tried to perform this role as her mother would have wanted her to perform it. It can therefore be assumed with a high degree of certainty that Lea performed this role with trepidation.

---

19 Marvin Carlson, *The Haunted Stage: The Theater as Memory Machine* (Ann Arbor, MI: University of Michigan Press, 2001), 7–8.

Another prominent role where you can certainly feel the spirit of her mother echoing in her was of course, the role of Mirele Efros. The role was written in New York in 1898 by Jacob Gordin for the actress Keni Liptzin, and was called *Mirele Efros: Di Yiddishe Koenigin Lear* (Mirele Efros, the Jewish Queen Lear).[20] The first actress to perform the role in Europe was Esther Rachel Kamińska. It can be said that she was the greatest Yiddish actress of the twentieth century. "Esther Rachel Kamińska, *Di Mame fon Yiddishn Teater*" (the mother of the Jewish Theater) is written on her tombstone. She created the typecast of the Jewish mother. Kamińska was one of the symbols of the 1905 revolution and was already considered a Jewish symbol when she played the role. Kamińska played the role as a *Yiddishe mama*, a Jew from a small town who falls to her knees when her children stab a metaphorical knife in her heart and she is forced to transfer her fortune to them. Her daughter, Ida Kamińska, also played the role. Hanna Rovina's performance took place in 1939 on the eve of the outbreak of World War II (the premiere was on July 19, 1939). Rovina echoed Esther Rachel's performance. She created a new Hebrew mother figure, one that is prouder and more noble, but still echoes the Yiddish mother figure, which falls apart when her sons and daughter-in-law claim rights to the family fortune. Rovina bursts into tears when she says, with the voice of a person who feels betrayed, defeated, and humiliated, "Oh, to the ears that hear this, because of money, you turned my house into hell, because of money... [*helplessly*] Good, good, I will give you all my possessions, take everything! Everything! Go away, go to sleep in peace [*sobs*]."[21]

Dina Koenig played the grandson Shlomele in *Mirele Efros* with Esther Rachel Kamińska, and in 1958, she played Mirele Efros at the State Theater in Bucharest. Lea did not see her mother in the role because, at that time, she had been expelled from the theater as a result of her request to immigrate to Israel. She was forbidden to come to the theater even as a spectator. When Lea was working on the role, neither Kamińska's nor Rovina's portrayal resonated with her.[22] Instead, she thought of her mother, the strong woman who struggled throughout life and supported her daughter and her mother who lived with them.

---

20 For more on the history of the play and major productions, see Goldberg and Levine-Keini, *The Yiddish Stage in Its Psychological and Juristic Aspects*, 27–50.
21 Kol Israel recording from the program *The Screen Rises*, 1957.
22 In this production, Lea Koenig and Miriam Zohar alternated between the roles of Mirele Efros and Machle, the servant. At the beginning of rehearsals, the image of Hanna Rovina in the role of Mirele Efros, a regal figure full of grandeur, resonated with Zohar. In the end, Mirele's character in Zohar's performance was more elegant and restrained, like an aristocratic lady, while Mirele of Lea's design was, as mentioned, a strong woman, less restrained and, at the same time, warmer. Regarding the design of the characters, see also Michael Handelzalts, "Last Night at the Theater: Fine, but for What?" [Hebrew], *Haaretz*, January 18, 1987.

The woman who managed to survive thanks to her theatrical talent and managed to keep a home even when her marriage fell apart, both during World War II and during the communist period in Romania. The woman who did not give up for a moment. Her daughter, who watched her in astonishment, understood, perhaps unconsciously, that, as a child, she was tasked with honoring her mother, bringing her pleasure and respect (and perhaps even admiration). When Lea played the role of Mirele Efros, she did not play the *Yiddishe mama*, the Jew from the *shtetl*, although she knew her well, but rather the feminist, strong, urban woman who, on her own, rebuilt her home after her husband's bankruptcy and managed to restore the family's good name while remaining noble and respectable. When Lea worked on the role, the significant thing she chose to build it on was the feminist aspect of a woman who survives adversity. Therefore, during the transfer of the property, Lea's Mirele Efros does not cry with pathos and does not break down. She transfers the property from a position of strength built on anger and insult. The transfer of the property, as Lea played it, came to say that this is what she wishes to do now. There is no surrender here and no collapse, but rather a brave decision. Therefore, when she is left alone at the end of the scene, her frame is small, but she is restrained and full of the inner truth of Lea Koenig, who salutes her heroine. In doing so, Lea turned the play from a melodrama, as it was customary to present it, into a contemporary and authentic drama relevant to this day.

Lea's life resonates in the play, as it did and still does in all the shows in which she performs. For Lea, the stage is an opportunity to recover memories and desires from her life, ventilate them, and sometimes even formulate and rework them. There is no doubt that Lea's Mirele Efros also resonates with Mother Courage, the woman who survives the war, whom Lea consciously compared to her mother, a mother who cared for her during the war and provided all her physical, spiritual, and nutritional needs throughout. In Lea's perception of Mother Courage, as is evident from the conversations with her, there is a clear connection between Mother Courage and her mother. Lea does not judge Mother Courage and does not think that she is a manipulative woman taking advantage of the war, as Brecht originally intended. Lea's Mother Courage is first and foremost dedicated to her mother's memory and honor. Lea describes the character of Mother Courage as "not cruel. Not at all. Mother Courage is above all a smart and sexy woman. She is a woman in every sense of the word. And her strength is that she uses the war to live, she doesn't understand that the war uses her as a human being. Mother Courage is trying to survive and, in the name of survival, she loses her children, but she continues on and continues to live, and I think that this momentum on which she continues, where she says that the war is such a terrible thing that it takes advantage of you even when you lose everything, is a very important thing."[23]

In light of the history of mother and daughter Koenig, there is no doubt that Dina's character resonated both in the role of Mother Courage and in the role of Mirele Efros.[24] In these two roles played by Lea, she echoed a mother who fights for her children, who tries to be strong and not break despite the difficulties that beset them, whether it is the death of her husband, the loss of the family fortune, or the children's attitude towards her (*Mirele Efros*), or whether it is the war, the need to make a living or the death of her children (*Mother Courage*). In both roles, the mother sacrifices herself and her life for her children and does not break, especially in the play *Mother Courage*; the mother does not achieve her intention. In both roles, survival is the ideal, there is no option to break, to fall or to fail. In other words, Lea performs in both roles a reconstruction of her private mother figure in all its complexity. There is a closing of a circle here, perhaps one of which Lea herself is not fully aware, of both of Lea's mother figures and of the mother-daughter relationship of the two. In my opinion, this is the reason why both plays were great successes with audiences and critics. The well-known theater critic Haim Gamzu summed things up with the words, "Mother Courage is the best role we have had the opportunity to see performed by Lea Koenig and she deserved the thunderous applause of the audience that was heard when the curtain came down."[25]

In view of the above, it is clear that Koenig graced the characters of Mother Courage and Mirele Efros with a completely unique rendition. This is even more evident in the character of Mirele Efros, where she played the character for the first time from a feminist point of view, a strong woman who goes through separation processes (separation-individuation) from her children during the play. Lea's acting was so different from the acting of the other actresses who played the role because she brought something very personal from within her, something very non-stereotypical, both in relation to femininity and in relation to mothers and daughters.[26]

---

23   See Chapter 6.
24   For more on Mirele Efros's character and the separation-individuation process between her and her children, according to the psychoanalytic theory of Margaret Mahler, see Goldberg and Levine-Keini, *The Yiddish Stage in Its Psychological and Juristic Aspects*, 27–50.
25   Haim Gamzu, "Mother Courage" [Hebrew], *Haaretz*, November 23, 1975.
26   In this matter lies, in my opinion, the difference between Lea's performance in the role of Mirele and that of Miriam Zohar, who brought her own personality to the role. And so, despite the identity in the *mise-en-scène*, the costumes, the text, and the other actors, the two created completely different characters, which caused some of the audience to come twice to the show to see each of them in the role of Mirele, the lady, and Machle, the servant. It should

Breakthroughs in Artistic Life in Israel

During Lea's career, we can name quite a few landmark breakthrough points that influenced culture in Israel in general and the world of theater in particular. First, Lea brought to the Hebrew stage the unique acting of Yiddish theater. A modern play, which is not full of pathos as was common among stage theater veterans. A modern realistic performance. Lea dared to bring comedy into a drama or tragedy with the understanding that even in the tragic moments of life, a comic and compassionate aspect can be discovered. For example, at a rally held in memory of the Yiddish writers who were murdered in the Soviet Union, Lea performed the sketch *Bei Nacht* (At night), by David Bergelson, in which a train ride in the Soviet Union is described. Bergelson described the speech of the people and, among other things, their snoring at night, saying it was like the rhythm of the rattling of the carriages. Zvi Stolper, who directed Lea, asked her to snore. Lea was afraid that the organizers of the event would rain fire and brimstone on her because people would laugh during a serious and sad ceremony. Her husband, who was a prisoner in the Vapniarka Concentration Camp during the war, claimed that even in the Holocaust there was humor, and in Yiddish they wrote both tragedies and comedies. Even in tragedy, there are moments of humor. The stage, Lea concluded, should reflect life in its full complexity and from an ideological perspective, so they chose this humorous performance for the event. Alongside her desire to be a Hebrew actress, Lea also contributed to Yiddish culture and the Yiddish language in the State of Israel. At times, her contribution to the language was groundbreaking, daring to introduce Yiddish into the strongholds of Hebrew Israeliness. As part of this, Lea performed in Yiddish at the Hammam Theater. Her performances there preceded the performance of *The Megillah* with the Burstein family in 1965. Interview evenings were held at the Hammam, and Lea was asked to perform songs in Yiddish with the composer Nurit Hirsh accompanying her on the piano.

Throughout her career, starting with the first interview, Lea didn't stop saying, without apology and without feelings of inferiority, that it was because she grew up and was educated at the Yiddish theater, she was able to bring the knowledge she had gained there to the Hebrew theater. Her career moved from Yiddish

---

be noted that part of the gimmick, which was even publicized within the framework of the PR campaign for the production, was the cooperation of the two actresses who became good friends after a big and painful fight that lasted almost ten years, a period of time in which they did not speak. On this matter, see Adi Noi, "The Talk of the Town: Because of one *Kaddish*, the Two Mireles did Not Speak to Each Other for Ten Years" [Hebrew], *Yedioth Ahronoth*, January 9, 1987, 11.

culture, in which she grew up, to Hebrew culture, which gave her an appreciation and respect; she adopted both into her repertoire and tried to balance them. Other milestones for Lea included when she participated in the first television drama series filmed in Israel, *Hedva and Shlomik*, and performed in quality films such as *Kadosh* by Amos Gitai or *The Testament* by Amichai Greenberg, and in popular films such as *Lupo*, *Lupo Goes to New York*, *Katz and Carrasso*, and other films by Menahem Golan. She performed, and performs to this day, in large theater halls and private living rooms and does not consider any performance to be disrespectful. For her, acting is the manifestation of everything, and everywhere she goes, she will always give her best. Side jobs, in her eyes, are a consequence of the actor's attitude towards the performance and they do not depend on the place or time in which the performance takes place. In doing so, Lea continues the tradition of Yiddish actors, who knew how to stand on any stage, whether it was a magnificent theater such as the Scala Theaters in Warsaw and Czernowitz, the State Theater in Bucharest, the Opera Theater in Odesa, or the Municipal Theater in Vilnius, or whether it is an improvised stage of planks on top of barrels in wine cellars or brothel yards. The Yiddish actors did everything for the audience: argued with them, made them laugh, made them cry, and gave their souls to them. Sometimes they did it for a nice sum of money, and sometimes for a meal, but their acting was always professional.

So too is Lea Koenig. From the first moment she entered the world of theater, from the moment her mother told her that she could be an actress, Lea has made sure to give her all when she goes on stage, to meet the strictest professional standards she set for herself, and to bring happiness and joy to her audience. But above all, to bring satisfaction and pride to her late mother because, in the end, to this day, Lea is very much her mother's daughter. All this baggage that Lea carries on her shoulders makes her, in my opinion, the top actress in Israel and a monumental and unique actress of her generation.

Truly the First Lady of the theater.

Appendices

Dina Koenig

A Short Biography*

Dina Koenig (August 6, 1907, Łódź, Poland–May 17, 1964, Bucharest, Romania) was one of the most important actresses in Yiddish theater. Both of Koenig's parents worked as tailors at the local theater in Łódź. Koenig was a 'child prodigy' in the theater. When she was only four years old, she played the role of the boy in the play *Broken Hearts* (*Gebrochene Hertzer*) by Libin. Julian Schwartz[1] told the story of how, in the play, there is a scene where the child is put to sleep. The actress Amelia Adler, the mother in the play, thought Koenig had really fallen asleep because she closed her eyes and did not open them even for a second. At the end of the scene, the child is supposed to shout, "Mom!" As the end of the scene approached, Amelia did not know what to do. Her heart, a mother's heart, did not allow her to wake the child and startle little Koenig. But on the other hand, if the child did not shout, "Mom!" it would destroy the act that sealed the show. However, just in time, with perfect precision, Koenig opened her eyes and shouted loudly, "Mom!" The audience in the hall burst into thunderous applause.

Julian Schwartz also shared how the writer Yitskhok Leybush Peretz came to one of the performances directed by Julius Adler at the Scala Theater in Łódź. Peretz came to the theater at the invitation of Adler, apparently to check the possibility of staging one of his plays. Koenig was playing the boy in Peretz's play *The Nurse*. During the play, Koenig looked at Peretz from the back of the stage

---

* This chapter is mainly a translation of the entry "Koenig, Dina" in Zalmen Zylbercweig's *Leksikon fun Yidishn Teater* (Lexicon of Yiddish theater). See *Lexicon of Yiddish Theater, Materials Collected and Edited by Zalmen Zylbercweig*, vol. 6 (Mexico City: Elisheva Farlag, 1969), 5200–5204. The entry, based on several sources mentioned at the end, was written by Zylbercweig, Julian Schwartz, and Abraham Kirschenbaum. The entry is presented here in Yaniv Goldberg's translation and adaptation. The references in the notes and the information in them are an addition of the translator, except for those at the end of which the source is indicated: [Zylbercweig] in square brackets.

1   Julian Schwartz, *Der Weg fun a Groyser Yidsher Aktrise*, July 8, 1964 [Zilbercweig].

and she turned to sing the song, "What is man? All earth and dust... today at home and tomorrow in the grave, mute and deaf." He applauded her and, when he came to thank the actors after the show, he gave Koenig a kiss, patted her head, and said to her, "*Maidele, west amol zayn a gute aktrise*" (Little girl, you'll be a good actress one day).[2] At the age of five, when girls usually start playing with dolls, Koenig, the child prodigy, performed various children's roles in different theater groups and in different genres: drama, operetta, vaudeville, and more. She was in love with the theater, watching the more experienced actors perform, and more than once, she got to hang out in the wings and snooze on the stage of the theater. Zalmen Zylbercweig said that, in his opinion, Julian Schwartz was exaggerating, that acting in various genres in which Koenig excelled came only at a later stage when she grew up and became a professional actress, not in her childhood. However, it must be mentioned that Koenig acted on stage as a child in the Yiddish theater because her parents were there most of the time due to their work as theater tailors. Every ruble the girl earned for the children's roles she played was essential to the family's livelihood.

Zylbercweig remembers Koenig in one of his plays. It was in 1914 at the Scala Theater in Łódź. Julius Adler staged the play *The Terrible Secrets*, by Zylbercweig and his brother Nathan, which was an adaptation of a sensational novel by L. Schreiber (A. L. Jacobovitch,) printed in the newspaper *Lodzer Togblatt* (Łódź's daily page). Koenig was, at the most, seven years old at the time and there was a role in the play for a boy named Yiddele. It was an important role in the play and Koenig made sure the audience gave her their full attention. Even back then, one could see that the blood of an actress ran through her veins.

In 1914 and 1915, Koenig sang songs in Yiddish and Polish, couplets and *chansons* at the Arcadia Cinema, accompanied by dances in various costumes sewn by her parents. Her theater teachers were Michael Michalescu (Yiddish poems), Bernstein, the director (poems in Polish and German), and the ballet teacher Nowitzki (dance.) Between 1916 and 1920, Koenig performed at the Yiddish theater in Łódź, where she created the following roles: Pistol in the play *Kean, ou Désordre et Génie* (Kean, or disorder and genius) based on the play by Alexandre Dumas and translated by Zylbercweig; Umschuld in *Every Woman*; Luft Boy in *The Rose from Istanbul*; and even took part in guest performances in various theater groups throughout Poland. Among other things, Koenig played the role of

---

2   Lea received the same compliment from her mother, and it is significant for her to this day.

the child Shlomele in the play *Mirele Efros* at Esther Rachel Kamińska's theater. Kamińska told her to keep the name Koenig as a stage name and not to change it.[3] Indeed, except for a short period during her marriage to Yosef Kamien when she was known as Koenig Kamien, she became famous as Koenig Koenig.[4]

In 1920, right after Julius Adler went to America, Koenig started singing in halls, cinemas, and various theaters. In the summer of 1923, Koenig joined David Zellmeister in Bucharest's garden theater, Theater Nouveau. She took part in the *Bucharest–New York* revue by Ben Eli and appeared in private entertainment evenings with her personal repertoire. Koenig also acted in the same year in the play *Hocus Pocus* by Ion Pribeagu, singing songs in Yiddish and Romanian such as, "I will Be Your Perfume," and "We are Brothers, I and the Rustling of the Lily Petals." In the same year, she also studied with the actor Rubinstein. On the recommendation of Pribeagu, Koenig joined the bar Alcazar De Tay in Bucharest, where she participated in cabarets as a singer and dancer. From there, she went back to Yiddish theater, where she performed with the actors Vera Kaniewska, Muni Serebrau, and Simcha and Naomi Natan.[5] (Later, Koenig would perform with them in the Vilna Troupe.)

Koenig played a second *soubrette* (a young dancer) and they traveled with the show *Berelle Busiak* throughout the country for a long concert tour that was a great success. Koenig was very popular in her repertoire of couplets and once, in town, when she played in the operetta *Sorelle, the Doctor*, the audience demanded after the curtain was lowered that she sing her popular couplet *Perfumol* (Perfume). The troupe's star, Vera Kaniewska, initially did not agree that Koenig should sing the couplet, as it had nothing to do with the play, but the audience did not calm down. They had to bring her outfit from the hotel for the couplet and Koenig was forced to sing it at the end of the show. The next day, they had to perform the *Canopy Dress*, but Kaniewska 'suddenly fell ill.' Simcha Natan and director Jean Polyakov managed to convince (with difficulty) Koenig to replace Kaniewska in the lead role. Koenig studied the role that entire day. From that moment, she started playing main roles. In the summer of 1924 in Czernowitz, Koenig acted in the play *The German House*, this time as the star. In the winter of 1924, Koenig played in the Tomis Hall in Bucharest in Ben Eli's revue *What, Who, When?*, a show with which they also traveled throughout

---

3 According to her daughter Lea Koenig.
4 In an advertisement in the newspaper *Lodzer Vekker*, March 8, 1929, she is called Dina Kamien Koenig. On June 5, 1931, in the same newspaper, she is called Dina Kamien again, but starting from June 26, 1931, she is called Dina Koenig.
5 The parents of the Yiddish and Hebrew actor Misha Natan.

the province. In Czernowitz, a group of hooligans tore up their sets and did not allow them to play. The troupe returned to Bucharest and Koenig performed there with Molly Picon and Clara Jung in several plays, among them *Tsipka Fire, Yankelle, Poopchen, Chancha in America,* and more.

In 1925, Koenig, already a famous actress throughout Romania, connected with the members of the Vilna Troupe who were on tour in Romania. Yosef Kamien was one of the members she met during this time. They fell in love and were married in the summer of 1927. Later, when they arrived in Lviv (Lemberg), she joined the Moskowitz Theater Troupe. However, she decided to leave them because they had her singing songs mainly and she wasn't doing as much acting as she wanted. It was around this time that she joined the Vilna Troupe. Koenig agreed to be a statist (background actor), for a year, after which she began to play significant roles, the first being on August 12, 1927, as the ruined bride in the play *The Experience*. Thereafter, she performed in many roles including Alecheko in *Yoshke Musikant* (Yoshke the musician) by Osip Dymov, *The Demon Train*, and *Periphery*.

The troupe went on a tour to perform in Austria, Czechoslovakia, and Romania under the direction of David Herman, Jacob Sternberg, and Eliyahu (Alex) Stein (Yosef Kamien's brother). Koenig played Jessica in *Shylock* (the Yiddish adaptation of Shakespeare's *The Merchant of Venice*) and Leah in *The Dybbuk* by S. An-sky. Everywhere they went, Koenig won the love of the audience and critics alike. In a review of the play, *Yiddenshtot* (The city of the Jews) by Aaron Zeitlin in November 28, 1929, which was staged in Grodno and directed by Michael Weichert, it was written about Kamien and Koenig that they embroidered the characters like a work of art.[6] About her role (barefoot dancer) in the play *Der Iker* (The main thing) by N. Yavreinov, directed by Kamien, it is written, "Among all the actors, Dina Kamien stood out in a good way, and with a heart full of emotion, she played her role, especially in the third and fourth acts as a maid in the furnished rooms."[7] Until 1940, Koenig played in the Czernowitz Folk Theater and performed in the Schneider Zal (Tailors' Hall), located on the border between the lower and upper part of the city of Czernowitz.[8] In 1940, Koenig fled with her daughter to Chisinau and there, at the Moldova State Theater, she acted in *Red Oranges* by Jacob Sternberg and *Kol Nidrei* by Peretz

---

6   Brizma, "Theater."
7   Nachman Meisel, "N. Yavreinov's 'Der Iker' in der Vilner Trope" [*The main thing* in the Vilna troupe], *Literarishe Bleter*, April 24, 1929, 349.
8   Later, her daughter Lea Koenig, would be invited to perform in the same hall, symbolizing the closing of a circle with her mother . . . Something Lea told me in a conversation I had with her.

Markish, both directed by Sternberg; and she played Mirele in Goldfaden's *The Witch* directed by Abba Lev and Tzeitel in *Tevye the Dairyman* directed by Albert Segalska. With the Nazi invasion, Koenig turned to Central Asia, where she performed in 1944 at the Revue Yiddish Theater in Tashkent and around the Soviet Union.

Koenig returned to Romania with her daughter in 1946, where she performed a little of her old repertoire and, in 1948, she was admitted to the Bucharest State Theater where she performed until her death. It is written about her acting that she improved and perfected her art at this theater. Her appearance went through a great artistic path that surely made her one of the greatest actresses in the theater in Romania. Koenig created a diverse gallery of characters in her seventeen years of acting in Bucharest. She played more than fifty roles in many different genres; Jews and non-Jews, and in all of them, she revealed her great talent, a gift from God. Her roles include Etti Mani in *Dos Groyse Gevins* (The jackpot) by Sholem Aleichem; Marfa Ignatyevna Kabanova in *The Storm* by Ostrovsky; Lady Milford in *Plot and Love* by Schiller; Mrs. Mamluk in *Professor Mamluk* by Friedrich Wolf; Mirele in *Mirele Efros* by Jacob Gordin; and the highlight of her roles was her last role, the mother, in *Mother Courage* by Brecht. It is also impossible to forget her reading evenings, her tragic and dramatic tone, and her fountain of charisma. In 1954, she received the Order for Cultural Merit from the Romanian People's Republic (RPR) for her long career and her artistic greatness, and, in 1956, she was rewarded with the honorary title of accomplished actress, also from the RPR.[9]

Dina Koenig died in Bucharest on May 17, 1964 (Shavuot 5724) from cancer. Thousands of people accompanied her on her final journey. She was eulogized by the representatives of the administration, by representatives of the artists from the Ministry of Culture, actors, musicians, the director of the Bucharest State Theater, Franz Auerbach, and the director Izo Shapira. At the cemetery, the Chief Rabbi of Romania, Rabbi Moshe Rosen, gave the eulogy. She was survived by her husband, the Yiddish actor Isak Havis (who died in Israel on May 8, 1991), and her daughter, the actress Lea Koenig.

---

9   Schwartz, *Der Weg fun a Groyser Yidsher Aktrisa*.

Yosef Kamien

A Short Biography*

Yosef (Osya, Oscar) Kamien[10] (March 19, 1900, Vilna–September 26, 1942, Uralsk) was one of the most important Yiddish actors in Eastern Europe between the two world wars and was an actor in the Vilna Troupe. His father was a secretary at a law firm. After Kamien finished high school, he joined a theater troupe and performed a German operetta in Vilna. He is the younger brother of actor Eliyahu (Alex/Alyusha) Stein. In 1918, he performed with Stein, Joseph Buloff, and other actors at the Yiddish theater in Vilna under the leadership of the actor Abraham Morewski. Morewski shared in his memoirs that Kamien came to the theater and brought with him a lot of pranks, charm, joy, and lively cheerfulness, and he liked him at first sight. Kamien excelled in the role of Count Mancini[11] and he created a character completely different from the one created by Buloff. In 1919, Kamien accompanied his brother, Buloff, and Morewski to Łódź, where they joined Abba Kompaneyets's dramatic Yiddish troupe to perform at the Polish theater. Here, Kamien appeared with Morewski in the plays *Shema Yisrael*, *Cain*, *Johannes Payer*, and *Days of Our Lives*. In 1920, the four actors continued to Warsaw and joined the Vilna Troupe, which was then in Warsaw. Kamien performed in the plays *Bar Yochai* and *Uriel Acosta*. Morewski described Kamien as fabulous in *Bar Yochai* and said that in the theater there are roles that are lost because they are performed by second-rate actors instead of the likes of Kamien.

Kamien left the Vilna Troupe several times and kept returning to it. When he was in the troupe, he excelled in the roles of a Cossack in the play *Kiddush HaShem* by Sholem Asch; Shalksnar in *Yiddenshtot* (The city of the Jews) by Aaron Zeitlin; as Hershel in the play *Hershel of Ostropol* by Moshe Livshitz; and Rabbi Tanhum in *Der Goylem* (The golem) by H. Leivick. Dr. Michael Weichert,

---

* This chapter is mainly a translation of the entry, "Kamien, Yosef [Osya]" in Zalmen Zylbercweig's *Leksikon fun Yidishn Teater* (*Lexicon of Yiddish Theater*). See *Lexicon of Yiddish Theater, Materials Collected and Edited by Zalmen Zylbercweig*, vol. 6 (Mexico City: Elisheva Farlag, 1969), 5295–5286. The entry, based on several sources mentioned at the end, was written by Zylbercweig, Julian Schwartz, and Abraham Kirschenbaum. The entry is presented here in Yaniv Goldberg's translation and adaptation. The references in the notes and the information in them are an addition of the translator, except for those at the end of which the source is indicated: [Zylbercweig] in square brackets.

10 Russian: *kamen* (Kamien); Yiddish: *stein*; English: stone.
11 A character in the play *He Who Gets Slapped* by Leonid Andreyev.

who directed the Vilna Troupe, spoke about Kamien's role in *Kiddush HaShem*: "Kamien, in his role as a Cossack, looked at Devoraleh as a saint who desired her and trembled because of her." At the Yiddish Social Theater in Riga, again under Weichert's direction, Kamien played the role of Mandel, the innkeeper, in *Kiddush HaShem*. Weichert admired how Kamien performed in the role of Shalksnar in *Yiddenshtot*. "Through his body, his gestures, his hands, and his feet, he expressed so much. He used his sharpened tongue and was brilliant with his graceful, yet cynical acting." In *Herschel of Ostropol*, Weichert claimed that Kamien failed to reach the audience; he acted well and was comical in a good way, but he lacked the depth of Herschel, the bittersweet humor, his concern for his livelihood, and the wisdom of a jester who knows several truths. Kamien played a gentile jester, a happy one who loved the bitter ale, and less of a Jewish jester.[12]

Compared to Weichert, the director who criticized Kamien for his role in *Herschel of Ostropol*, Elchanan Zeitlin (Aaron's brother) wrote in his review that Kamien created a character who impressed with his honesty and power of persuasion. "This is one of Kamien's greatest roles, a real work, which brings him respect and recognition. A strange kind of sadness looms over this sad and loved character, Herschel, performed by Kamien. It is a mixture of humor and bitter human tragedy. A mix of joke and paradox with bloody seriousness and truth. Kamien earned, without a doubt, the thunderous applause[13] for his role as Herschel. The play with Kamien in the lead was a considerable success and Kamien became a favorite of theater goers all over Poland.[14] In April 1928, Kamien directed the comedy drama *Der Iker* (The main thing) by Nikolai Yavreinov.[15] Nachman Meisel wrote about it in his review. "The Vilna Troupe gave comedy greater weight than drama. They bent the drama and sharpened and highlighted the comedy, so the result was a happy and cheerful show. The tragic and dramatic element was sometimes exaggerated and grotesque . . .

---

12 Michael Weichert, *Memoirs* (Tel Aviv: Menora, 1961), vol. 2, 170 [Zilberzweig].
13 Elchanan Zeitlin, "Herschel of Ostropol—A Naye Glantz Leistung fun di 'Vilner,'" *Grodner Moment Express*, October 17, 1930, 5.
14 Ezra Lahad, "The Vilna Troupe is Seventy," *Bama* 111 (1988): 18.
15 Nikolai Yavreinov (1879–1953), Russian director and playwright, devised a method of acting according to which each person has an unconscious instinct to present to others as well as to oneself, to create and embody different characters. Through this concept, the hostile and sometimes boring world can be made familiar, friendly, interesting, happy, and full of life and creativity. According to Yavreinov, the unconscious instinct can be turned into a technique of awareness, which will allow you to reach a very high level of acting and personal development.

Deserving of mention is the actress Dina Koenig, who played with emotion and with all her heart."[16]

The troupe returned to perform *The Golem* with Kamien in the role of Rabbi Tanhum. On December 18, 1929, while the band was traveling from Lida (where the troupe performed for two days), just twenty-two kilometers from Grodno, the bus in which the actors were traveling was going up a mountain when a wheel suddenly broke off and the bus flipped on its side. Fortunately, the driver was able to stop the bus from overturning completely. The actors were startled, but not physically harmed. Three actors began walking to the nearby village (about six kilometers) to call Grodno and ask them to send another bus. Meanwhile, a truck had passed by and the two drivers had managed to put the wheel back on, so the troupe arrived safely in Grodno. The three actors who had gone to call for help arrived in Grodno with the bus that had been sent to help them...[17]

In December 1930, Kamien once again retired from the Vilna Troupe and, with David Herman and Dina Koenig, founded the Kinstlerischen Teater (Artistic Theater) in Lodz, which would present better Yiddish and European plays. The troupe was financed by a group of Herman's friends in Lodz. Their first performance was *Wen Bloot Redt (Di Rase)* (When blood speaks/The race), a drama in three acts by the Dutch playwright Jan Fabricius, directed by Herman. At the same time, the Vilna Troupe was in Vilnius.[18] In October 1932, Kamien performed with the actress Lydia Pototska, in Chisinau. At the end of that year, together with the actors Jacob Weisslitz, Dina Koenig, and David Licht, he appeared in Warsaw at the Warsaw Literary Association in the play *Wen Bloot Redt (Di Rase)*. In February 1933, he performed in Yitskhok Leybush Peretz's play, *At Night in the Old Marketplace*, with Weisslitz and also directed the Goldfaden Association Troupe in Stanyslaviv (now Ivano-Frankivsk).

By this time, Kamien was suffering terribly from pain in his leg and, in 1935, he travelled to Vienna for surgery, where his leg had to be amputated.

---

16 Nachman Meisel, "N. Yavreinov's 'Der Iker' in der Vilner Trope" [*The main thing* in the Vilna Troupe], *Literarishe Bleter*, April 24, 1929, 349 [Zilbercweig].
17 "Di 'Vilner Trope' Schier Nicht Oomgekoomen in an Auto Catastrophe," *Grodner Moment Express*, December 19, 1929, 8. The article opens with the words, "We can thank God for the Vilna Troupe," and ends with the words, "This is how the Jewish actors torture themselves on the way of their artistic wanderings." And see also "Di Vilner Trope Schier Oomgekoomen in an Auto Catastrophe," *Haynt*, December 23, 1929, 5.
18 Nachman Meisel, "Fun Woch Tzu Woch" [From week to week], *Literaryshe Bletter*, January 9, 1931, 17 (Zayt 33).

This made it difficult for him to perform in the theater, so he began, sometimes alone and sometimes with his actor brother, Alex Stein, to hold reading evenings and present short excerpts from dramatic plays. On September 13, 1935, an evening was held in his honor in Vilna.[19] The poet Itzik Manger, said that he heard Kamien at the reading evening of *The Good Soldier Švejk* (*Schweik* or *Schwejk*) by Jaroslav Hašek. He describes the event as an unusual experience. "It was a first-class acting creation. No make-up, no costumes, no scenery, and no stage! Theater! I saw *The Good Soldier Švejk* on several stages. I saw the great actor Fullenberg in the role. I saw the motion picture and I give you my word that what Kamien did was as good as anything I've seen, if not better. I dare to say that Kamien's creation was genius. He doesn't read, he performs. It is a great victory."[20]

Between 1937 and 1938, Kamien held Arab readings in Romania. He appeared in Czernowitz at the Scala Theater in the upper city[21] and there his daughter, Lea Koenig, saw him for the last time.[22] In 1939, before the Nazi invasion of Poland, Kamien performed in Warsaw with the duo Dzigan and Shumacher in the revue *Nadir oon Wein Nischt* (Take it and don't cry). He could no longer perform on stage, but he was brilliant in his readings and performed musical numbers wonderfully, including songs and excerpts from dramatic works.[23] With the outbreak of World War II, Kamien fled with his new woman, the singer, Nadia Kareni (died in Israel), to Bialystok. There, in 1940, he fell ill with typhus, but fought and again managed to overcome his illness. After he recovered, Kamien went out with Kareni and cantor Moshe Koussevitzky to 'Brigade Concerts' in the surrounding cities and towns. Koussevitzky sang operatic arias and folk songs in Yiddish and Yosef Kamien did the readings. The shows were very successful and especially successful was the reading, *Port of Shanghai* by Moshe Taft. The trips were conducted under difficult conditions and Kamien's strong body finally succumbed to the disease. Not until his last breath did the joy of life leave him.[24]

---

19 Ibid., September 13, 1935, 13.
20 See Zylbercweig, *Lexicon of Yiddish Theater, Materials Collected and Edited by Zalmen Zylbercweig*, vol. 6 (Mexico City: Elisheva Farlag, 1969), 5293.
21 Nachman Meisel, "Fun Woch tzu Woch," *Literaryshe Bletter*, December 4, 1936, 14.
22 According to a conversation with Lea Koenig.
23 Nachman Maisel, *Geven Amol a Lebn* (Buenos Aires: Central Farband fun Poilishe Yidden in Argentina, 1951), 275 [Zilbercweig].
24 Jonas Torkov, *Farloshene Stern* [Extinguished stars], vol. 2 (Buenos Aires: Central Farband fun Poilishe Yidden in Argentina, 1953), 187–191 [Zilbercweig].

Kamien died on September 26, 1942 (15 Tishrei 5702) in Uralsk, Kazakhstan. He left behind an only daughter, actress Lea Koenig.

This is how Jonas Turkow summed up his character. "Yosef Kamien was one of the best Yiddish actors, the most fundamental and juiciest that the Jewish people have had. Yosef Kamien, the beautiful, strong, elegant, and peaceful man was not so lucky in his personal life. With his first wife, a girl from Vilna who was not an actress, he married young and divorced young."[25] Even with his actress wife, Dina Koenig, he did not live happily. During this time, they had to amputate his leg. He was a chronic smoker and got nicotine poisoning that concentrated in his toe, but nothing helped. He had to have surgery, which was funded by the Goldfaden Association from Stanyslaviv, where he worked as a director. During the surgery, his leg was amputated. Later on, the couple divorced, but even though he had lost his leg, he didn't lose his sense of humor and he used to joke about the 'stupid surgery' he had had. He could no longer act, even though a play was written especially for him, which he performed for a short time. The Goldfaden Association took care of financing an artificial leg (prosthesis) and he then started to perform at reading evenings with tremendous success.

Kamien used to joke with his friends that, when he sat down, he looked like a real gentleman. After the operation, Kamien fell ill with other diseases including diabetes, kidney disease, dysentery, and heart disease. He invested all his strength in the reading evenings, which weakened his heart. Besides his talent, Kamien was full of grace and warmth in his acting. He was also a good person and a beloved friend. He was an artistic individual who cannot be compared to anyone else because Yosef Kamien was unique, he was the one and only.[26]

---

25 According to his daughter Lea Koenig, her father's marriage to her mother, Dina Koenig, was his first marriage. He had never been married before.
26 Torkov, *Farloshene Stern* [Zilbercweig].

Lea Koenig's Theater Roles

Romania

	Year	Show	Playwright	Director	Role
	All plays were performed in Yiddish.				
1	1949	*Der Frender Shotn* (The foreign shadow)	Konstantin Simonov	George Teodorescu	Lena
2	1949	*Der Oytzer* (The treasure)	Sholem Aleichem	Moshe Rubinger	Esther and statist (background actor)
3	1950	*Tevye der Milkhiker* (Tevye the dairyman)	Sholem Aleichem. Adapted by Beno Poplicker	Maurizio Sekler	Chava
4	1951	*Dos Folk Zingt* (People sing)	Musical revue	B. Lebly	
5	1951	*Di Kishuf Macherin* (The witch)	Abraham Goldfaden	B. Lebly and Dina Koenig	Statist (background actor)
6	1951	*Der Yunger Partner* (The young partner)	A. Ferventziye	Rado Meiron	
7	1952	Hershele Ostropoler (Hershel of Ostropol)	Moshe Gershenzon	B. Lebly	
8	1952	*Platoon Krechet*	Alexander Korneichuk	Rado Meiron	The daughter
9	1952	*Hasia di Yessoyme* (Hasia the orphan)	Jacob Gordin	Rado Meiron	Hasia
10	1953	*Der Eingeredter Kranker* (The imaginary invalid)	Molière	George Teodorescu	Toinette
11	1953	*Mit a Lid Oyf di Lipn* (With a song on the lips)	Musical revue by Zvi Stolper and Moshe Balan	Sevilla Pastor and Dina Koenig	
12	1953	*Greenwald Mishpuche* (Greenwold family)	Leibush Brookstein	Izo Shapira	
13	1954	*Perzenleche Motivn* (Personal motives)	Stefan Horya	Nelo Bochevsky	

	Year	Show	Playwright	Director	Role
14	1954	*Mit Pfefer un Mit Saltz* (With salt and pepper)	Musical revue by Zvi Stolper and Moshe Balan	Nelo Bochevsky	
15	1955	*Blondzhende Shtern* (Wandering stars)	Sholem Aleichem	Beno Popliker	Pipchen
16	1955	*Shach-Mat* (Checkmate)	Musical revue by Zvi Stolper and Moshe Balan	Maurizio Sekler	
17	1956	*Lomir Lachn* (Let's laugh)	Musical revue by Berg and Flavius	Maurizio Sekler	
18	1956	*Masoes Binyomin HaShlishi* (The travels of Benjamin III)	Mendele Mocher Sforim	Maurizio Sekler	A young peasant
19	1956	*A Goldfaden Cholem* (A Goldfaden dream)	Jacob Rothbaum according to Izik Manger, Abraham Goldfaden, Rothbaum, Fenster, and Einbinder	Jacob Rothbaum	Tzipkele
20	1956	*Familie Kovacs* (The Kovacs family)	Chava Novak	Nelo Bochevsky	The daughter (Dina Koenig played the mother and Hirshl Stolper played the son)
21	1957	*Dos Togbuch fun Anne Frank* (The diary of Anne Frank)	Frances Goodrich and Albert Hackett	George Teodorescu	Anne Frank
22	1957	*Tevye der Milkhiker* (Tevye the dairyman)	Sholem Aleichem Adapted by Beno Poplicker	Beno Poplicker	Chava
23	1957	*Der Gan Eden auf Der Erd* (Heaven on Earth)	Musical revue by Zvi Stolper and Moshe Balan	N. Raphael	

(Continued)

	Year	Show	Playwright	Director	Role
24	1957	Der Shturem (The storm)	Alexander Ostrovsky	Franz Auerbach	Katerina
In 1958, Lea is expelled from the theater after her request to immigrate to Israel. Therefore, she didn't perform that year and was not allowed to attend the theater either.					
25	1959	Di Efentleche Meinung (The public point of view)	Orel Starin	Franz Auerbach	
26	1960	Di Heldn Zenen in Zal (The stars in the theater hall)	Orel Starin	Franz Auerbach	
27	1961	A Million far a Shmeichl (A million for a smile)	Anatoly Sofronov	George Teodorescu	Olga Petrovna Kartashyova

Note: Lea had participated in all the plays staged at the State Theater in Bucharest since 1949. The plays in which she performed only ensemble roles have not been included in this list. The complete list of performances is in the book *A Hundred Years of Yiddish Theater in Romania* by Israil Bercovici.[27]

Israel

	Year	Show	Playwright	Director	Role
All the plays were staged at the Habima National Theater, except for those specifically stated otherwise. All plays were performed in Hebrew, except where stated otherwise.					
28	1962	Master Puntila and His Man Matti	Bertold Brecht	Shmuel Bonim	Eva Puntila
29	1962	Bereshit (Genesis)	Aharon Megged	Amnon Kabatchnik	Chava and Istahar
30	1962	War and Peace	Lev Tolstoy, adapted by Erwin Piscator and Guntram Prüfer, contributor, Alfred Neuman	Julius Gelner	Maria
31	1963	The End of the Race	Peter Ustinov	Abraham Asau	Stella
32	1964	The Parisian	Henry Becque	Joel Silberg	Clotilde
33	1965	Wisdom Lies in the Pocket (Chochma Ligt in Keshene, Yiddish)	Revue by Zvi Stolper	Zvi Stolper	

---

27   Israil Bercovici, *One Hundred Years of Yiddish Theater in Romania* (Bucharest: Criterion, 1976), 283–306.

	Year	Show	Playwright	Director	Role
34	1965	*The Back Street* (*Di Zaytike Gasse*, Yiddish)	Fanny Hurst	Zvi Stolper	Rea Smith
35	1965	*The Silver Wedding* (*Di Zilberne Chaseneh*, Yiddish)	Somerset Maugham	Zvi Stolper	The woman
36	1965	*Doing Wonders: Helen Keller* (*Helen Keller*, Yiddish)	William Gibbens	Zvi Stolper	The teacher and Sullivan
37	1965	*The Witch* (*Di Kishuf Macherin*, Yiddish)	Abraham Goldfaden	Zvi Stolper	The witch
38	1966	*The Subject Was Roses*	Frank D. Gilroy	Avraham Ninio	Netty Cleary
39	1967	*Tango*	Slawomir Mrozek	Alexander Berdini	Eleonora
In 1968, Lea goes on a Yiddish concert tour abroad.					
40	1968	*Bereshit* (Genesis, private production in Yiddish, performed in South America)	Aharon Megged	Zvi Stolper	Chava and Istahar
41	1969	*Neither by Day Nor by Night*	Abraham Raz	Arnon Tamir	Mrs Sokolova (alternately with Miriam Bernstein Cohen)
42	1969	*The Terrace* (Haifa Theater)	Jean Genet	Leonard Schach	Irma
43	1969	*A Lost Letter* (Haifa Theater)	Ion Luca Caragiale	David Esrig	Zoe Trahanache
44	1970	*The Shoemaker's Holiday*	Thomas Dekker	David William	Margery Eyre
45	1970	*The Chairs*	Eugène Ionesco	David Levin	The Old Woman
46	1971	*Colombe*	Jean Anouilh	Theodore Toma	Madame Alexandra
47	1972	*The Independence Night of Mr. Israel Sheffy*	Abraham Raz	Misha Asherov	Chana Sheffy
48	1972	*A Picnic for Two*	Aldo Nicolaj	Zvi Stolper	Miriam
49	1973	*Catch the Thief*	Yosef Tommy Lapid	Niko Nitai	Yaffa Kimmel
50	1974	*Wedding*	Yosef Bar Yosef	Tom Lewy	Heftziba
51	1975	*Mother Courage and her Children*	Bertold Brecht	David Levin	Mother Courage

(Continued)

	Year	Show	Playwright	Director	Role
52	1976	Kaddish	Alan Ginsberg	Hanan Snir	Naomi
53	1976	The Italian Straw Hat	Eugène Labiche and Marc-Michel	Omri Nitzan	Baroness De Champigny
54	1976	Richard III	William Shakespeare	David Levin	Margaret
55	1977	His Reputation Precedes Him	Ephraim Kishon	Avraham David	Masha
56	1978	The Shadow Box	Michael Cristofer	Hanan Snir	Maggie
57	1978	Winter Funeral	Hanoch Levin	Hanoch Levin	Shratzia
58	1979	A Simple Story	Shmuel Yosef Agnon	Yossi Israeli	Cirl
59	1979	The Father	August Strindberg	Omri Nitzan	Laura
60	1980	The Marriage Contract (HaKetubah)	Ephraim Kishon	Hy Kalus	Shifra
61	1981	Filumena	Eduardo De Filippo	Miki Gurevich	Filumena
62	1982	Romulus the Great	Friedrich Dürrenmatt	David Levin	Julia
63	1982	Grocery Store	Hillel Mittelpunkt	Amit Gazit	Mrs. Laiche
64	1983	Passion Play	Peter Nichols	Nancy Diuguid	Nell
65	1983	Hamlet	William Shakespeare	Dino Ceaunescu	Gertrude
66	1984	Brighton Beach Memoirs	Neil Simon	Amit Gazit	Kate Jerome
67	1984 & 1985	A Pair from Heaven (private production in Yiddish and English, performed abroad)	Yiddish poets and writers	Zvi Stolper	
68	1986	Sunset	Isaac Babel	Yuri Lyubimov	Yevdokia Kholodenko
69	1986	The Farm	Franz Kreutz	Nola Chilton	The peasant
70	1986	Mirele Efros	Jacob Gordin	Amit Gazit	Alternately Mirele and Machle, the servant
71	1987	Broadway Bound	Neil Simon	Amit Gazit	Kate Jerome
72	1988	John Gabriel Borkman	Henrik Ibsen	Jack Messinger	Ella Rentheim
73	1988	The Cherry Orchard	Anton Chekhov	Omri Nitzan	Lyubov Andreyevna Ranevskaya

	Year	Show	Playwright	Director	Role
74	1989	*The Labor of Life*	Hanoch Levin	Miki Gurevich	Leviva
75	1989	*Gold*	Yosef Bar Yosef	Ofira Henig	Sima Wald
76	1990	*Blood Wedding*	Federico Garcia Lorca	Hanan Snir	The bridegroom's mother
77	1991	*Arsenic and Old Lace*	Joseph Kesselring	Roni Pinkovich	Abby Brewster
78	1992	*Stars without Sky*	Various Yiddish poets and writers	Zvi Stolper	One-woman show
79	1993	*The Floating Light Bulb*	Woody Allen	Ilan Eldad	Enid
80	1993	*When the Messiah Comes* (*Az Mashiach vet Kumen*, private production in Yiddish)	Musical Revue	Zvi Stolper	
81	1994	*Stars without Sky* (*Stern un Himmel*, private production in Yiddish, performed abroad)	Various Yiddish poets and writers	Zvi Stolper	One-woman show
82	1994	*The Old Lady's Visit*	Friedrich Dürrenmatt	Omri Nitzan	Claire Zachanassian
83	1995	*Harold and Maude* (Beit Lessin Theater)	Colin Higgins	Itzik Weingarten	Maude
84	1996	*The Importance of Being Earnest*	Oscar Wilde	Andrew Manley	Lady Bracknell
85	1997	*Three Tall Women*	Edward Albee	Jack Messinger	Woman A
86	1997	*Habima Stories*	A revue of the Habima plays over the years, edited by Dori Parnas	Roni Ninio	
87	1998	*Sonia Mushkat*	Savyon Liebrecht	Itzik Weingarten	Lydia
88	1999	*A Tour Guide to Warsaw*	Hillel Mittelpunkt	Hillel Mittelpunkt	Marga
89	2001	*Love Letters* (Be'er Sheva Theater and Givatayim Theater)	A. R. Gurney	Yossi Alfi	
90	2001	*Quartet* (rendered as *A Birthday for Giuseppe*)	Ronald Harwood	Moshe Perlstein	Cissy

(Continued)

	Year	Show	Playwright	Director	Role
91	2001	The House of Bernarda Alba	Federico Garcia Lorca	Ilan Ronen	Poncia
92	2002	Everybody Loves Opal	John Patrick	Roni Pinkovich	Opal
93	2003	The Full Monty	Terrence McNally	Steven Dexter	Janet Burmeister
94	2004	Butterfly are Free	Leonard Gershe	Tatiana Canlis Olier	Mrs. Baker
95	2004	Oscar and the Lady in Pink	Éric-Emmanuel Schmitt	Itzik Weingarten	Rosa (one-woman show)
96	2005	The Cemetery Club	Ivan Menchell	Ilan Eldad	Lucille
97	2006	Autumn Sonata	Ingmar Bergman	Itzik Weingarten	Charlotte (the mother)
98	2007	Driving Miss Daisy	Alfred Uhry	Itzik Weingarten	Daisy
99	2008	The Life before Us	Romain Gary	Itzik Weingarten	Madame Rosa
100	2010	Morris Shimel (Habima Theater and Haifa Theater)	Hanoch Levin	Yael Ronen	Tollebreina
101	2011	Neither by Day Nor by Night	Abraham Raz	Roy Horovitz	Mrs. Sokolova
102	2012	Arsenic and Old Lace	Joseph Kesselring	Moshe Kepten	Abby Brewster
103	2012	Little Gem	Elaine Murphy	Roy Horovitz	Kay
104	2013	A Time for Love (Et Dodim)	Roi Rashkes	Itzik Weingarten	The mother
105	2013	A Tour Guide to Warsaw (Shpatsir Bagleiter iber Warsaw, Yiddish, Yiddishspiel Theater)	Hillel Mittelpunkt	Hillel Mittelpunkt	Marga
106	2015	The Velocity of Autumn	Eric Coble	Itzik Weingarten	Alexandra
107	2015	What are We Going to Do about Jenny?	Donald R. Wilde	Hillel Mittelpunkt	Jenny
108	2016	Quartet (HaSifriya Theater)	Dan Clancy	Roy Horovitz	Judy
109	2017	Three Sisters	Anton Chekhov	Hanan Snir	Olga
110	2018	King Lear	William Shakespeare	Gadi Roll	King Lear

	Year	Show	Playwright	Director	Role
111	2018	Behind the Fence	Hayim Nahman Bialik	Moshe Kepten	Mrs. Shakoripin-shchika
112	2019	Mikveh	Hadar Galron	Rafi Niv	Shoshanna Devorah, the old balanit
In 2020, due to the pandemic, there were no theater performances in Israel.					
113	2021	My Zakopane	Uri Egoz	Roy Horovitz	Goldie
114	2022	Women's Minyan	Naomi Ragen	Lilach Segal	Fruma
115	2023	A Tour Guide to Warsaw (The Hebrew Theater)	Hillel Mittelpunkt	Hillel Mittelpunkt	Marga
116	2023	Marzipans	Maya Heffner	Mor Frank	Ada
117	2025	An Evening with Lea Koenig (An Ovnt mit Lea Koenig, Yiddish, Yiddishpiel Theater)	Various Yiddish poets and writers	Yaniv Shimon Goldberg	One-woman show
118	2025	Little Gem	Elaine Murphy	Lilach Segal	Key

Lea Koenig's Music Albums

	Year	Name	Poets and composers	Record Company	Producer
1	2023	Dos Mol oyf Yiddish (This time in Yiddish)	Various artists in Yiddish	Indi publishing	Yaniv Goldberg
2	2024	Mayn Veg (My way)	Various artists in Yiddish and Hebrew	Indi publishing	Yaniv Goldberg

From Lea's Photo Album

All photos courtesy Lea Koenig unless stated otherwise.

Dina Koenig as a child prodigy in the role of Yiddele in the play *Di Shrekliche Soydes* (The terrible secrets) by L. Schreiber

Dina Koenig as Tsipka in the play *Tsipka Fire* at the Yiddish theater in Czernowitz

From Lea's Photo Album | 215

Dina Koenig and Yosef Kamien after their marriage

Yosef Kamien and his daughter, Lea Koenig

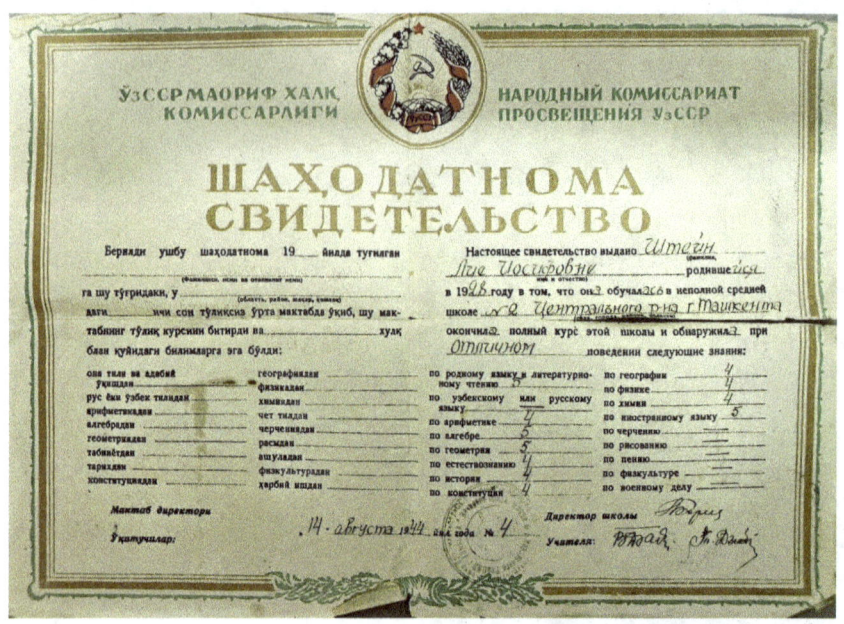

Lea Koenig's school diploma from School No. 2 in Tashkent, Uzbekistan, received on August 14, 1944, during World War II

Zvi Stolper and Lea Koenig after their wedding in Bucharest

From Lea's Photo Album | 217

Dina Koenig and Isak Havis

Lea Koenig's house at 5 Shkolna Street in Czernowitz. Photo: Yaniv Goldberg

The bridge near the house. Photo: Yaniv Goldberg

Advertisement for Yosef Kamien's last show with Shimon Dzigan and Israel Schumacher, June 1939

From left to right: Dina Koenig, Isak Havis, and Lea Koenig at a concert at the State Jewish Theater in Bucharest

Mirele Efros. From left to right: Judith Kronenfeld as Sheindele, Mano Ripple as Dunya, Dina Koenig as Mirele Efros, and Yankele Alperin as Yosele.
The State Jewish Theater in Bucharest

A concert in the Romanian periphery. From left to right: Miku Lazarowitz (accordion player), Liku Segal (drummer), Dina Koenig, Isak Havis, Shimon Wolfenson (violinist), Bibiana Goldenthal (singer), Beno Popliker, and musician not identified.
The State Jewish Theater in Bucharest

The Foreign Shadow. Lea Koenig as Lena, a Russian soldier, her first role.
The State Jewish Theater in Bucharest

From Lea's Photo Album | 221

Tevye the Dairyman. From left to right: Idit Horowitz as Hodel, Lea Koenig as Chava, Sadie Glick as Zeitl, Dina Koenig as Golda, and Isak Havis as Tevye (standing). The State Jewish Theater in Bucharest

The Kovacs Family. From left to right: Lea and Dina Koenig. The State Jewish Theater in Bucharest

Hasia the Orphan. Lea Koenig in the role of the orphan, Hasia. The State Jewish Theater in Bucharest

Hasia the Orphan. Dina Koenig as Freida Trachtenberg. The State Jewish Theater in Bucharest

From Lea's Photo Album | 223

Checkmate. All the characters in the picture are Lea Koenig in different roles in the play.
The State Jewish Theater in Bucharest

Checkmate. Lea Koenig as a child.
The State Jewish Theater in Bucharest

The Imaginary Invalid.
Lea Koenig in the role of Toinette.
The State Jewish Theater in Bucharest

The Diary of Anne Frank. From left to right:
Lea Koenig in the role of Anne Frank
and Samuel Fischler in the role of Anne's father.
The State Jewish Theater in Bucharest

The Diary of Anne Frank. From left to right: Beno Popliker as Peter's father, Sonya Gorman as Peter's mother, Leonie Waldman as Anne's sister, Hanna Rieber as Anne's mother, Lea Koenig in the role of Anne Frank, and Samuel Becker in the role of Dusseldorf. The State Jewish Theater in Bucharest

The director George Teodorescu, who directed Lea in the plays *The Diary of Anne Frank* and *The Imaginary Invalid*

Zvi Stolper and Lea Koenig upon their arrival in Israel

Lea Koenig learning Hebrew at the *ulpan* at Beit HaPoalot in Petach Tikva

From Lea's Photo Album | 227

Lea Koenig and Hanna Rovina

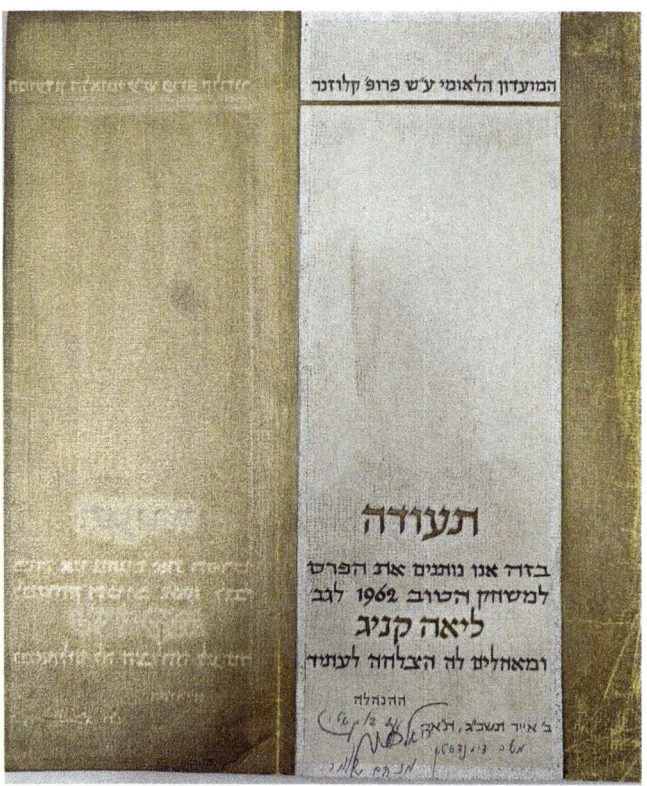

Klausner Prize award for Lea Koenig

Klausner Prize ceremony. Lea Koenig and a representative of the award committee

Klausner Prize ceremony. From left to right: A representative of the award committee, Lea Koenig, Dov Ber Malkin, Yehoshua Bertonov, and Avraham Ninio (standing)

From Lea's Photo Album | 229

Lea Koenig and Zvi Stolper (right) on tour in Melbourne, Australia

Lea Koenig and Zvi Stolper. Photo: Gérard Allon

Bereshit. From left to right: Yehoshua Bertonov in the role of the garden's owner (God), Nahum Buchman in the role of Adam, and Lea Koenig as Eve. Habima National Theater. Photo: Mirlin Yaron, courtesy of the Habima National Theater

Bereshit. From left to right: Raphael Klachkin in the role of the snake and Lea Koenig in the role of Eve. Habima National Theater. Photo: Mirlin Yaron, courtesy of the Habima National Theater

From Lea's Photo Album | 231

The Chairs. From left to right: Shlomo Bar Shavit, the old man, and Lea Koenig, the old woman. Habima National Theater. Photo: Yaakov Agur, courtesy of the Israeli Center for the Documentation of the Performing Arts, Tel Aviv University

Back Street. Lea Koenig.
Photo: Photo Mackey

Mother Courage.
Lea Koenig.
Habima National Theater.
Photo: Gérard Allon

Mother(s) Courage. From left to right: Dina Koenig as Mother Courage,
Lea Koenig as Mother Courage. Image editing: Avshalom Gil-Ad.
Photo courtesy of Yaniv S. Goldberg

From Lea's Photo Album | 233

Kaddish. Lea Koenig. Habima National Theater. Photo: Gérard Allon

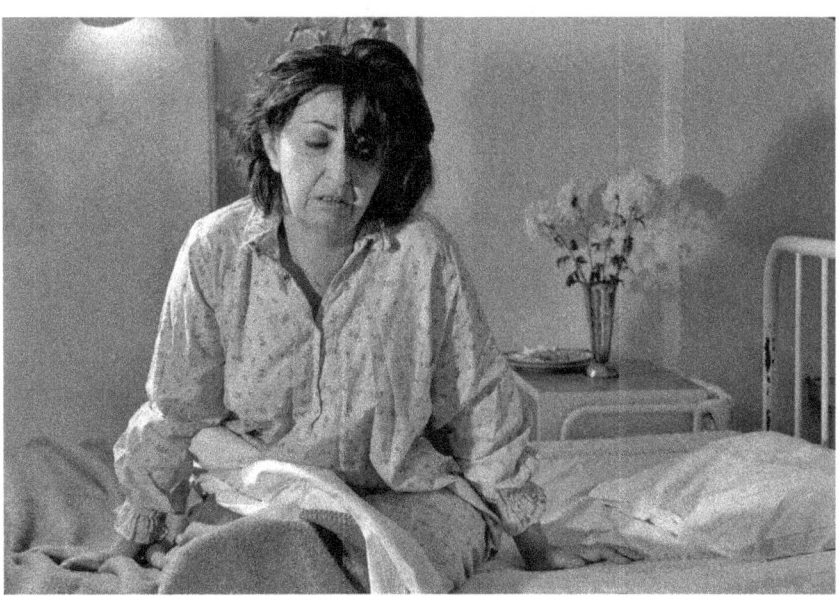

Kaddish. Lea Koenig. Habima National Theater. Photo: Gérard Allon

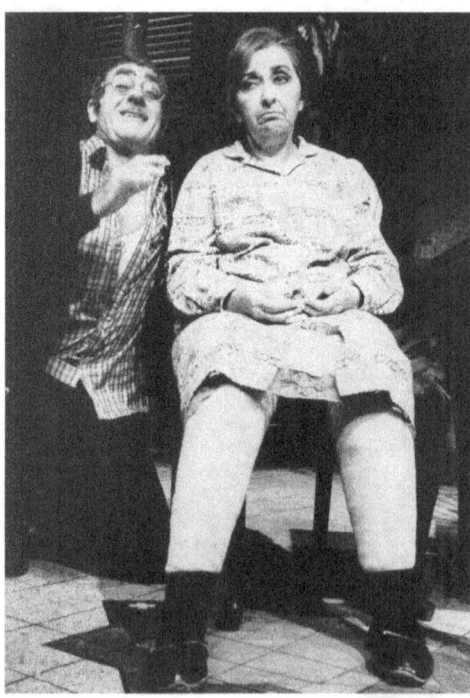

Grocery Store.
Lea Koenig as Mrs. Laiche
and Nahum Buchman as Yossel.
Habima National Theater.
Photo: Rachel Hirsch

The Labor of Life.
Nissim Azikri as Yona
and Lea Koenig as Leviva.
Habima National Theater.
Photo: Pesi Girsch

Winter Funeral. From left to right: Lea Koenig as Shratzia and Shlomo Bar Shavit as Tsitzkeva. Habima National Theater. Photo: Yaakov Agur, courtesy of the Israeli Center for the Documentation of the Performing Arts, Tel Aviv University

Mirele Efros. From left to right: Miriam Zohar in the role of Machle, the servant, and Lea Koenig as Mirele Efros. Habima National Theater. Photo: Yechiam Gal

Mirele Efros. L-R: Rivka Gur as Hanna Devorah, Yael Pearl as Sheindele, Mosco Alkalai as Nahumtze, Ami Weinberg as Yosele, Miriam Zohar as Mahle, Lea Koenig as Mirele Efros, Shmuel Rodansky as Shalmon, and Shimon Cohen as Dunya.
Photo: Yechiam Gal, courtesy of Habima National Theater

Driving Miss Daisy. From left to right: Lea Koenig as Miss Daisy and Jacob Cohen as Hoke Colburn, the driver. Habima National Theater. Photo: Gérard Allon

The Life before Us. Lea Koenig as Madame Rosa and Oshri Cohen as Momo. Habima National Theater. Photo: Gérard Allon

Morris Shimel. From left to right: Deborah Kidder as Telegreptcia, Lea Koenig as Tollebreina, and Avi Kushnir as Morris Shimel. Habima National Theater. Photo: Gérard Allon

The Velocity of Autumn. From left to right: Tomer Sharon as Chris and Lea Koenig as Alexandra. Habima National Theater. Photo: Gérard Allon

From Lea's Photo Album | 239

Behind the Fence. Yigal Sadeh as Hanina Lippa and Lea Koenig as Mrs. Shakoripinshchika. Habima National Theater. Photo: Gérard Allon

Behind the Fence.
Lea Koenig as Mrs. Shakoripinshchika.
Habima National Theater.
Photo: Gérard Allon

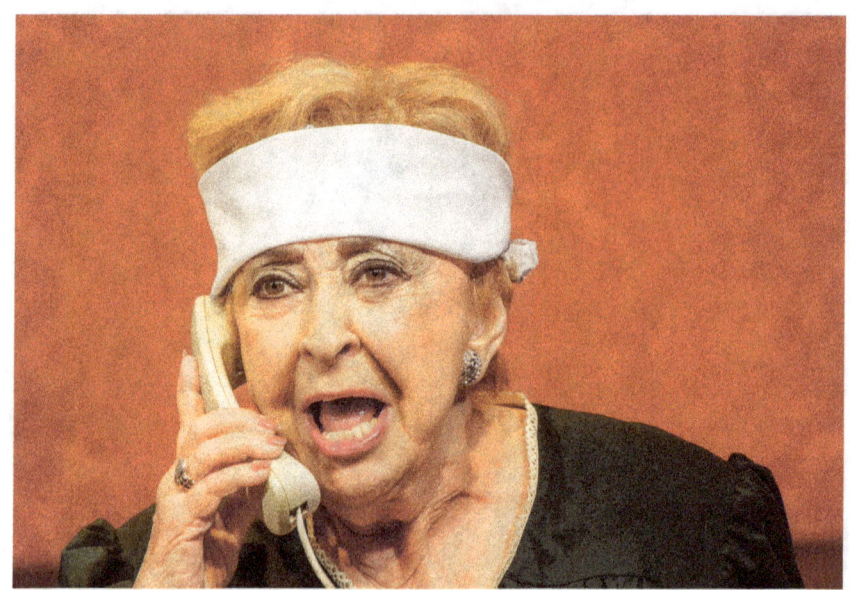

A Tour Guide to Warsaw (Yiddish). Lea Koenig as Marga Weissberg. Yiddishspiel Theater.
Photo: Gérard Allon

A Tour Guide to Warsaw (Hebrew).
Lea Koenig as Marga Weissberg.
Habima National Theater.
Photo: Gérard Allon

Three Tall Women. From left to right: Tatiana Canellis Ollier as Woman B, Lea Koenig as Woman A, and Hila Vidor as Woman C. Habima National Theater. Photo: Gérard Allon

Actors' Studio in honor of Lea Koenig and in memory of Zvi Stolper, Bar-Ilan University, 2014. From left to right: Natan Hecht, Miri Reznik, Dr. Yaniv Goldberg (moderator and initiator of the event), Lea Koenig, Orna Rotberg, Ami Weinberg, Rabbi Prof. Daniel Hershkowitz (then president of Bar-Ilan University). Photo: Meshulam Levy

Ceremony naming the street next to the Givatayim Theater in honor of Lea Koenig, Givatayim 2020. From left to right: mayor of Givatayim, Ran Kunik, Lea Koenig, and then CEO of Habima National Theater, Noam Semel. Photo: Givatayim Municipality spokesperson

Lea Koenig and her first Yiddish record, *Dos Mol oyf Yiddish* (This time in Yiddish), released on November 30, 2023, with Yaniv S. Goldberg, who produced it

Bibliography

Hebrew and Yiddish Sources (Translated)

Altshuler, Mordechai (ed.). *The Jewish Theater in the Soviet Union: Studies, Theories, Documents.* Jerusalem: Hebrew University, 1996.
Aridor, Edna. *The Story of a House: Beit HaHalutzot–Beit HaOlot, 1939–1976.* Tel Aviv: Naamat Publishing House, Department of Movement Education and the Next Generation, 1982.
Bercovici, Israil. *A Hundred Years of Yiddish Theater in Romania.* Bucharest: Criterion, 1975.
Finkel, Shimon. *On the Margins of Totality: Hesitations about Artistic Mission.* Tel Aviv: Eked, 1976.
Goldberg, Yaniv. "'You are not my groom': A Feminist Reading of the Play *The Dybbuk—Between Two Worlds* by S. An-sky." *Jerusalem Studies in Hebrew Literature* 27 (2014): 133–153.
Krasney, Ariela. *The Badchan.* Ramat Gan: Bar-Ilan University Press, 1998.
Lahad, Ezra. "The Vilna Troupe is Seventy," *Bama* 111 (1988): 5–29.
Maisel, Nachman. *There was a Life Once.* Buenos Aires: Central Farband fun Poilishe Yidden in Argentina, 1951.
Manger, Itzik, Jonas Torkov, and Moshe Perenson (eds.). *Yiddish Theater in Europe Between the Two World Wars,* vol. 1: *Poland.* New York: Altveltlecher Yiddisher Kultur Congress, 1968.
Noverstern, Avraham. *Here Live the Jewish People: Yiddish Literature in the United States.* Jerusalem: Magnes Press, 2015.
Rozik, Eli. *Basics of Play Analysis.* Tel Aviv: Or Am, 1992.
Stanislavski, Konstantin. *My Life in Art.* Tel Aviv: Masada, 1942.
Steinlauf, Michael. "The Jewish Theater in Poland." In *Existence and Fracture of Polish Jews across Their Generations,* edited by Israel Bartal and Israel Gutman, vol. 2, 327–349. Jerusalem: Zalman Shazar Center for Jewish History, 2001.
Torkov, Jonas. *Extinguished Stars,* vol. 2. Buenos Aires: Central Farband fun Poilishe Yidden in Argentina, 1953.
Weichert, Michael. *Memoirs,* vol. 2. Tel Aviv: Menora, 1961.
Zylbercweig, Zalmen. *Lexicon of Yiddish Theater. Materials Collected and Edited by Zalmen Zylbercweig,* vol. 6. Mexico City: Elisheva Farlag, 1969.

English and Other Sources

Bragg, Melvyn. *Richard Burton: A Life.* Boston, MA: Little, Brown and Company, 1988.
Caranfil, Tudor. *Istoria Cinematografiei în Capodopere: Vîrstele Peliculei,* vol. 2. Iași: Polirom, 2009.
Carlson, Marvin. *The Haunted Stage: The Theater as Memory Machine.* Ann Arbor, MI: University of Michigan Press, 2001.

Goldberg, Yaniv, and Noga Levine-Keini. *The Yiddish Stage in its Psychological and Juristic Aspects.* Newcastle upon Tyne: Cambridge Scholars Publishing, 2023.

Hartmann, Heinz. *Ego Psychology and the Problem of Adaptation.* New York: International Universities Press, 1958.

Temkine, Pierre. "Auf den Spuren von Godot: Eine literarische Ermittlung" [Following the traces of Godot: A literary investigation]. In *Warten auf Godot: Das Absurde und die Geschichte* [*Waiting for Godot*: The absurd and history], edited by Pierre Temkine, Denis Thouard, and Tim Trzaskalik, 29–42. 2nd ed. Berlin: Matthes & Seitz, 2009.

Newspaper and Magazine Articles

Al HaMishmar (Hebrew)
- Yosef Yambor. "Behind the Scenes—*Master Puntila* at Habima." January 19, 1962, 7.

Grodner Moment Express (Yiddish)
- Dr. Brizma. "Theater." November 28, 1929.
- "Di 'Vilner Trope' Schier Nicht Oomgekoomen in an Auto Catastrophe" [The "Vilner Troupe" Almost Vanished in a Car Accident]. December 19, 1929, 8.
- Zeitlin, Elchanan. "Herschel of Ostropol—A Naye Glantz Leistung fun di 'Vilner Trope'" [Herschel of Ostropol—A New Bright Achievement of the "Vilner Troupe"]. October 17, 1930.

Davar (Hebrew)
- L. G. [Leah Goldberg]. "'Mirele Efros' at 'Habima.'" July 26, 1939, 4.
- Wallach, Aliza. "Lea Courage." November 7, 1975, 30.
- Shapira, Reuven. "Shabbos in Malabes." August 1, 1980, 14.

Dvar HaPoelet (Hebrew)
- Goldberg, Leah. "Hanna Rovina (After Her Appearance in *Mirele Efros*)." August 15, 1939, 167–168.

Haaretz (Hebrew)
- Gamzu, Haim. "Mother Courage." November 23, 1975.
- Handelzalts, Michael. "Last Night at the Theater: Fine, but for What?" January 18, 1987.
- Shabtai, Nano. "King Lear, a Timeless and Relevant Shakespeare, as well as the Talent of Lea Koenig." January 20, 2019. https://www.haaretz.co.il/gallery/theater/theater-review/. premium-MAGAZINE-1.6853315. Last accessed date: March 30, 2025.

HaTzofe (Hebrew)
- Feuerstein, Emil. "*Master Puntila and His Man Matti* at Habima." January 26, 1961, 8.
- ———. "Lea Koenig in Tragedy and Comedy." February 26, 1965, 12. Courtesy of Historical Press Archive, the National Library, in partnership with Tel Aviv University.

Haynt (Yiddish)
- "Di Vilner Trope Schier Oomgekoomen in an Auto Catastrophe." December 23, 1929, 5.

LaMerhav (Hebrew)
- Z. C. [Zvia Cohen, editor of the section for women and home]. "Lea Koenig Again." May 26, 1966, 3.

Literaryshe Bletter (Yiddish)
- Meisel, Nachman. "N. Yavreinov's 'Der Iker' in der Vilner Trope". Nos. 17–18. April 24, 1929, 349.
- ——. "From Week to Week." No. 2 (349). January 9, 1931, 17 (Zayt 33).
- ——. "From Week to Week." No. 37 (592). September 13, 1935, 13 (Zayt 597).
- ——. "From Week to Week." No 49 (656). December 4, 1936, 14 (Zayt 786).

Lodzer Vekker (Yiddish)
- Di Vilner Troupe. "Kinstlerisher Frimorgn" [Artistic Morning] (advertisement). March 8, 1929.
- "About Herman's Theater." June 5, 1931.
- "Jacob Pregger's 'Experience' at David Herman's Theater." June 26, 1931.

Ma'ariv (Hebrew)
- "The Night of the Executed Poets." March 16, 1952, 2.
- Ben Ami, Nachman. "Master Puntila and His Man Matti." January 18, 1962, 8.
- Haelyon, Yaakov. "Screen and Mask." June 6, 1974, 25.
- Gelblum, Aryeh. "Yossi Courage in Habima." July 14, 1975, 5.
- Na'eh, Buki. "The Religious People Shouted Outside." February 26, 1984, 1–2.
- Advertisement on behalf of the Habima National Theater. April 19, 1989, Entertainment section, 4.

Yedioth Ahronoth (Hebrew)
- Noi, Adi. "The Talk of the Town: Because of One *Kaddish*, the Two Mireles did Not Speak to Each Other for Ten Years." January 9, 1987, 11.

Literary Sources

Gordin, Jacob. *Mirele Efros, the Jewish Queen Lear*. New York: no publisher found, 1898.
Levin, Hanoch. *The Labor of Life and Others*. Tel Aviv: The United Kibbutz Publishing House, 1991.
Mendele Mocher Sforim. *Collected Writings*, vol. 1. Krakow: Va'ad HaYovel, 1909.
Playbill of the Vilna Troupe's *The Dybbuk* for the *Shloshim* of S. An-Sky. Warsaw, 1920.
Sholem Aleichem. *Wandering Stars*. Serialized in Warsaw newspapers from 1909 to 1911. Warsaw: Vilner Falag fun B. Kletskin, 1922.

Electronic Sources

Actors' Studio with actress Lea Koenig. Bar-Ilan University. Moderated by Dr. Yaniv S. Goldberg. January 31, 2012. Video recording.

Actors' Studio with actor Yehuda Efroni on the occasion of receiving a Lifetime Achievement Award from the Brookdale Program. Bar-Ilan University. Moderated by Dr. Yaniv S. Goldberg. March 18, 2013. Video recording.

Actors' Studio with actress Dvora Kedar on the occasion of her receiving an honorary doctorate degree from Bar-Ilan University. Moderated by Dr. Yaniv S. Goldberg. April 23, 2017. Video recording.

Habima Theater Archive. http://archive.habima.co.il. Last accessed date: March 30, 2025.

In the State of the Jews [Hebrew]. Episode 3, "It Sounds Better in Yiddish." Written by Anat Zeltzer and Modi Bar-On. Channel 1, Matar Productions, 2003–2004. https://vimeo.com/155535096. Last accessed date: March 30, 2025.

Mabat Sheini, "Jews for Pigs." Directed by Eyal Tavor, edited by Roi Ben Ami. Channel 1, December 14, 2011. https://www.youtube.com/watch?v=KeXLic0am2Q. Last accessed date: March 30, 2025.

Mirele Efros [Hebrew]. Written by Jacob Gordin, directed by Michael Ohad. Audio recording from the program *The Screen Rises*. Kol Israel radio station, 1957.

www.ingramcontent.com/pod-product-compliance
Lightning Source LLC
Chambersburg PA
CBHW061346300426
44116CB00011B/2008